Howard Gilbert
January 21, 1980

CIVILIZATION *and* OLD FRIENDS

CIVILIZATION

AND

OLD FRIENDS

Clive Bell

TWO VOLUMES IN ONE

THE UNIVERSITY OF CHICAGO PRESS
CHICAGO AND LONDON

Civilization was originally published in 1928,
and *Old Friends* in 1956, both by Chatto & Windus, London

The University of Chicago Press, Chicago 60637
The University of Chicago Press, Ltd., London
© 1973 by The University of Chicago
Old Friends © 1956 by Clive Bell
Printed in the United States of America
International Standard Book Number: 0-226-04206-5 (clothbound)
Library of Congress Catalog Card Number: 73-85850

CIVILIZATION

CONTENTS

DEDICATION TO VIRGINIA WOOLF

Dearest Virginia,

If I do this essay the honour of dedication to you, it is not only, nor chiefly, because by the spell of your name I might hope to charm my readers. Not that I should be ashamed to owe that or any other benefit to our friendship; but in truth my motive happens to be more honourable and more interesting. It is that you alone of my friends were in at the birth and have followed the fortunes of this backward and ill-starred child. You alone know that it was the first conceived of all my brood, and that all the rest (except some collections of articles)have, in a sense, come out of it. Its conception dates from our nonage. You remember, Virginia, we were mostly socialists in those days. We were concerned for the fate of humanity. And from that concern sprang first the idea, then the rough draft, of what was to be, of course, my magnum opus, *a book to deal with nothing less than every significant aspect of our age, a book to be called* The New Renaissance.

'It was a childish phantasy,' as I imagine Hood says somewhere; but childish as I was I realized even then that to explain where we were it would be necessary to demonstrate whence we had come. The New Renaissance *was to have given a picture of contemporary art, thought, and social organization by tracing the history of those manifestations of civility from earliest times to the present — to*

9

1909 *say. But by* 1911 *I was a little wiser—a little more grown-up at any rate—and I perceived that my subject was unmanageable. Wherefore, inspired by the first and second Post-Impressionist Exhibitions, I cut out of my* New Renaissance *a section and published it in the spring of* 1914 *under the simple and comprehensive title* Art.

Then came the war. And the war, with its political and economic consequences has, as you will soon perceive, modified my ideas considerably. Indeed the difference between this essay and the book about which I used to chatter in your workroom in Fitzroy Square is to be attributed mainly to that differentiating event. For, though the comedy—the spectacle, I mean, of millions of men and women trying by means of political and social organization to get what they more or less believe they want, and calling what they believe they want good—remains, the illumination is new. By the autumn of 1918 *I had begun to see things differently; my opinions and beliefs had changed. The things that had seemed valuable as ends seemed so still, but much of what I had taken for possible means to those ends seemed nonsense. I saw the old problem anew; and, for a moment, my vision appeared sharp and perhaps interesting. So that autumn I pulled out the dirty manuscript and began to re-write.*

Fate still was waiting for me, for it rather. Early in 1919 *I found myself, through no fault of my own, a professional art-critic and an almost professional* homme d'esprit. *Again the* opus *was abandoned. Only I extracted from it another chapter, published under the title* 'On British Freedom,' *which made a short, and in my opinion admirable, tract, which no one marked. And yet I would still be talking; which is why I have carried to this quie-*

DEDICATION

tude the 1918 *manuscript and from it extracted an essay on civilization.*

You shall hear no more of The New Renaissance. *What remained of the manuscript after this had been extracted fed, some months ago, the central heater. Here is the gist of the old familiar argument, modified by the war, and I think by nothing else. For since the war, the Russian revolution and the Italian* coup d'état, *nothing has happened, and I have read nothing, seriously to alter my conception of civilization or of the means by which it might be attained. Here are the paralipomena of my better thoughts and days, gathered together, unified I hope, well bound and printed certainly, and laid at your feet, dearest Virginia, by your affectionate friend,*

CLIVE BELL.

CASSIS, *April* 1927.

11

I

INTRODUCTION

SINCE from August 1914 to November 1918 Great Britain and her Allies were fighting for civilization it cannot, I suppose, be impertinent to enquire what precisely civilization may be. 'Liberty' and 'Justice' have always been reckoned expensive words, but that 'Civilization' could cost as much as I forget how many millions a day came as a surprise to many thoughtful tax-payers. The story of this word's rise to the highest place amongst British war aims is so curious that, even were it less relevant, I should be tempted to tell it; and in fact only by telling can I explain how this essay took final shape.

'You are fighting for civilization,' cried the wisest and best of those leaders who led us into war, and the very soldiers took up the cry, 'Join up, for civilization's sake.' Startled by this sudden enthusiasm for an abstraction in which till then politicians and recruiting-sergeants had manifested little or no interest, I, in my turn, began to cry: 'And what is civilization?' I did not cry aloud, be sure: at that time, for crying things of that sort aloud, one was sent to prison. But now that it is no longer criminal, nor unpatriotic even, to ask questions, I intend to enquire what this thing is for which we fought and for which we pay. I propose to investigate the nature of our leading war-aim. Whether my search will end in discovery and — if it does — whether what is discovered will bear any likeness to the Treaty of Versailles remains to be seen.

CIVILIZATION

If I remember right, England entered the war because Germany had violated a treaty, it being held that a European war was preferable to an unavenged injustice —*fiat justitia, ruat caelum,* let justice be done though it bring the house down. The unqualified acceptance of this formidable doctrine may well have aroused in reflective minds a sense of insecurity, which sense may have in duced those publicists and politicians who had to justify to chapel-goers and liberal newspaper-readers our declaration of war to back the moral with a religious motive. Whatever the cause, that was what happened. Someone, possibly Mr. Lloyd George himself, more probably Mr. Horatio Bottomley, struck out the daring figure — 'The Cross versus Krupps.' And as from the first the newspapers had welcomed the war as Armageddon, it stood to reason that Kaiser Wilhelm II. was Antichrist. Positively there was something Neronic about him, an alleged taste for music maybe. Besides there were prophecies, signs, and portents in the sky, and the angels pullulating at Mons, all which tended to prove that God was for us and very likely that we were against the devil. And yet, remembering His Imperial Majesty's engaging habit of pressing into the hands of young ladies a little book called *Talks with Jesus,* some of us found the identification unconvincing. Was it quite courteous either to insist on the dogmatic issue, when the French republic was officially agnostic and the Mikado of the Shinto persuasion? And was it prudent to involve the God of the Christians too deeply in a quarrel where French infidels, Japanese miscreants, Moslems and Parsees from India, and cannibals from Senegal, were banded against that pillar of the Catholic Church, the late Emperor of Austria? So, just when we were beginning to wonder whether the war could be

14

exactly described as a crusade, some cautious and cultivated person, a writer in *The Times Literary Supplement*
I surmise, discovered that what the Allies were really up
against was Nietzsche.

That discovery was, at first, a great success. Nietzsche
was a butt for the high outrageous mettle of every one of
us. That he was a German and a poet sufficed to put him
wrong with the ruling class; and since he was said to have
despised mediocrity the middle and lower had some
grounds for disliking him. Down with Nietzsche! Ah,
that was fun, drubbing the nasty blackguard, the man
who presumed to sneer at liberals without admiring liber-
al-unionists. He was an epileptic, it seemed, a scrofulous
fellow, and no gentleman. We told the working men a-
bout him, we told them about his being the prophet of
German imperialism, the poet of Prussia and the lickspit-
tle of the Junkers. And were anyone who had comprom-
ised himself by dabbling in German literature so unpatriotic as to call our scholarship in question, we called him a
traitor and shut him up. Those were the days, the best of
1914, when France and England were defending Paris
against Nietzsche and the Russian steam-roller was catch-
ing him in the back.

And yet this holding of the fort against Nietzsche was
not wholly satisfying either. For one thing it seemed depressing to be on the defensive everywhere. For another
Nietzsche was so difficult to pronounce; and besides it
seemed odd to be fighting against someone of whose existence, six months earlier, not one in ten thousand had
heard. We wanted not merely to be fighting against
things; something we wanted to be fighting for. For
what? Belgium seemed too small, not to say grubby,
Christianity indiscreet, the balance of power old-fash-

ioned, ourselves improbable. We longed for a resonant, elevating and yet familiar objective; something which Christians and Agnostics, Liberals, Conservatives and Socialists, those who had always liked war and those who on principle detested it, those who doted on Marie Corelli and those who thought better of Mr. Wells, those who loved whiskey and those who preferred Lady Astor, those, in a word, who took their opinions from *The Daily News* and those who took them from *The Daily Express* could all feel proud and pleased to make other people die for. And then it was that to some more comprehensive mind, to someone enjoying a sense of history and his own importance, to the Prime Minister or Professor Gilbert Murray I dare say, came the fine and final revelation that what we were fighting for was Civilization: and then to me this urgent query — 'And what is this civilization for which we fight?'

An exact definition I do not hope to give: already I have outgrown that glorious certainty which enabled me in sixty thousand words to tell the world precisely what was art. Yet, as a British general might have stuck the butt end of his cane into a map of France, observing bluffly — 'Your objective must be somewhere hereabouts,' so I, perhaps, can make a smudge on the chart of general ideas and say — 'Civilization lies about there.'

To begin with what is dull and obvious, it seems reasonable to suppose that civilization is good. Were it not we should hardly have been expected to pay so much for it. And if good, it must be good either as an end or as a means. Now, unless when we speak of 'a highly civilized society' we mean the Ideal or Absolute Perfection or Heaven civilization is not the end; and the fact that we do commonly speak of the defects and vices of civilization seems to show that to most of us it is no more than a means. Heaven transcends civility: and a society might be perfectly civilized and yet fall short of the ideal. From which it follows that what I am going to describe, or attempt to describe, is not absolute good but a particular means to good. To estimate its value will be my business later. For the present, we need agree only that, since civilization is good, and since good states of mind are generally allowed alone to be good as ends, civilization is presumably a means to good states of mind: which is of course another reason for rejoicing that those who were fighting for it were those who won the war.

To say that civilization is a means to good is not, be it noted, the same as saying that it is the only means. This I feel bound to mention because of late the opinion has gained ground that unless a means to good be the sole means, it is not a means at all. It is thus that science has fallen into disfavour with a school of thinkers, or perhaps I should say writers, for no better reason than that, in the opinion of these and indeed of most people, a world in which there was nothing but science would be deficient in passion and beauty. The notion that passion and beauty and science may all be good is, I know not why, abhorrent to the romantic neo-Mumbo Jumbo mind both here and abroad. Certainly civilization is not the only means to good. Life, since it is a necessary means to states of mind of any sort, is a means to good: sun and rain, because they are means to life, are means to good also. Certainly, life, sun, and rain are also means to civilization, since without them civilizatiion could not come into being; but they are not the same as civilization, neither are they means to good only in so far as they are means to civilization. In fact, life, sun, rain, bread, wine, beauty, science and civilization are all means to good; and the thing to bear in mind is, that while beauty is a direct means to good, and civilization a mediate, sun, rain and life itself are remote, though essential, means.

I should not have wasted ink and paper on this proposition had I not foreseen that it would lead to another, identical as it happens, yet by the very people who have accepted it in its first and more obvious form sometimes overlooked, especially when they are urging us to do this or that in the interests of civilization: not being the *only* means to good, civilization can not be *any* means to good. Of course, if civilization were the only means to good, it would follow that anything which made for good was a part of civilization. But as civilization is not, it behoves us to pick and choose correctly. In suitable hands, and at the right moment, gin and the Bible are means to good undoubtedly; yet it is a question how far European traders and missionaries are justified in calling what they carry into savage countries civilization. Irrational and uncompromising belief, blind patriotism and loyalty, have often been means to sublime states of mind, to good therefore; but they are not civilization, and to civilization more often than not have proved inimical. Civilization is a particular means to good: and we must be careful not to assume that anything we like or respect is a part of it. We must not assume that it contains all our favourite virtues. We may vastly prefer eating a slice of roast mutton to studying metaphysics; yet it would be rash on that account only to take it for granted that the first was the more civilized of these two admirable occupations. Civilization, which is not the only means to good, which is not any means to good, is a particular means which, on the authority of allied statesmen, and on grounds in my opinion more solid, we may take to be immensely important. Even so we are far from discovering what it is.

The past participle 'civilized' (**Lat.** adj. *civilis*), as those who devoted their best years to the study of these things have the advantage of knowing, is correctly as well as commonly predicated of a state or society (*civitas*). Till the middle of the eighteenth century a Frenchman for *'civilisé'* would have written *'policé,'* and *polis,* you know, means city. When we speak of a civilized age we mean that the society which flourished in that age was civilized. Most commonly and most correctly 'civilization' or 'civility' is attributed to an organized agglomeration of human beings. Less commonly, and rather less correctly, is it predicated of persons — citizens (*cives*). But even a mind unsharpened on the whetstone of gerunds and verbs in *mi* will guess that in fact civilization must be the product of civilized individuals, and that any attempt to understand the nature of the thing or account for its existence leads inevitably and directly to human beings who create and maintain it. Further, unaided common sense will tell us that about individuals we have a chance of making statements more profitable and more probable far than any we can hope to make about an entity so vague and multifarious as a state or society. There is some getting at a man: you can say something fairly definite about the desires and idiosyncrasies of John Smith or Wei Sing; but what for certain can be said about those of Great Britain or China? When we talk of 'China's honour' or 'England's interests,' it is impossible we should mean anything precise, and unlikely that we mean anything at all. Not all the inhabitants of the British Isles have the same interests, neither have all Chinamen the same feelings. But we might be able to name with confidence the ruling passion of a particular Chinaman and trace with assurance a line of conduct that would be favourable to Smith. Had England refrained from declaring war on Germany England, as everyone knows, could never again have held up her head, but I dare say Smith would have kept his nose in the air.

This being so, you might expect me to begin my enquiry into the nature of civilization by attempting to discover what constitutes a civilized man. That would be the logical order; I am debarred from following it by a fact. The fact is that whereas it is pretty generally agreed that certain societies have been civilized, and even highly civilized, there is no such consensus of opinion about persons. My grand object being to discover what civilization is, my first endeavour should be to discover characteristics peculiar to admittedly civilized entities. If before examining the entity 'civilized individual' I examine 'the civilized society,' that will be because of the latter we have universally recognized types.

I shall begin with neither. I shall begin with entities universally reckoned uncivilized; for by doing justice to the characteristics of these I ought to arrive at certain negative conclusions of fundamental importance. I shall know what civilization is not. No characteristic of a barbarous society can possibly be a peculiarity of civilized societies. It cannot be one of those distinguishing characteristics, of those characteristics for which I am looking, which differentiate civility from barbarism. It cannot be of the essence of civility. Not until I have discovered what civilization is not, shall I attempt by seeking its essence in universally accepted types to discover what it is. When in those types I have found — if I can find — common characteristics, not to be found in barbarous societies, I shall have done the first part of my job. I shall have discovered the distinguishing characteristics of civilization.

I am going to elaborate a theory. That theory, if I am to take my readers with me, must be based on assumptions which seem to them fair. I must, that is to say, deduce the peculiar characteristics of civilization from a consideration of entities admittedly civilized and admittedly uncivilized. Now, as I have said, the only entities about the civility or barbarism of which there is a real consensus of opinion are societies: wherefore it is to societies, and not to individuals, that I must look for my distinguishing characteristics. These found, I can go on to consider their source which can be only in the minds of men and women. A group of these, as we shall see, is the veritable fountain. And if we are to push our speculations so far as to enquire whether by cultivating the cause one might hope to magnify the effect — whether, in fact, one might increase civilization — inevitably we shall find ourselves wondering by what means might be produced and maintained greater numbers of highly civilized people. But for the present I must go to societies for my characteristics; for amongst societies alone are to be found specimens unanimously voted savage and others generally reckoned civilized. Two or three, at any rate, there are the high civility of which is not contested by any reasonably well-educated person. These shall be my paragons: to those other three or four, which often are, or have been, reckoned 'highly civilized,' but of which the claims to that title are seriously and on solid grounds disputed I will not go.

Just as there are admittedly civilized societies, there are societies which all the world agrees to call barbarous. These you may admire; you may like them — or think you

21

like them — better than you like civilized societies; but by consent so common are they reckoned savage that anthropologists go to them for some indication of the state of primitive man during those centuries or millenniums when he was ceasing to be a brute or at any rate passing from the palæolithic to the neolithic stage. These admirable anthropologists have made minute studies of the manners and beliefs of the most barbarous of these barbarous peoples; and it is from their studies that I hope to learn at least what civilization is not. Remember, no characteristic, no matter how honourable, can, if possessed by savage communities, possibly be a distinguishing characteristic of civility. Civilized societies may share such characteristics of course: they may possess them either as attributes common to humanity or as relics of barbarism. Also, these characteristics may be valuable and attractive, and far from being peculiar to savages may be possessed by many or most highly civilized people: but because they are not peculiar to civilized societies they will not help us to a definition. Though certain characteristics shared with savages were common to all civilized societies, they would not be distinctive; and distinctive characteristics — peculiarities — are what we are looking for. We want characteristics which are common to all highly civilized societies and which savages are without. Only by disentangling these can we hope to learn what civilization is.

My first business, then, will be to clear the ground. I must eliminate those characteristics that might possibly be taken for tokens of civility were they not shared with the lowest and most undeveloped of savage tribes. To this end I must write a learned chapter, at the foot of whose pages some readers, justly suspicious of my erudition, will look for a forest of notes. They will be disappointed. In so slight and superficial an essay copious footnotes would be out of place. A few there must be; but a few only. For the mass of information in my next chapter I have gone to that classic work, Westermarck's *Origin and Development of the Moral Ideas.* Here the suspicious reader will find warrant for every fact adduced; and here he will find, what is more, a masterly account of the faith and morals of savage peoples, based on monumental learning, supported by innumerable references, and illustrated by fascinating anecdotes. As for footnotes, my objection to them in light literature is, partly that they distract the eye, partly that too often they are a device for shirking the detestable labour of working hard lumps of raw matter into form. If the habit of reprinting articles is to be suffered these long adscititious footnotes must be suffered too. To journalism claiming immortality they are the inevitable complement. But in a light essay which purports to have been conceived as a whole from the first word to the last they are generally a sign of weakness and hardly to be tolerated. It is not that I dislike a show of erudition. On the contrary I am as conscious as another of the considerable dignity conferred on the page by a judicious citation or an imposing name; also the hopeful convert to my views shall not fail to be comforted and confirmed in his faith by meeting, in the text, with some fine ones. But only when I have to make one of those statements that jerk from an unfriendly reader the ejaculation — 'liar,' shall I be at pains, by means of an asterisk, to guide the insult home.

Just now I tried to please this sort of reader by calling my essay slight and superficial. Slight, in every sense, assuredly it will be. Probably in the same way it will be superficial; but when I used the word I was thinking chiefly of its most modern connotation. I meant that I was going to try to be intelligible. I sympathize with those writers who have been obliged by poverty or the exigencies of military service to dispense with education, and I quite understand why they discountenance those who object it has been to express ideas as simply, clearly, and briefly as possible. Such desperate methods would reduce the longest books of many of our best prophets to a very few pages; for when there is no butter to spread you cannot even spread it thin. In such dearth the only thing to do is to dig mysteriously into the loaf, which in literature is called being profound. And though there are readers who, having gone down to the bottom of the pit and there failed to discover the smallest speck of margarine, will venture to call such profundities empty, in the brisker parts of Europe and America the profound style is generally held in honour. In me, however, the airs of a mole or a miner would be mere affectation. Besides, unlike modern poetry and philosophy and philosophic fiction, an essay of this sort cannot hope to appeal to that great public which, in quest of like, brushes aside all hairsplitting distinctions between sense and nonsense. I dare not be profound. And frankly this essay would have been written with all the shallow lucidity of Montesquieu, Hume or Voltaire had the essayist known the secret of their superficiality.

Because I wish to be understood I shall try to be intelligible; for the same reason I shall repeat myself. Long ago I might have learnt from the hoardings that to say the same thing over and over again is the way to convince; but when I was younger, being rather silly about my fellow-creatures, I used to believe that to convey to them one's meaning one had only to state it clearly and once. There was someone in Messrs. Chatto and Windus's publishing house as green as I, who, after reading the MS. of my first book, *Art*, hinted with great delicacy that on one point — the definition of a work of art — I had perhaps insisted excessively. So I had: as a private and exceptional human being 'the reader' was perfectly right, but as a publisher he was wrong. For the public I had not been repetitious enough; and to this day able critics in England and America continue to assert that by 'a work of art' I mean precisely what I said so often I did not mean. Well, I have learnt my lesson. Wherefore, anyone who may notice that in this essay I say the same thing several times over, will be so kind I hope as to attribute the author's tediousness to a peculiarity of readers in general — a peculiarity, I need hardly say, not shared by the particular lady or gentleman who happens to be reading these words.

II

WHAT CIVILIZATION IS NOT

RESPECT for the rights of property is not peculiar to civilized societies. That the brutes have no such respect is true, neither have they flint implements; savage human beings have both, which distinguishes them from the brutes but does not make them civilized. Flint implements and respect for the rights of property may be means to civilization: but no more than flint implements can a sense of those rights be considered a peculiarity of civilization. A contrary opinion has been held by many rich and thoughtful men; but Westermarck tells us that numerous savage tribes have as nice a sense of mine and thine as any English magistrate. Theft would seem to have been almost unknown amongst North American Indians till the coming of the whites, who, in justice be it said, did their best to counteract any moral laxity they might have imported by sending missionaries to remind the natives that eternal punishment awaits those who break the eighth commandment. It must not be supposed, however, that a belief in God and a future life is confined to the civilized,—not here have we our first characteristic; on the contrary, most savage races have a lively faith in God and many make a practice of eating him. The very lowest Australian bushfolk—the most barbarous perhaps of barbarous creatures—'believe in the existence of a supreme being who is a moral lawgiver and judge.' They even call him 'Father' and worship him

26

in the character of an elderly gentleman. Savages are rarely atheists: like us 'they entertain the larger hope.'

At public meetings I have heard ladies say that the measure of a people's civility is the position it accords to women; as the one is high or low so will be the other. This, however, is not the case. From the Bushmen, Andaman Islanders, and Veddahs, than whom no men are much nearer brutes, says Westermarck, women get more consideration that they got from the Athenians in the time of Aristotle. While the uxorious, albeit cannibalistic, males of many savage tribes regard their wives as little less than equals, in those notoriously civilized ages of Tang and Sung the Chinese seem to have regarded theirs as little better than livestock. Indeed, it is clear that many cannibals possess an infinitude of domestic virtues, being kindly, honest, and industrious, generous within their own tribe and hospitable to strangers; whence it seems to follow that even the merits of the British proletariat are not peculiar to civilized societies. The truthfulness of savages has often astounded explorers. The Veddahs of Ceylon are said to be models of veracity, and both Andaman Islanders and Bushmen 'regard lying as a great sin.' On the other hand, the Greeks and Cretans, it will be remembered, had a poor reputation in this respect; while on the continent of Europe the distinctive epithet reserved for Great Britain is 'perfidious.' Not only truthful, many savages are clean. The Megé, a miserable people of the Gold Coast, subject to the savage Monbuttu, 'wash two or three times a day' and wash all over. I wonder how many Europeans from the end of the Roman Empire to the accession of Queen Victoria washed themselves all over once a year.

27

CIVILIZATION

In the important matter of sexual morality the practice of many backward peoples may well provoke our envy. Like Boswell they 'look with horror on adultery.' The forest tribes of Brazil, for instance, are inflexibly monogamous, and so are several of the tribes of California. It seems sad and rather strange that Professor Westermarck should yet have to describe these as 'a humble and lowly race . . . one of the lowest on earth.' 'The Kardok do not allow bigamy even to a chief; and though a man may own as many women for slaves as he can purchase he brings obloquy on himself if he cohabits with more than one.' It is as though a married man should go to bed with his cook. I am not quite sure what the professor means when he says that 'Among the Veddahs and Andaman Islanders monogamy is as rigidly insisted upon as anywhere in Europe;' but, at any rate, the natives of Kar Nicobar are irreproachable. These respectable savages 'have but one wife and look upon unchastity as a very deadly sin.' With them as with many other savage tribes it is punished by banishment or death. 'It is noteworthy,' says Westermarck, 'that to this group of peoples' (the group that feels quite nicely in these matters) 'belong savages of so low a type as the Veddahs of Ceylon, the Igorrotes of Luzon, and certain Australian tribes.' It is noteworthy, he might have added, that whereas unchastity is regarded as a heinous crime by the most abject savages, in the most glorious ages of the world it has been regarded as a peccadillo at worst. Unlike the natives of Kar Nicobar, the most thoughtful and sensitive people in the most brilliant epochs of history have been blind to the horrid sinfulness of fornication. Plato advocated communism in women. Chastity was of small account in the circle of Alcibiades, the court of Hadrian, the Medici gardens, or the salons where Voltaire, Helvétius, and Diderot gave shape to a new intellectual order and preached the philosophy of pleasure. Socrates and Shakespeare, Raphael and Titian, Caesar and Napoleon, the Duke of Wellington and George Eliot herself appear to have led lives that would have rendered them unfit for the best Igorrotes society in Luzon. In the great periods of Chinese history things, I fear, were no better. So, as the natives of Kar Nicobar look upon unchastity as a very deadly sin, we are forced to conclude that chastity is not one of the distinguishing characteristics of civilization.

Let us not flatter ourselves by supposing that patriotism is a peculiarly civilized virtue. The North American Indians are renowned for it, Carver going so far as to say of the Naudowessies — 'the honour of their tribe, and the welfare of their nation, is the first and most predominant emotion of their hearts.' Of the Yorubas of West Africa Mr. MacGregor writes: 'No race of men could be more devoted to their country'; yet, unless I mistake, this tribe has been suspected of eating missionaries. 'Solomon Islanders not seldom die from homesickness on their way to the Fiji or Queensland plantations.' While, according to Mr. Williams, a Fijian, who, having visited the United States, began, at his chief's request, to enumerate the respects in which that country was superior to his own, was promptly put to silence by an indignant audience with cries of 'he is a prating impudent fellow: kill him.' However it may be with chastity, it is clear that as pure a flame of patriotism burns in the Fiji Islands as in any part of Europe. And though few modern nations have much to learn from them, many famous peoples of old might have profited by their example. For instance, the Chinese, soon after the time of Confucius, were learning from their philosophers that we ought to love all men equally: 'according to the Hindu work, Panchatantra, it is the thought of little-minded persons to consider whether a man is one of ourselves or an alien': and Democritus of Abdera held that 'every country is accessible to a wise man, and that a good soul's fatherland is the whole earth.' The later Cyrenaics and Cynics denounced patriotism as ridiculous, and their doctrine developed into that benign Stoic cosmopolitanism which was the religion of Seneca, Epictetus and Marcus Aurelius. 'Il est clair qu'un pays ne peut gagner (he is talking of war) sans qu'un autre perd, et qu'il ne peut vaincre sans faire des malheureux,' was the final judgment of Voltaire.

I think we must take it as settled that neither a sense of the rights of property, nor candour, nor cleanliness, nor belief in God, the future life and eternal justice, nor chivalry, nor chastity, nor patriotism even are amongst the distinguishing characteristics of civilization, which is, nevertheless, a means to good and a potent one. Obviously the essence of civilization is something to which savages have not attained; wherefore it cannot consist in primitive virtues. The antithesis between the noble savage and the civilized man which has been current these two hundred years implies a general recognition of the fact that civilization is not a natural product. We should expect it rather to have to do with those last acquisitions of humanity—self-consciousness and the critical spirit. We should expect it to be the result of education. Civilization is something artificial.

There lingers on, however, a school of thought, drawn chiefly from the half-educated and bumptious smattering a little science, according to which civilization consists in absolute submission to Nature's law.[1] 'Leave it to Nature'

30

is their motto: the brute and vegetable kingdoms are the exemplars of civility. Men have made a mess of it, they say, by not allowing the fittest to survive: we shall not be truly civilized till we leave the weak to die and recognize formally that might is right. The fit shall inherit the earth. The question is, of course, who are the fit? If the physically inferior have succeeded in so organizing society that overwhelming policemen hold the muscular under-graduates of London University in awe, may it not be be-cause the physically inferior are the mentally superior? Cunning quite as much as guts, if we may trust the text-books, has done the work of evolution. After all, that puny mammal, man, has fared better in the struggle for existence than the majestic mammoth. And even a-mongst men, perhaps the fittest to survive have survived. It begins to look as if the naturalist's argument stultified itself. If the survival of the fittest be a law of nature we may assume that the fittest to survive do survive. If, as seems not improbable, war is to become the normal con-dition of humanity, the future will be with those crafty weaklings who adapt themselves to their circumstances by devising means of evading military service, just as in the glacial period those species survived which learnt to pro-tect themselves from the sharpness of the climate. 'You have tampered with Nature's Law,' say the science stu-dents; 'It is our nature to,' we reply.

All this, I fear, will strike the downright biologist as sophistic and vicious; and if he realizes that he is getting the worst of the argument he will most likely fall back on morality. Few can take a higher moral tone than your half-baked man of science, who will brand remorselessly as sloppy, shifty, dishonest, cowardly, mean, silly, senti-mental and altogether pernicious those who believe we ought not to expose rickety children, strangle consumptive artists, or have our loves chosen for us by Professor Ray Lankester. 'We ought,' they exclaim indignantly: but here, again, are they not stultifying themselves? There is no 'ought' in Nature; only 'is.' When the biologist says that we ought not to tamper with Nature he introduces a non-naturalistic, an ethical, criterion. But if ethics are to be used as arguments in favour of Nature's law, with equal propriety they may be used as arguments against. We may say that it would offend our moral sense to murder babies and ailing poets and all those who cannot hope to attain the B1 standard of efficiency: such action, we may say, would not in our judgment make for good states of mind. 'Very well,' says the science student grimly, 'but be sure that if man refuses to obey the law of Nature man will perish.' 'And if,' we reply, 'the sole end and purpose of man's existence be but to continue his species, if the individual have no value save as a means to that end, does it matter?' That any given race of apes should become extinct signifies not a straw; and if man is to live for no other purpose than that for which apes live, his continued existence becomes equally unimportant. Once admit, however, that man exists for some other purpose than that of continuing his species and the whole Imperial Institute quivers to its foundations, since it may be precisely on account of those other purposes that we protect the weak and respect the individual.

The dilemma whose horns I have been furbishing for the benefit of the South Kensington science student is this: either, whatever is, is right; or, man knows better than Nature. In the first case there can be nothing to grumble about; in the latter the biologist must find better grounds for grumbling. The mastodon, having failed in his struggle for existence, goes out. Very well, some other species, carrying on the mastodon's mission, race preservation, takes his place. All is well. If the race of South Kensingtonians perish and one more biologically efficient take its place, where is the harm in that? All is well; Nature's purpose is served. Why should we put ourselves about to preserve the South Kensingtonians unless we believe that their purpose is different from and finer than that of Nature? 'And why,' interjects the reader, 'should you be betrayed by irritation into long-windedness? Surely two sentences would have sufficed to convince anyone that by a civilized society we do not mean a species perfectly organized for its own preservation? What about the pismires?'

There remain one or two other things which it may be just worth pointing out that civilization is not. For instance, elaborate mechanical contrivances are not, as some have supposed, of its essence. It would be worse than stupid, it would be unpatriotic, to hold that Germany, just before the war, was more highly civilized than France, yet in the application of science to industry the Germans surpassed all nations, except perhaps the people of the United States. No one imagines that Melbourne is today as highly civilized as was Athens in the time of Pericles, and we may be sure that the last to make such a mistake would be the best educated inhabitants of that great, electric-lit, train-served, tram-ridden city. Many Frenchmen admit, unwillingly, that even Paris at the present day is less highly civilized than Periclean Athens; but not only all Frenchmen, all educated Americans too, would agree that modern Paris is more highly civilized than New York. It is not denied, however, that in means of communication and transport, in sanitary arrangements and lighting, Paris is still behind the times.

Soon after the Russo-Japanese war I took to dine at a restaurant in Soho, where a dozen very young intellectuals were in the habit of meeting once a week, one of those charmingly modest British officers who have lived so long in a world where it is their duty to be stupid that they have quite forgotten how intelligent they are. We fell, I recollect, to discussing the subject of this essay — 'What is civilization?' Fabianism was a good deal to the fore just then, and some of us were sure that no society could be described as civilized where provision was not made for paupers, invalids, and lunatics; others (ladies were of the party) felt that in a civilized community every adult would have a vote; others again that a truly civilized people would give every poet and artist five hundred a year and establish picture galleries in the provincial towns; others — but perhaps what the others said would not seem so interesting now as it did then. What my soldier said was this: 'I can't tell you what civilization is, but I can tell you when a state is said to be civilized. People who understand these things assure me that for hundreds of years Japan has had an exquisite art and a considerable literature, but the newspaspers never told us that Japan was highly civilized till she had fought and beaten a first-class European power.' The irony was well placed; but the gallant captain himself would have been the last to maintain that proficiency in arms was really a test of civilization. I know he would have denied as strenuously as the merest milksop that the barbarians who overran the Roman empire were civilized, or that the Tartars who overthrew the Sung dynasty and in Central Asia ruined

34

Mahometan culture were anything better than a pack of brutes. With a couple of instances I could have persuaded him. The philanthropists might have been confronted with those examples which just now confounded, or should have confounded, the people who measure civility by mechanical development. And, as for the person who held that a civilized society is one where every adult has a vote, he (or she) was talking manifest nonsense. Political institutions may, or may not, be means to civilization; they cannot be of its essence. Many savage tribes are ruled by despotic chiefs, others appear to be democratic. Athens in her prime was an oligarchy of free citizens, supported by voteless slaves; France, in the eighteenth century, an almost unlimited monarchy. Civilization, we may be sure, has to do with something more fundamental than forms of government.

I have now succeeded, to my own satisfaction, in showing that certain characteristics which are sometimes mistaken for peculiarities of civilization are, in fact, nothing of the sort. I have tried to eliminate the unessential. The primitive virtues are seen to be compatible with barbarism: jellyfish conform to Nature's law: no particular type of political institutions is common to civilized or to barbarous societies: savage hordes have gained great victories and conquered powerful States: and — though here I was trespassing on ground that belongs to a later chapter — not all those societies which educated opinion universally recognizes as having been highly civilized have brought mechanical invention or philanthropic organization to a particularly high state of efficiency. It is these societies, universally recognized by educated opinion as highly civilized, that in my next chapter I must scour for common and peculiar characteristics. Such character-

35

istics I shall take to be the essentials of civilization. Anyone, therefore, who does not share the general, educated opinion as to the high civility of those societies will, since he denies my premises, see no necessity in my conclusions. For him this essay can have no more than an academic interest. I do assume, on the strength of a consensus of educated opinion which amounts almost to unanimity, the high civility of three different societies. I do not assume, nor dream of assuming, that they alone have been highly civilized. I have chosen the three about the high civility of which there appears to be no dispute, and about which I happen to know something. There are societies with strong claims to be considered highly civilized, against whose claims, however, strong arguments are often adduced. Clearly to them I ought not to go for characteristics. Others there are, of which the civility is taken for granted, but about which, it turns out on examination, we know so little that hardly any characteristics can with certainty be ascribed to them. Nevertheless, many people I feel sure will insist on adding to my list, and them I will beg not to quarrel with my conclusions until they have seen whether the characteristics common to my three typical civilizations are not shared by those that they would add. Even if they find it necessary to amend by addition or subtraction my list of civilized characteristics, I see no reason why our difference should be considered fundamental. Between us there may still remain enough common ground to sustain my definition. We shall see.

III

THE PARAGONS

OLD-FASHIONED historians who had a pleasant tidy way of dealing with the past used to plot out from that wilderness four periods of high civilization: the Athenian (the Ionian we should say, if we were exact, which I have no intention of being), from the battle of Marathon, 480 B.C., to the death of Alexander, 323; the first and second centuries of the Roman empire; Italy in the fifteenth and early sixteenth centuries; and France from the end of the Fronde (1653) to the writer's own time if, like Voltaire, he was writing in the eighteenth century, to the Revolution if he was writing in the nineteenth. I suppose no educated man or woman alive would deny the high civility of three out of these four; but many would demur at the name of Rome, while others would wish to add Tang and Sung and what is vaguely known, or rather talked of, as Persian civilization. First on the list almost all would agree to place the Athenian; but whereas some would limit this social masterpiece to that little span of sixty dazzling years which lies between 480 and 420 and is called the age of Pericles, others would protract it to Aristotle and Alexander and stretch it back to Solon. In my admiration for the sixth century, for its sculpture which I consider the supreme manifestation of the Greek plastic genius, for its intellectual ardour from which all serious modern thought descends, I yield to none: nevertheless I share the general disinclination to call the sixth century highly civilized, whereas unhesitatingly I bestow that title on the fifth and without much demur on the fourth. In this feeling, shared I believe by most educated people, lies an important implication: the civilization of an age, we feel, is not to be measured entirely by the beauty of its art or the splendour of its thought. We feel—I, at any rate, feel—that the era of high Athenian civility opens not before Marathon; while, painfully aware though I am of the inferiority, not so much in particular genius as in general alertness, of the post-war period, I cannot admit that the epoch closes before the death of Aristotle (322). From Solon to the final repulse of the Persians seems to me, and to most people I think, a great but not completely civilized age; from the fall of the Athenian democracy to the conquests of Alexander a less great but more highly civilized. Be that as it may, no one is now likely to refuse whatever honour the title 'highly civilized' may be supposed to confer to the age of Plato, the later Aristophanes, Praxiteles, and Aristotle. Few will deny that it is an essential part of that great Athenian civilization to which I shall return again and again, which, indeed, anyone who hopes to discover the nature of civilization must study profoundly and with an open mind.

The claim of any period in Roman history to a place amongst the great ages of civilization is certain to meet nowadays with fervent and effective opposition. No Roman period will be found amongst my paragons; but were I to summarize here the arguments that have convinced me that none is admissible, clearly I should have to anticipate conclusions at which I hope presently to arrive. Since we have not yet decided what are the characteristics of civilization I cannot presume to say that Rome was without them. All I can do is to adumbrate the evidence which has led me to think poorly of the Roman mind and sensibility: and, be it noted, not all of this need, nor indeed will, turn out to be valid against Rome's claim to high civility. It is the fact that her claim is seriously disputed by very many whose dissent is not to be disregarded that makes it improper for me to draw inferences from her history. I will not, however, be so disingenuous as to pretend that I do not share their unfavourable opinion. I will give my reasons, or some of them, at once; but why exactly I consider that Rome was never highly civilized will become apparent only in the course of my essay.

Voltaire held that it was in the first century of the empire that Roman culture reached high-water mark; but an admirer today would prefer to take his stand on the second, I fancy. The barbarism and brutality of the Republic became obvious to historians long ago — so obvious that sharp students began to grow suspicious of later ages. Having begun to wonder whether it was probable that the quality of life had been changed essentially by Caesar's adventure or Cato's *beau geste,* they soon discovered that under the earlier emperors Roman society remained much what it had been in the days of the Republic. For this reason it is the second century, the years between the accession of Nerva and the death of Marcus Aurelius, which is now held by that melting minority which still believes in Roma Dea to have been an age of sweetness and light. A larger and younger school, in which I claim a modest place on the sizar's bench, holds that in all her political transformations Rome remained essentially brutal and uninteresting. In her literature, art, thought and general culture we find nothing of value which is not a dull echo of Greece. To us the vast majority of Latin writers seem never to have conceived of their language as a means of self-expression, but to have used it much as do sixth-form boys, making versions instead of expressing themselves. The bulk of Latin literature has unmistakably the air of an exercise. Roman writers, for the most part, aspired to produce books that should be like books; the notion of writing to express one's own thoughts and feelings was unnatural to them. Wherefore, turning from Homer to Virgil, or from Sophocles to Seneca, is like turning from *Pilgrim's Progress* to a parish sermon. Homer and Sophocles wrote because they had something to say, Virgil and Seneca because it seemed right to say something. Except Catullus and Lucretius what Latin authors have conveyed to us a sense of any real experience? One or two no doubt. Has a single Roman sculptor expressed anything at all? Not that I am aware of. Roman philosophy reminds one of an exceptionally high-toned debate in the House of Commons. The argument, as a rule, is fairly well conducted, but it never brings one within measurable distance of the heart of the matter, and philosophy which is not even trying to reach those parts is apt to be uninteresting. And if their philosophy (e.g. *De Amicitia*, or Seneca's *De Providentia*) reminds one of parliamentary debates, their private correspondence recalls the smoking-room conversation of Victorian senators. It is friendly, sensible, and urbane; never intimate, witty, or romantic. Though Tacitus had his epigrams and Juvenal his invective, of intimacy, wit, and romance the Romans, in general, knew nothing. They could talk reasonably about practical affairs, as reasonably as prefects at public schools. They had jokes, opinions, indignation, appetite. They respected, as does the better sort of English business man, those honourable and

40

friendly obligations that bind man to man in offices and law-courts, in railway-carriages and on the links. But never, never, did they get close to anything that matters; and that is why the strong smell of Rome rolling across the ages reminds me at best of the House of Commons and political dinner-parties, at worst of petrol and patchouli, plush and new leather.

For anything I can see the Romans were incapable of passionate love, profound aesthetic emotion, subtle thought, charming conversation, or attractive vices. They had no sense of the reality of the world of thought and feeling. Such culture as they managed to get they got in the second century, and it was purely Greek: a handful of Greek writers and thinkers illustrate dimly that age. How little this thought leavened the Roman lump may be inferred from the fact that superstition was then so gross that, according to Renan, the better minds were drawn to Christianity chiefly on account of its comparative reasonableness. It was in the second century that Roman law, the greatest and most beneficent product of the empire, was given its familiar character — it was not codified, of course, till more than three hundred years later. Now Roman law, as we know it, is essentially Greek: the eminent jurisconsults, who were Stoics to a man, modifying and developing along lines indicated by their philosophical doctrine the older Roman theories, substituting for the *jus reipublicae* the *jus gentium*. As for Roman taste: it is within the knowledge, as they say, of all tourists that Hadrian, one of the most refined and Hellenized of Roman rulers, built himself at Tivoli a villa which, in description, reminds one oddly of the worst escapades of modern millionaires. The good Gregorovius is agog; '. . . this villa' (says he), 'built according to his (Hadrian's) own

41

design, was the copy and reflexion of the most beautiful things which he had admired in the world. The names of buildings in Athens were given to special parts of the villa. The Lyceum, the Academy, the Prytaneum, the Poecile, even the vale of Tempe with the Peneus flowing through it, and Elysium and Tartarus were all there. One part was consecrated to the wonders of the Nile and was called Canopus after the enchanting pleasure-grounds of the Alexandrians . . . . At a sign from the Emperor these groves, valleys, and halls would become alive with the mythology of Olympus; processions of priests would make pilgrimages to Canopus, Tartarus and Elysium would become peopled with shades from Homer, swarms of bacchantes might wander through the vale of Tempe, choruses of Euripides might be heard in the Greek theatre, and in sham fight the fleets would repeat the battle with Xerxes.' If only it had all gone by electricity it would have been perfect.

That the influence of Rome on the world was enormous no one would deny: nor should one deny that it was in many ways beneficent. That, however, does not prove that the Romans were highly civilized, seeing that as much could be said for the German barbarians who overran and ruined the empire. Just what we owe to Rome is still matter of dispute. But that many competent judges deny her claim to high civilization is unquestionable; wherefore I could not, if I would, draw from her history acceptable data.

Between the death of Boccaccio (1375) and the sack of Rome (1527) the Italians are generally allowed to have attained to a very high pitch of civilization, with which allowance I assuredly find no fault. There are those who murmur against the political methods of the age; and to them I would, in the first place, point out that we are not yet sure that political morality is an essential feature of high civilization; in the second, that political assassination may be a substitute for war, and that the murder of one is generally to be preferred to the murder of thousands. Certainly, amongst the intelligent and cultivated Italians of the Renaissance contempt for brute force was greater than it is amongst Italians today, a comparison which is not, I suppose, much to the purpose.

It cannot be denied that in the fifteenth century Italian writing of which a great part was in Latin suffered from precisely those faults we have deplored in Roman. Rather than a means of expression it is an act of culture, an erudite performance, bearing about the same relation to literature that reading family prayers does to religion. 'Il trecento diceva, il quattrocento chiacchierava,' say the cognoscenti. Not but what the fifteenth century had writers who meant it: Boiardo, Pulci, Sacchetti, and Lorenzo himself. For the visual arts of the Renaissance I presume no apology is required: but people easily forget the seriousness of that age's attempt to give science a foundation in fact. Physics, medicine, and anatomy were again studied by Europeans, and, towards the end of our period, had been pushed almost to the point at which the Greeks left them: geometry and physics were picked up at that point and carried forward: while zoology and botany, I am given to understand, were once again taken seriously. To play the Renaissance off against the middle ages is to deal oneself too strong a hand. But if you have the courage to examine the philosophic syncretisms of the Medicean Platonists you will find that, silly as they are, they conceal beneath their mountainous quilts of metaphysical goose-down an infantile clutching at truth which

distinguishes them from the lucubrations of Roman philosophers who merely restate familiar fallacies with the
complacent and cumbrous air of one who discharges a
moral obligation. Lucretius himself was not original, but
he was exceptional. On the whole, it is true that the men
and women of the Renaissance were concerned intensely
with things that have a real existence in that high world
of thought and feeling which we call spiritual, whereas
almost all that was significant in Roman thought was
concerned with the practical. Rare exceptions apart, the
adventures of the Roman mind in the upper regions were
about as interesting as are the ecstasies of tourists in picture galleries.

It will be objected that the Renaissance was a superstitious age, addicted to astrology and nonsense of that sort,
which is as true as that the scientific spirit was then wider
awake than it had been in Europe since the fourth century B.C. Also, the best minds resisted. Already in the
fourteenth century Petrarch had made an effective stand,
and in the fifteenth Pico della Mirandola seems to have
carried opinion with him in his famous attack on the
mystery-mongers.[2] The novelists, their prince Franco
Sacchetti in the van, poke fun at soothsayers and impos-
tors; and Giovanni Villani says, 'No constellation can
subjugate either the free will of man, or the counsels of
God.' 'How happy,' remarks Guicciardini, 'are the as-
trologers, who are believed if they tell one truth to a hundred lies, while other people lose all credit if they tell one
lie to a hundred truths.' That in general the effect of the
Renaissance was to provoke 'scepticism' is clear, the difficulty is to determine precisely to what this 'scepticism'
amounted. The Inquisition called it 'atheism,' and
stamped it out ruthlessly after 1527, with the aid of the

black Spaniards. If I might generalize from particular cases of which I know something (but which happen to be French) I should say that there were two brands of Renaissance scepticism: an airy Voltairianism not incompatible with a certain amount of mild superstition of which Bonaventure des Périers may serve as a specimen, and a rather dour uncompromising atheism, quite free from supernaturalism, though not from philanthropic superstitions, of which Etienne Dolet — a martyr to truth if ever there was one — stands as type. According to Calvin, Dolet 'méprisait ostensiblement l'Evangile,' and declared that 'la vie de l'âme ne differait en rien de celle des chiens et des pourceaux.' But, indeed, superstition and other vices notwithstanding, the claim of the Italian Renaissance to high civility is not seriously opposed; and M. de Gobineau, than whom no one has better understood its intellectual life can put into the mouth of Lucrezia Borgia the following judgment, 'Il n'existe de grand dans ce monde que l'amour des arts, l'amour des choses de l'esprit, l'amour de ceux qu'on aime.' She is speaking for her age.

The other example of which I can make use without much fear of contradiction is the civilization which flourished in France during *le grand siècle* and the eighteenth century. From 1660 to 1789 is an age less glorious than that of Pericles but hardly less renowned. It is the common opinion, and that it should be so is significant, that whereas the second half of the seventeenth century and early part of the eighteenth is the greater, the second half of the the eighteenth (which ends in 1789) is the more civilized. So here again we have evidence that educated people distinguish between a great age and a civilized, or rather recognize that grandeur and civilization, though by no means incompatible, are not synonymous. What is more, though it is probable that during the first half of this period—from the Restoration to the death of George I.—England played as great a part in the world as France, though it is certain that her intellectual triumphs and literary output were at least equal to anything that was being done elsewhere, though her military achievements· were prodigious, no one would dream of suggesting that England was at that time as highly civilized as her neighbour. And, in passing, may I record the irrelevant but I think not uninteresting fact, that, during the first part of this period, when creatively and intellectually England was more than a match for her rival, England was not yet what France was still, a great imperial power. It was after the peace of Paris, in 1763, that France became intellectually paramount, though her empire had fallen into the hands of the English who had India and America to console them for the loss of Milton, Dryden, Congreve, Marvell, Prior, Pope, Swift, Newton, Boyle, Bentley, and Locke.

There are two or three periods, reputed highly civilized, about which European historians have said little because they know nothing. Under the Tang dynasty (*circa* 600-900 A.D.), and even more under the Sung (960-1279), it looks as though the Chinese had attained a state of exquisite refinement. But our knowledge of both is so meagre, so miserably bare of detail, that the attempt to deduce from either the peculiar characteristics of civilization is one on which only a half-educated journalist passing himself off as a historian would venture. We have Chinese art—paintings, sculpture, ceramics—and certainly it seems fair to assume that the men who created, and still more the men and women who appreciated, such things were in the highest degree civilized: for

THE PARAGONS

Chinese art, and Sung art especially, is not only good but civilized — a distinction on which I shall soon have to dwell. We have Chinese poetry and some prose — in translations. But, for my part, I refuse to draw inferences from translations because no one can tell how much of himself a modern translator may not have worked, unconsciously, into an ancient text. The fact is, Chinese social and political history has been neglected by European scholars; wherefore we, puzzled and misled by a completely unfamiliar temperament and point of view, cannot hope to gain from the scraps of information that come our way any clear idea of how a cultivated Chinese lady or gentleman of the Tang or Sung epoch would have thought or felt about the things that touch and interest us most. It is childish to suppose that from a few pots and pictures, poems, travellers' tales and records (these in translations too) we can conjure up a valid vision of his or her way of life and habits of mind. About the lives of citizens of Periclean Athens, about the Florentines of the Renaissance, and about eighteenth-century Parisians we know enough to be able, by an effort of imagination, to make ourselves a picture. We can even get a rough notion of what our lives lived amongst them would have been. We can imagine our surroundings. We can conjecture, perhaps, how our friends would have spoken and behaved, and how we should have reacted to what they did and said. Such feats of fancy though difficult are not impossible. But to see himself, precisely and with conviction, drinking tea and conversing with a party of cultivated mandarins and their young ladies, about the year 1150, in the sacred city of Hangchow, is, I am persuaded, a feat beyond the fancy of any modern Occidental.

Similar considerations forbid me scouring Persia for instances. That there were one or two periods of high civilization in what is vaguely called Persia is possible and even probable; but to conjure up a definite vision of life at Ispahan, Rhages, or Bagdad (which is not in Persia by the way) is beyond the scope of my knowledge or the power of my fancy. Also, I have noticed that those to whom the task comes most easy have, as often as not, no sure opinion as to where and when the Persia of their dreams existed. The Abbasid empire at the height of its glory stretched from Bokhara to the Mediterranean and from the Causasus to the extremity of Arabia. That this empire, centering on Bagdad and ruled about the year 800 by Haroun al-Raschid, supported a considerable civilization is clear enough to all the gorgeous East school, and not less so perhaps to those precisians who distinguish it from a quite different civilization which flourished in the eleventh and twelfth centuries, and was made illustrious by the school of Firdousi and by Omar Khayyám. And what do we know of either? There is a vast literature, some part of which has been translated: but, since the reputation of Persian poetry stands high with those who know the language, I assume that such translations as I have read are faithless to the text. In the eighteenth century the admirable Jones laid a foundation on which Persian history might have been built: but I can think of no modern writer on mediæval Persia who has succeeded in making the subject real to himself even; and I dare say one gets a better idea of how things were in the tenth and eleventh centuries at Bagdad or Ispahan from M. Dozy's *Histoire des Musulmans d'Espagne* than from any modern book that purports to treat of Asia. There was a great art? Yes; but unluckily it is the product of different ages and cultures. There is the Sassanian art of the fifth and sixth centuries, running on, with its exquisite textiles,

long after the Arab conquest into the tenth. There exist a
few superb paintings of the thirteenth century—the age
of Genghis Khan—revealing Sung and Sassanian influences; and the early thirteenth century is also the familiar age of Rhages pottery. In the fourteenth come Timour, and Háfiz, and Sultanabad ware. But the ordinary
Persian art with which most people are fairly well acquainted is the Sefevean art of the sixteenth and seventeenth centuries. It is to this art, and to the seventeenth-
century court of Shah Abbas, that our picturesque authors, painters, and stage-managers go first for their vision
of Persian life; and by confounding Persia with the Kali-
fate, by mixing up Sassanian textiles of the sixth century
with Samanid poetry of the eleventh, by installing the
Rhages potters and Háfiz at the court of Shah Abbas, and
confusing the Shah with the great Mogul, they obtain a
sweet and viscid compound which they are pleased to call
Persian civilization. And if they can bring home from the
Levant some Turkish cloaks and trousers in which to send
their wives to dinner-parties dressed as Persian princes, so
much the better for them. But to me, ignorant of the
language, and aware of all these things, to form an idea
of Persian civilization seems a difficult, if not impossible
task. Wherefore, in my search for civilized characteristics
I shall say nothing about the almond trees of Samarkand
or the bulbuls that almost invariably sing in them.

Fifth and fourth century Athens, then, Renaissance Italy, and France from Fronde to Revolution, shall be our
paragons: their claim to high civility is undisputed, and
we happen to know something about them. My immediate purpose is to discover characteristics which are common to them and are not possessed by notoriously savage
tribes. If my quest prove something less desperate than

the proverbial hunt in a bottle of hay that will be because I have already given myself a hint. For, discussing the characteristics of abject savages I said — and no one contradicted me I think — that the first step a savage takes towards civilization — I was speaking of moral characteristics of course — is the acquisition of self-consciousness and a habit of reflection. These are not the distinguishing qualities of high civility of course: they are much too common. But it is true to say that an almost complete lack of self-consciousness — other than that brute self-consciousness which a dog will sometimes manifest when he knows he is being stared at — and of even a rudimentary critical sense is what distinguishes the lowest barbarians from the rest of mankind. It is a broad anthropological distinction comparable with that drawn by biologists between animal and vegetable, and helpful only as a point of departure. But refine these qualities, and Self-Consciousness, which leads to examination and comparison of states of mind, will give you the Sense of Values, while the Critical Spirit, universally applied, leads on to the Enthronment of Reason as ultimate arbiter in questions of fact. Here we have characteristics which not savages only, but all inferior societies are without; and in ransacking my paragons of civility for common and peculiar qualities I shall expect to find that all spring from one or the other.

My notion is that a Sense of Values and Reason Enthroned are the parent qualities of high civilization, and that the search for characteristics that I am about to undertake will resolve itself into a search for their children. Very likely someone will discover that, right though I may be so far as I go, I have not gone far enough, that there exist other ancestors and other offspring. That will not necessarily invalidate my conclusions: my essay will be proved incomplete but not necessarily incorrect. If, after examining my characteristics, someone discovers others common and peculiar to high civilizations, clearly I shall have to add them to my list. But only the demonstration that some of those in my list were shared by barbarous peoples would force me to abandon my position.

A sense of values, as I understand the term, is possessed only by those who are capable of sacrificing obvious and immediate goods to the more subtle and remote. People who deliberately sacrificed comfort to beauty—with no practical or superstitious end in view—would appear to me to possess a sense of values. To prefer a liberal to a technical education, an education that teaches how to live rather than one that teaches how to gain, is another manifestation of this highly civilized sense. Reason is to my mind enthroned when there is a prevalent opinion that everything requires, and must ultimately admit of, a rational explanation and justification. But it must not be supposed that when I call a society reasonable, or say that it possesses a sense of values, I mean that all the individuals who compose that society habitually act and think reasonably or feel subtly. Reason may be enthroned in a society where hundreds of thousands are given to the grossest superstition. To call a people reasonable or discriminating is no more exact a generalization than to call a people fair or dark. Also, the enthronement of reason will give different results in different conditions. At Athens it gave elementary speculations as to the meaning of good and the nature of matter, in the eighteenth century it produced religious scepticism and a taste for political economy. What we are about to deal in are the tendencies of vague entities—of societies. We cannot hope,

51

therefore, to make generalizations that will admit of no exceptions.

We must bear in mind that there never has been a perfect civilization. If we conceive the sense of values and enthronement of reason as the parent qualities from which descend civilized characteristics, we must figure these characteristics as a basketful of slippery marbles of which each civilization has grasped what it could. The sense of values and the critical spirit have spawned a heap of Possibilities: of these some have never been grasped; others have been grasped by every society that has raised itself a little above sheer barbarism; while a few — refinements for the most part of qualities which all civilized societies have clutched at — are so polished and elusive that they have slipped through most fingers and yet have been held more or less firmly in a few favoured hands. These favoured and prehensile hands are the groups, the societies, which we agree to call 'highly civilized.' And it is to the discovery and description of the rare and runaway qualities they have grasped, and for a time made their own, that I am about to address myself. Utterly savage tribes, be it noted, have grasped none.

The enthronement of reason as prime arbiter in life is impossible in savage communities for several reasons, of which one of the most obvious is that in savage communities conditions are too precarious and, as a rule, the struggle for existence too acute to admit of the necessary subordination of the instincts of self and family preservation. In fact, the man with a gun is far better equipped for self-preservation than the man with a club, but the savage has never lived in conditions favourable to that sustained and obstinate reflection which alone can lead to such complicated mechanical inventions as guns. The savage who stops to think runs a considerable risk of stopping altogether. So, like the birds and Sir John Falstaff, he acts on instinct; and on instinct he depends so much that reason has very little chance of coming effectively into play. The ascendancy of instinct is fatal to reason. Similarly savages cannot have a nice sense of values: no Eskimo can realize that the ultimate value of a sonnet is greater than that of a roasted egg, because the immediate value to him of a roasted egg is altogether too pressing and palpable. In vain do you demonstrate to one living under present threat of death by starvation or frost-bite the superiority of a liberal over a purely practical education. Before he can appreciate good states of mind he must have some security of person. And so the judgments of savages are mostly instinctive and their beliefs traditional, while their tastes are founded on too limited an experience to admit of fine discriminations. The savage who begins to criticize intellectually the customs and conventions of his tribe soon ceases to exist or ceases to be savage: he has taken a long step towards civilization. So has he who begins, ever so dimly, to perceive that the true value of things is their value as means to states of mind. But so long as a man remains natural and follows instinct he will not go far towards civilization. Civilization comes of reflection and education. Civilization is artificial.

THEIR CHARACTERISTICS: THE SENSE OF VALUES

IF a dozen tolerably educated people (I am becoming a little tiresome about this epithet 'educated,' but by omitting it I stultify my argument) were asked to name the preeminent characteristic of the Athenian mind, eleven would be likely to reply 'love of knowledge' or 'of truth' or 'curiosity' or 'belief in the intellect' or 'reasonableness' or something of that sort. The twelfth, however, with an air of superior subtlety, might well maintain that what really made the Athenians Attic was their exquisite sense of values. What is more, the eleven, so soon as they had got over their pardonable vexation, would almost certainly agree that all were right, that reasonableness and a sense of values were the twin characteristics of Athens in her prime. *Sōphrosunē* (sweet reasonableness) and *spoudaiotēs* (appropriate seriousness) were, as every schoolboy who begins his education on the classical side is informed, the qualities that distinguished Greek life, thought and art: the one is Reason, sweetened by a Sense of Values, the other a Sense of Values, hardened and pointed by Reason. The very word 'classical,' whose first meaning, according to my dictionary, is 'pertaining to ancient Greece or Rome (her ape),' suggests reasonableness and taste. And these qualities which, with their children, were the distinguishing characteristics of Ath-

ens, we shall find, unless I mistake, distinguishing every
age of high civilization.

Athenian respect for art and thought is proverbial.
That story of a sculptor who, accused of torturing a
youth — and torture in the eyes of the Athenians was an
abominable crime — admitted the charge, but, having
produced in defence the superb statue for which the con-
tortions of his model had served was acquitted — that
story, I say, though certainly fabulous, illustrates the impression left on the ages by Athenian aestheticism. At
Lesbos the effigy of Sappho, whose name is mentioned
with reluctance in the nicest English homes, adorned the
coins; for by the Lesbians 'the supreme head of song' was
accounted the supreme glory of the state. And, by the
way, a pathetic relic of Italian civility is to be discovered
in the fact that the head of Salvator Rosa, the only
painter, I will not say of merit, but of repute, that Naples
ever produced, still decorates the notes of the Banco di
Napoli. The respect paid by Athens to things of the intellect is notorious. An open-minded and severely intellectual discussion of every question that came into their
heads seems to have been one of their principal occupations. 'Ce peuple, rieur et curieux,' says Michelet, 'plus
qu'aucun jeu d'athlète estime l'ironie socratique.' And
who can forget that extraordinary thing which happened
at Athens in the year 404 B.C., the performance, in the
state theatre and at public cost, of the *Lysistrata?* Not
only was Athens in the throes of what, for once, may
fairly be described as 'a life and death struggle,' she had
just suffered the crushing disaster before Syracuse which
was to lead to her final ruin. War-fever was raging. Not
the less did the Athenian state give in the public theatre,
at the public expense, this violently anti-militarist and

anti-patriotic play. That the army was ridiculed, patriotic sentiments held cheap, Spy-hunters and Spartaneaters mocked, and the leaders of the democracy mercilessly flayed made no difference. Was the *Lysistrata* the best comedy of the year? That was the question. If so, it ought to receive the prize and a public performance. And performed it was. I can recall nothing in history that manifests more brilliantly a public sense of values.

At Athens the moneys set apart for the theatre were made sacred and inviolate. Not unnaturally, perhaps, did a public which could appreciate the profoundest tragedies and subtlest comedies make art the first charge on the exchequer. The citizen who lived in conditions of simplicity which a British coal-miner would consider derogatory to his human dignity, grudged nothing that was to be spent on the production of plays, the erection of statues, or the construction of temples. And that reminds me of something I should have said in my first chapter: amongst the many things civilization is not—it is not comfort. That savages live uncomfortably proves nothing; for I am not saying that discomfort is but that comfort is not characteristic. The life of an Athenian, so rich and complex in thought and feeling, was in most material blessings indecently deficient. Of civilization, as the shop-walker understands it, the Athenians had next to none; and I am glad to see that Mr. Wells has had the honesty to confess his contempt for such ungenteel people. The richest citizens seem often to have slept on the dining-room chairs—to be sure they were benches almost—wrapping themselves up in their ulsters like so many third-class passengers. The houses of the Athenians were small, unpretentious, and devoid of labour-saving devices: domestic conveniences there were

56

none. The furniture and utensils were scanty and plain, and would have provoked the patronizing pity or moral indignation of a class-conscious dustman. And this indifference to comfort was not peculiar to the highly civilized citizens of Athens. Who has not heard English and American tourists animadvert on the extreme inconvenience, draughtiness, and publicity of Italian palaces? The Renaissance had luxury and magnificence and for comfort cared little. Comfort came in with the middle classes. In the eighteenth century the French aristocracy still maintained a tradition of style, keeping *le confort anglais* at a distance; and thirty years ago it was still a general complaint that travelling in France was spoilt by the lack of domestic amenity. They are changing all that now, which, however, is none of my present business. My business is to note that this civilized unwillingness to sacrifice style to comfort is an inevitable consequence of the sense of values.

Hardly less notorious than the aestheticism and intellectuality of Athens is the extraordinary honour paid by the Italians of the Renaissance to poets and painters, philosophers and scholars. The Florentines, at that time the most ardent politicians in Europe, yet felt that their art was the greatest glory of their state. In Tuscany the merits of painters and sculptors were canvassed as hotly as in Yorkshire are those of footballers and jockeys. All Italy could not do honour enough to Petrarch, and Boccaccio, Brunelleschi and Mantegna, Bembo and Bibbiena, Politian, Ariosto, Raphael, Michael Angelo and Titian. Indeed, it is no exaggeration to say that, though they had known and admired such extraordinary figures as Lorenzo the Magnificent, Savonarola, Caesar Borgia, Julius II. and Leo X., the Italians of the early sixteenth century, in Rome and Florence at any rate, regarded Raphael and Michael Angelo as the supreme expressions of their country's genius. Such men were honoured above kings and princes: but, what is much more important, art — not artists but art — was honoured above trade, politics and war. Let us confess at once, that, though the honour paid to art and thought was as just as it was splendid, the homage paid to individuals was excessive. How should an age of which one of the chief characteristics was a frenzied cult of the individual not deify almost its great men? An over-emphatic assertion of personality was not so much amiss either in people who had only just escaped from the oppression of the middle ages to learn, in the words of Leon Battista Alberti, that 'Men can do all things if they will.' For a thousand heavy years Europe had crouched under a dogma which bade man consider himself a miserable reprobate incapable by nature of right thinking, feeling, or acting. His humanity he was to hold loathsome, the assertion of his personality a tremendous crime: so they had been telling him for a thousand years. And now, suddenly, by the discovery of Greek art and thought, he was made aware that man is the measure of all, that he can and must think and feel and act for himself, that it is for him to create his circumstances, and, mastering nature, to devise and carry out vast experiments. What wonder if men, realizing on a sudden that in the ancient world man had been, that in the new world he could be, master of his fate; that the human intellect is sole judge of truth; that the human will can make and unmake law and custom, changing what had seemed to be the predestined order of the universe; — what wonder, I say, if the Italians of the Renaissance, drunk with the revelation of man as the master and measure of all, paid honours wellnigh divine to those superb examples of their race visible amongst them, creating beauty, dissipating ignorance, exuding force, changing the very conditions of life and enriching its content?

In her sense of the supreme importance of art and thought, which is the first and fairest consequence of a sense of values, Renaissance Italy yields hardly to Athens herself. 'Il n'existe de grand dans ce monde que l'amour des arts, l'amour des choses de l'esprit, l'amour de ceux qu'on aime': it shall stand as her motto. Though the bent of the eighteenth century's mind was not essentially different, in one important respect that age was quite unlike the Renaissance or the age of Pericles. The eighteenth century was not greatly creative. The creative impulse came earlier—in the seventeenth: the later period when civilization was at its highest was devoted rather to speculation and contemplation. So here again is evidence that the essential characteristic of a highly civilized society is not that it is creative, but that it is appreciative: savages create furiously. The eighteenth century understood the importance of art; and its taste, though limited, was pure enough. In the minor and domestic arts it could discriminate finely; and the rich were willing to pay for beauty not in cash only but in time and trouble. The rich men and women of the eighteenth century cultivated their taste. The poor, as I hope presently to show, so long as to be poor means to be unfree and uneducated, are concerned actively with civilization only in so far as by their labours they make it possible, and, passively, in so far as their manners, habits, opinions and sentiments are coloured by it. For the positive and unmistakable characteristics of civilization it is useless to go to Athenian slaves or French peasants. How far it may be possible in the

CIVILIZATION

future for whole populations to become civilized is a question I must reserve for my last chapter.

At present I am dealing with the eighteenth century, an age in which the fire that glowed on the heights radiated to the upper middle class and perhaps just warmed the lower. I can hardly think it went further though, in the opinion of Buckle, who may be reckoned a pretty good judge and no flatterer of any age but his own, 'one of the leading characteristics of the eighteenth century, and one which pre-eminently distinguished it from all that preceded, was a craving after knowledge on the part of those classes from which knowledge had hitherto been shut out.'3 Knowledge was the grand desideratum: the eighteenth century, though it respected art, reserved its finest enthusiasm for things of the intellect. Athens had excelled in literature, the plastic arts, science, and philosophy, and her enthusiasm for all had been boundless; the Renaissance which excelled in visual art and erudition reserved its most fiery admiration for these; while the generous heart of the eighteenth century, obeying the same instinct, thrilled most intensely to the triumphs of the speculative intelligence. Mathematical, philosophical, and scientific investigation came first; and an age which prided itself on philanthropy naturally set store by political science and economy—studies still in their fresh and attractive infancy—wherein, they believed, not unreasonably perhaps, lay the keys that one day would unlock the gates of Utopia. The story of David Hume's success in Paris gives an idea of the tone of polite society. His appointment as secretary to the British Embassy was an international event. *Tout Paris* was at his feet, slightly at the annoyance of Mr. Walpole, who seems to have felt that this highly civilized society perhaps underrated the value of a good accent and aristocratic connections. I shall not insist on the honours paid to Voltaire, Buffon, or the memory of Newton; but I will just venture to remind my readers that these French ladies and gentlemen did actually read the authors they admired.

From this sense of values, from the intellectual curiosity of the *beau monde,* flowed a consequence which has for ever endeared the eighteenth century to civilized people: these studious fine ladies and gentlemen were not to be bullied or bored. They were not the sort to put up with a crack-brain style or erudite prolixity. They insisted that their teachers—Catherine the Great was fond of styling herself 'élève de Voltaire'—should express themselves in pleasant and perspicuous language. So much deference was Science expected to pay, if not to beauty, at least to *ton.* The eighteenth century had standards, and it liked to see them respected. Nor were these standards confined to the writing of prose: the eighteenth century had standards in life. Indeed, it is a mark of civilized ages that they maintain standards below which things must not fall. This comes of having a sense of values.[4]

Have you never heard a great good-humoured fellow, replete with a fabulously expensive dinner in an impressively ill-furnished and overlit restaurant, excited by Saumur (recommended as Perrier Jouet, 1911), and a great deal of poor conversation half-drowned by even noisier music, observe, as he permits the slovenly waiter to choose him the longest cigar, 'That will do, sonny; the best's good enough for me'? That sort of thing happens when people have lost their standards: also, there are now but two or three restaurants in London where it is an unqualified pleasure to dine. The best is not good enough for one who has standards, who knows precisely what he wants and insists on getting it. The modern Englishman apparently has none: to go to the most ostentatious shop and there buy the most expensive thing is all that he can do. Fifty years ago the nice housewife still prided herself on knowing the right place for everything. There was a little man in a back street who imported just the coffee she liked, another who blended tea to perfection, a third who had the secret of smoking hams. All have vanished now; and the housewife betakes herself to the stores. The March Hare's paradox has ceased to be paradoxical: no longer do we insist on getting what we like, we like what we get. It is a small thing, perhaps, that you may dine at any of the half-dozen 'smartest' restaurants in London, pay a couple of pounds for your meal, and be sure that a French commercial traveller, bred to the old standards of the provincial ordinary, would have sent for the cook and given him a scolding. Consider, however, the cause: it is not that the most expensive English restaurants fail to engage the most expensive French *chefs*; they are engaged, but they soon fall below the mark because there is no one to keep them up to it. The clients have no standards. It is a small thing: but that way barbarism lies.

When I say that civilization insists on standards I am not falling into that antiquated error of supposing that civilization is something which imposes a grievous uniformity on the individual. The critics and scholars of the Victorian age, too coarse and insensitive to appreciate Racine and Poussin, explained the inferiority of these artists to Tennyson and Turner by the fact that they were products of an excessive civilization which made impossible free personal expression and put an absolute veto on experiment and development. Highly civilized ages, so the story ran, insisted on absolute uniformity: they were stiff and rigid. As a matter of fact, artists have experimented quite as freely in civilized as in other ages : you may pick instances where you please. At Athens, within a little more than a hundred years, there was a change from the archaic style in sculpture to the Phidian, and from the Phidian to the Praxitelean ; in literature from Aeschylus to Sophocles, and from Sophocles to the new comedy. In Italy the beginning of the fifteenth century saw a revolution in painting — the end of the Giottesque movement and the discoveries of Masaccio, Castagno, and Mantegna, while before the sack of Rome Raphael and Michael Angelo had again modified the tradition and founded a new school. Every student of French literature knows that the admirers of Corneille were surprised and even shocked by the style of Racine, and the development of eighteenth out of seventeenth century prose is what no extension lecturer suffers his victims to ignore. The rise of a school of sentiment and nature in the second half of the eighteenth century was generally expatiated on, out of national vanity I presume, by those very critics who denounced the static uniformity of that age. They did not know, perhaps, that at about the same time Gluck and his followers were giving almost as sharp a turn to the musical tradition as was to be given a hundred years later by Wagner.

Civilized ages do no doubt tend to respect tradition in art as in other things ; and there is a danger that respect for tradition may degenerate into worship of conventions, which — unlike tradition which is the expression of accumulated experience — are no more than the tricks and habits of a recent past standardized for general use. On the other hand, in civilized ages there will be a sensitive and cultivated public, in sympathy with the artist, and disposed to allow him to know best what is best for himself. Such a public will not easily be gulled into mistaking an accepted formula for the great tradition. Neither Masaccio and his followers, nor the school of early eighteenth-century prose-writers, nor towards the close of that century the early Romantics, had to join in such bitter battles as those that raged round the names of Hugo, Wagner, Rossetti, Mallarmé, and Cézanne. Because in civilized ages the public was less brutally insensitive than it was in the nineteenth century, because circumstances were less exasperatingly unsympathetic, the artist was not often driven into noisy and wasteful protest. No genuine artist is a protestant by nature. The role is forced on him by the malevolence of his contemporaries. And protestantism is the bane of art, for he who begins in protesting is in danger of ending on a tub. Civilization tends to make protestation unnecessary.

The uniformity of highly civilized ages, such as it is, though it may have disadvantages of which presently I must speak, is not fatal to art. Partly it is, no doubt, the consequence of a formidable and instructed public opinion not lightly to be disregarded; largely, it comes of the fact that artists, finding themselves in a well-disposed world, are relieved from the necessity of making spectacular protests. Between artist and public in a highly civilized society there is a good deal of common ground which the former has no reason to suspect of being treacherous or to despise as being probably barren. On the contrary, he assumes sympathy and understanding; and because a civilized public is less likely than another to mistake the debris of moribund movements for tradition, he feels no intolerable fear of having his hands tied with conventions. In a highly civilized age the artist is neither hostile to nor mistrustful of tradition, but helps himself freely to whatever it can give. And another cause of apparent uniformity in highly civilized ages is to be found in another characteristic of highly civilized societies, a characteristic which springs partly from a sense of values, partly from reasonableness, and is closely related to the civilized insistence on standards: highly civilized societies are polite.

Good manners are an amenity the value of which people with a sense of values will not under-estimate. But good manners come also of that reasonableness which is the other prime characteristic of civilization, since from reasonableness come open-mindedness, a willingness to listen to what others have to say, and a distaste for dictatorial methods. As, however, I am now trying to describe the defluents of the civilized sense of values, I shall not trespass on ground I propose to cover in another chapter. We will, if you please, leave reasonableness and her children alone. It is clear that a sense of values which seeks to extract from life the best that it can give will of itself insure politeness—his best being what no man parts with for anything less.[5] Also, one possessing a sense of values will not fail to appreciate the sheer intrinsic superiority of courteous over emphatic and ill-bred behaviour. How this civilized taste for urbanity will affect young, original and enterprising artists will depend to some extent on their temperaments. But there are always two ways of compassing a change, the intelligent and seemly, and the blackguardly and strident. Civilized people prefer the former.

I am not, of course, being so silly as to pretend that the artists of civilized ages are superior to those of uncivilized. Art can flourish in either; it can turn either to account. We do feel that some artists are highly civilized,

CIVILIZATION

Phidias, Sophocles, Aristophanes, Raphael, Racine, Molière, Poussin, Milton, Wren, Jane Austen, and Mozart; we do feel that others are not, the builders of the Gothic cathedrals, Villon, Shakespeare, Rembrandt, Blake, Wordsworth, Emily Brontë, Whitman, Turner, Wagner, and the Congolese fetish-makers: we cannot say that one set is superior to the other. The fact is, the difference between them is not fundamental: it is a matter of means, not of ends. The end of art is the same everywhere and at all times — the perfect expression of a peculiar state of aesthetic ecstacy or, as I should say, the creation of significant form. It is in the means by which they achieve this end, in their attitude to and their attack on the problem, that civilized artists differ from uncivilized. Art is one of the two most personal things in the world. Wherefore, fully to appreciate the peculiarities of civilized art, we should have to consider those of the civilized individual; and as this individual is presently to have a whole chapter to himself I think we may allow the civilized artist to wait his turn. For the moment I need say only that it is foolish to suppose that civilized artists are either superior or inferior to uncivilized, and no wiser to maintain that civilization is either favourable or unfavourable to art. Of our three typical societies two were extraordinarily creative, the third ordinarily so. Civilization is neither favourable nor unfavourable: but, because different temperaments thrive in different atmospheres, it seems probable that civilization may be the one or the other to particular artists. How many mute, inglorious Miltons, Raphaels, and Mozarts may not have lost heart and gone under in the savage insecurity of the dark ages? And may not the eighteenth century, which clipped the wings of Blake, have crushed the fluttering aspirations of a dozen Gothically-minded geniuses and laughed some budding Wagner or Webster out of all idea of self-expression?

The popular theory that high civilizations necessarily impose uniformity on individuals is what popular theories generally are: consider the Renaissance. Nevertheless where the standard of culture and intelligence is high, clearly the exceptional person will be less inclined and less likely to distinguish himself from the mass than where it is low. Thus there may arise a tendency to uniformity. This is a danger of civilization; but a mere glance at history suffices to show that it is not a characteristic. A danger it is however. And as I wish to be fair, and as I have insisted from the first that civilization was not the ideal I shall, with your leave, devote a few pages to trying to show, by means of an example, just what this danger amounts to. Let us consider the case of France and England.

An Englishman of any superiority must stand on his own feet, becuase there is nothing about him on which he could deign to lean.[6] He must make his own way, because all public roads lead through intolerably dreary country to intellectual slums and garden suburbs. The life of a first-rate English man or woman is one long assertion of his or her personality in the face of unsympathetic or actively hostile circumstances. An English boy born with fine sensibility, a peculiar feeling for art, or an absolutely first-rate intelligence, finds himself from the outset at loggerheads with the world in which he is to live. For him there can be no question of accepting those national conventions which express what is meanest in a distasteful society. To begin with, he will not go to church or chapel on Sundays: it might be different were it a question of going to Mass. The hearty conventions of family life which make almost impossible relations at all intimate or subtle arouse in him nothing but a longing for escape. He will be reared, probably, in an atmosphere where all thought that leads to no practical end is despised, or gets, at most, a perfunctory compliment when some great man, who in the teeth of opposition has won to a European reputation, is duly rewarded with a title or an obituary column in *The Times*. As for artists, they, unless they happen to have achieved commercial success or canonization in some public gallery, are pretty sure to be family jokes. Thus, all his finer feelings will be constantly outraged; and he will live a truculent, shamefaced misfit, with *John Bull* under his nose and *Punch* round the corner, till, at some public school, a course of compulsory games and the Arnold tradition either breaks his spirit or makes him a rebel for life.

In violent opposition to most of what surrounds him, any greatly gifted, and tough, English youth is likely to become more and more aware of himself and his own isolation. Meanwhile, his French compeer is having rough corners gently obliterated by contact with a well-oiled whetstone, and is growing daily more conscious of solidarity with his accomplices in a peculiar and gracious secret. France, in fact, has still a civilization. The English lad grows more and more individualistic. Daily he becomes more eccentric, more adventurous and more of 'a character.' Very easily will he snap all conventional cables and, learning to rely entirely on himself, trust only to his own sense of what is good and true and beautiful. This personal sense is all that he has to follow; and in following it he will meet with no conventional obstacle that he need hesitate for one moment to demolish. English civilization, or what passes for civilization, is so smug and hypocritical, so grossly Philistine, and at bottom so brutal, that every first-rate Englishman necessarily becomes an outlaw. He grows by kicking; and his personality flourishes, unhampered by sympathetic, clinging conventions, nor much — and this is important too — by the inquisitorial tyranny of Government: for, till the beginning of the war at any rate, an Englishman who dared to defy the conventions had less than a Frenchman to fear from the laws. As a result of all this, England is not a pleasant country to live in for anyone who has a sense of beauty or humour, a taste for social amenities, and a thin skin: on the other hand, we have that magnificently unmitigated individualism and independence which have enabled particular Englishmen of genius to create the greatest literature in all history and elaborate the most original, profound and fearless thought in modern.

If it takes two to make a quarrel it takes as many to make a bargain; and if even the best Frenchmen are willing to make terms with society, that must be because society has something to offer them worth accepting. What French society has to offer is French civilization. Conventions are limitations on thought, feeling, and action; and, as such, the enemies of originality and character, hateful, therfore, to men richly endowed with either. French conventions, however, have a pleasant air of liberality, and France offers to those who will be bound by them partnership in the least imperfect of modern civilizations. The bribe is tempting. Also, the pill itself is nicely coated. Feel thus, think thus, act thus, says the French tradition, not for moral, still less for utilitarian, reasons, but for aesthetic. Stick to the rules, not because they are right or profitable, but because they are seemly — nay, beautiful. We are not telling you to be respectable, we are inviting you not to be a lout. We are

69

offering you, free of charge, a trademark that carries credit all the world over. 'How French he (or she) is!' Many a foreigner would give his eyes to have as much said of him.

In noting the consequence of this French respect for the rules, we have to register profit and loss. What France has lost in colour she has gained in fertility; and in a universal Honours List for intellectual and artistic prowess the number of French names would be out of all proportion to the size and wealth of the country. Furthermore, it is this traditional basis that has kept French culture up to a certain level of excellence. France has never been without standards. Therefore it has been to France that the rest of Europe has always looked for some measure of fine thinking, delicate feeling, and general amenity. Without her conventionality it may be doubted whether France could have remained so long the centre of civilization. On the other hand, it is true that the picture presented by French history offers comparatively few colossal achievements or stupendous characters. With the latter, indeed, it is remarkably ill supplied: and whereas most of the great and many of the secondary English writers, thinkers, and artists have been great 'characters,' the slightly monotonous good sense and refinement of French literary and artistic life is broken only by a few massive and surprising figures. I cannot doubt that a certain number of Frenchmen, born with a promise of high originality, never succeed in being or expressing themselves completely, because they are enticed by the charms of the French tradition into accepting conventions and conforming to rules. 'C'est convenu,' 'C'est inadmissible' are phrases that start much too readily to the tongues of intelligent and well-educated Frenchmen. That is because they have never been compelled, as their English compeers have, to think and feel and find a way for themselves on pain of having to pass their lives imprisoned, like Chinese male-factors, in a box where they can neither lie nor sit nor stand nor lean nor kneel, nor do anything but wallow. And so I admit that gifted young Frenchmen accept conventions and rules of life because these, in France, are not patently absurd or shocking; and they are not patently absurd or shocking, I admit, because they are the relics of a civilized tradition : what I will not admit is that this is a serious charge against civilization.

Turn from modern France and consider the great age of Greece. It was as prolific almost as seventeenth-century England in vivid and original characters. Neither is the Italian Renaissance a conspicuous example of moral and intellectual conformity. If France, which for the last three hundred years has been the most highly civilized country in Europe, impresses us by a plethora of first-rate minds and a diffusion of culture rather than by a crowd of gorgeous minds and amazing characters, that may have as much to do with the temper of the race as with anything else. It is probable that France owes her deficiency, such as it is, not more to excess of civilization than England owes her exuberance to lack of it. Barbarism will not of itself provoke genius and character and a turn for self-expression in language; but hitherto England has cherished something which may account for much, and that is a respect for privacy superior far to anything enjoyed by Continental countries. The English eccentric, the crank, the genius, driven by the prevailing atmosphere into odd holes and corners, has there been suffered to exist and develop much as he chose. That is why the reputation of England as a nursery of originality and character stands, and deserves to stand, high. It stands yet; but it may not stand much longer. There is a movement to undermine it. This

71

toleration of oddity is anisocratic. Englishmen should learn to conform; they should be compelled to develop along judiciously laid grooves. Discipline and compulsion have come more than ever into fashion since England in contempt of her traditions accepted compulsory service. And if the season-ticket holders on one hand, and the trade unions on the other, succeed in doing their worst, it is probable that within a few decades England, disgarlanded of genius, character, and originality, will appear naked in her normal barbarity, an objective of universal merriment and contempt. She will have eliminated her individualism; but she will not be the more civilized for that.

He who possesses a sense of values cannot be a Philistine; he will value art and thought and knowledge for their own sakes, not for their possible utility. When I say for their own sakes, I mean, of course, as direct means to good states of mind which alone are good as ends. No one now imagines that a work of art lying on an uninhabited island has absolute value, or doubts that its potential value lies in the fact that it can at any moment become a means to a state of mind of superlative excellence. Works of art being direct means to aesthetic ecstasy are direct means to good. And the disinterested pursuit and perception of scientific and philosophical truth, as they provoke analogous states of emotional intensity, may be assigned to the same class. But the value of knowledge is different. Knowledge is not a direct means to good: its action is remote. An exact knowledge of the dates of the Kings and Queens of England will put no one into a flutter. Knowledge is a food of infinite potential value which must be assimilated by the intellect and imagination before it can become positively valuable. Only when it has been so assimilated does it become a direct means to good states of

THE SENSE OF VALUES

mind; but without this food both intellect and imagination tend to grow stunted and wry, are in danger even of starving to death.

It is the nourishing quality in knowledge that people with a sense of values most esteem; though obviously it has a practical importance as well: knowledge makes it possible to build motor-cars and mend legs. What is peculiar to civilized people is, in the first place, that they are capable of recognizing the value of knowledge as a means to exquisite spiritual states, and, in the second, that they esteem this value above any remote, utilitarian virtue. Beauty, of course, has no practical value whatever. A good picture may promote useful conduct, but a bad one is as likely and more to achieve the same result. It is the mark of a barbarian — a Philistine — that, having no sense of values, failing to discriminate between ends and means and between direct means and remote, he wants to know what is the use of art and speculation and pure science. The reply that they are direct, or almost direct, means to emotional states of the highest value and intensity for obvious reasons does not impress him. Useless to tell him that these are the keys that unlock the gates of Paradise, unless somehow you can give him a taste for Paradise. And how can you give him that? Only, I suppose, by giving him a glimpse of Paradise. And how a glimpse is to be given I am sure I do not know; but I conceive it is what education ought to do. If teachers could somehow make ordinary boys and girls grasp the quite simple fact that, though the world may seem to offer nothing better than a little money and a great deal of work, any one of them can, if he or she will, have a life full of downright, delectable pleasures; if teachers could make them realize that the delight of being alone in a bed-sitting room with an alert, well-trained, and well-stocked mind and a book, is greater than that of owning yachts and race-horses, and that the thrill of a great picture or a quartet by Mozart is keener (and it is an honest sensualist who says it) than that of the first sip of a glass of champagne; if the teachers could do this, the teachers, I think, would have solved the central problem of humanity. I cannot solve it: I can but say that the only people who possess the key to this palace of pleasures are the people who know how to value art and thought for their own sakes and knowledge as an instrument of culture.

The disinterestedness of the Greeks in their pursuit of truth has been made a reproach to them by the Philistines. Mathematical speculation and the study of geometry they pushed to a point that still astonishes those who are competent to measure the ground covered; in metaphysical, ethical, and political thought they are our masters; while in the theory of mechanics they went far enough to throw out, by way of parergon, a model steam-engine, but, to the horror of succeeding ages, did not trouble to exploit the invention. They never made a locomotive, gunpowder, or even a spinning-jenny. They sought truth for its own sake, and as a means to culture, not as a means to power and comfort. What is more, those who sought it for material benefits and personal profit they despised, holding such base exertions beneath the dignity of free men and incompatible with the finest life. It may surprise some scholars even to learn that at Athens it was thought dishonouring to take an active part in trade, yet both Plato and Aristotle affirm it. The Athenians wished to live richly rather than to be rich; which is why we reckon them the most highly civilized people in history.

To the Athenians the idea that a thing of beauty requires other justification than its beautifulness did at times occur; chiefly, perhaps, because to the Athenian mind there were very few ideas that did not. The Italians of the Renaissance were less thoughtful. It must be confessed, however, that in the later eighteenth century the French abused the art of painting shamelessly. The pictures of Greuze, for instance, were unblushingly recommended as moral pick-me-ups, stimulating sensibility, and provoking pity. As a result, there are still people of taste who cannot bring themselves to see what an excellent painter Greuze really was. The eighteenth century, as already I have admitted, was sounder on truth than on beauty; just as the Renaissance was sounder on beauty than on truth. And yet the latter's respect for pure, disinterested scholarship was true, and has been made a truism by Browning's fantastic verse:

'That low man seeks a little thing to do,
    Sees it and does it:
This high man, with a great thing to pursue,
    Dies ere he knows it.
That low man goes on adding one to one,
    His hundred's soon hit:
This high man, aiming at a million,
    Misses an unit.
That, has the world here—should he need the next,
    Let the world mind him!
This, throws himself on God, and unperplexed
    Seeking shall find Him.
So, with the throttling hands of Death at strife,
    Ground he at grammar;
Still, thro' the rattle, parts of speech were rife:

CIVILIZATION

While he could stammer
He settled *Hoti's* business —let it be!
Properly based *Oun* —
Gave us the doctrine of the enclitic *De*,
Dead from the waist down.'

That, whatever else it may be, is the antithesis of Philistinism: it is a life spent in the pursuit of 'useless knowledge.' The grammarian is at once superb and slightly ridiculous; but what makes him ridiculous is not his disregard of common values but a maniacal concentration on one good thing to the neglect of all others. The specialist is never completely civilized. The eighteenth century could be as unpractical as the Renaissance. Amongst the lower intellectual orders it is still fashionable to reproach that charming age with having devoted itself to such purely speculative sciences as mathematics and geometry, rather than to the more useful Biology and Chemistry. Important mechanical discoveries were made in the age of reason, but the best minds took very little interest in them. The only 'useful' sciences that got much flattering attention were Political Science and Political Economy, which I am so old-fashioned as still to regard as useful. Few historians fail to ascribe the doctrinaire character of the French Revolution to the century's preoccupation with abstractions. A generation brought up on Darwin and Spenser, they think, could never have been so remorselessly uncompromising, so absurdly theoretical. I know not what the remnants of the Russian *bourgeoisie* will say to that.

From a sense of values comes that desire for, and belief in, liberal education which no civilized age has been without. The richest and fullest life obtainable, a life which contains the maximum of vivid and exquisite experiences, is the end of every civilized man's desire. Because he desires it he aims at complete self-development and complete self-expression : and these are to be achieved only by those who have learnt to think and feel and discriminate, to let the intellect play freely round every subject, and the emotions respond appropriately to all stimuli. Knowledge in addition is needed; for without knowledge the intellect remains the slave of prejudice and superstition, while the emotions sicken on a monotonous and cannibalistic diet. The civilized man desires an education which shall be as direct a means as possible to what alone is good as an end. He cultivates his powers of thinking and feeling, pursues truth and acquires knowledge, not for any practical value that these may possess, but for themselves, or — that I may distinguish him sharply from the date-collector and competition-winner — for their power of revealing the rich and complex possibilities of life. The Philistine, wanting the sense of values, expects education to show him the way to wealth and power, things which are valuable only in so far as they are more or less remote means to that ultimate good whither liberal education leads direct. Liberal education teaches us to enjoy life; practical education to acquire things that may enable us or someone else to enjoy it.

To few things did an Athenian attach greater importance than to the education of his son. When, for a short time, the Mityleneans became masters of the sea, they thought the greatest punishment they could inflict on disobedient allies was to deprive them of their schools. With the exception of rhetoric and the use of arms, no part, I think, of the Athenian curriculum aimed directly at practical results. Italy was heir to Greece : and there can be no fairer testimony to the strength and taste of the Renaissance than that for almost four hundred years it committed the governing classes of Europe to an education that was liberal so far as it went. On this fundamental question of education we know exactly what was the best mind of Italy; for Baldassare Castiglione, having treated the subject with admirable thoroughness, has summed up his arguments and illustrations thus: 'Il vero e principal ornamento dell' animo in ciascuno penso io che siano le lettere.' In the new curriculum there was, of course, plenty of dust and ashes; but the tradition inherited by the Renaissance from Greece, was after all based on Greek, and therein differed completely from the pedantic futilities of the middle age. By the study of Greek letters and philosophy the young *élite* of all nations was at least given the chance of acquiring those things that are best worth having. Europe had a traditional education that was essentially liberal. The tradition went unchallenged through the seventeenth and eighteenth centuries, though in the latter the curriculum was brought up to date, without being vulgarized, by a more general and systematic teaching of mathematics and geometry. In the nineteenth, with the industrial revolution, the rise of the middle classes, the religion of money-making sometimes called 'the gospel of work,' and the passion for 'getting on,' it was violently attacked and began visibly to wane. During what is called by Mr. H. G. Wells 'the tragic happenings of the last few years,'[7] and by liberally educated people 'the war,' it perished.

A sense of values and the power of discriminating between ends and means suffice to make a man an individualist. To be sure that other parent quality, the enthronement of reason, also breeds a sense of the supreme importance of the individual; but as in considering the civilized man's desire for self-development we have come near this highly civilized characteristic, we may as well deal with it at once. Anyone who realizes that the sole good as an end is a good state of mind, and that there are no grounds for supposing that such a thing as a collective mind exists, will naturally set store by the individual in whom alone absolute good is to be found. For such a one to forget that all generalizations must ultimately be tested by the experience of individuals would be unpardonable, seeing that to talk about the good of the herd, as though it were something different from the good of the individuals who compose the herd, is recognized even by politicians, when it suits their purpose, as barbarous folly. Thus, British statesmen, apt though they are to speak of British interests as though they were different from the interests of the people who live in Britain, were profoundly shocked by the extravagances of German journalists who exalted above the individual German the German state. The state cannot be an end in itself: it can be no more than a means to those good states of mind which alone are good as ends, and are to be found only in individuals.

The Athenians were often put to it to reconcile the rights of the citizen with the needs of the city; but at any rate until years of war had begun to coarsen their sense of values they generally succeeded in preserving free play for personality, thereby making possible that civilization which remains the wonder and glory of the Western world. Of Athenian liberty, however, I shall have so much to say in the next chapter, when I come to discuss the eldest child of reason, Tolerance, that for the moment I will ask the reader to take it for granted. Here I will observe only that the Greeks were in some sort the

inventors of individualism. In a world of Oriental superstition and servitude, they first stood up to assert the personal significance of the educated, intelligent citizen. To
them first came the idea that a man with senses, emotions, and a brain was the master of a universe; that the
world was his oyster which, with intelligence and courage, he could open; that the individual intellect is a
match for the powers of nature; that every man who can
feel and think is a king.

The Italians of the Renaissance felt so acutely the importance of the individual as the chief source of all that is
thrilling, significant, and splendid, that, as I have admitted, in their glorification of personality they pushed, perhaps, too far. Not content with claiming for the individual complete liberty of expression and experiment, they
cultivated personality to a point at which it became hu-
bris and egotism: worse still, they sometimes took these
essentially barbarous traits for personal distinction. The
more perfectly civilized ages of Pericles and Voltaire
never made that mistake: good manners and sociability,
characteristics which develop as civilized societies become
more and more appreciative of the pleasures of conversation, abated in these the individualistic tendency to
aggressive self-assertion. But that all three were intensely
individualistic will not be disputed. The individualism of
the Greeks is, perhaps, best seen in their philosophy, and
that of the Renaissance in its extravagance. It is unnec-
cssary, I presume, to prove that the eighteenth century
was individualistic by showing how all that mass of political thought which culminated in the Revolution based
itself on the rights of man and his peculiar significance as
a human being.

THE SENSE OF VALUES

About something which follows necessarily from individualism, though quite as much from the individualism born of reason as of that which springs from a sense of values — about Cosmopolitanism I mean, perhaps a word should be said. No intelligent individualist is likely to feel much affection for the state, which, in fact, he regards as, at best, a dangerous makeshift. A tendency towards cosmopolitanism, based on individualism, a movement of liberation from the herd instinct, is the unfailing accompaniment of an advance in civility: indeed, it might stand almost for its measure. Over the savage herd instinct bears absolute sway; the savage has the dimmest notion of values that transcend the tribe and no sympathies outside it. But a civilized man sympathizes with other civilized men no matter where they were born or to what race they belong and feels uneasy with brutes and philistines though they be his blood-relations living in the same parish. I am not going to prove by instances the cosmopolitanism of the eighteenth century; only to appease the curiosity of any ignorant person who in the way of business may be obliged to read this book I will give one quotation from an eminent authority:

'Il reste à signaler un caractère de la philosophie du xviiie siècle, qui dépend de tous les autres ou s'y relie: elle est cosmopolite, et elle donne naissance a une litterature cosmopolite. . . . Les armées du roi étaient battues par un Prussien: mais ce Prussien parlait français, et il était plus pareil à nous qu'un grenadier qui mourait pour lui. Ainsi le vainqueur de Rosbach rendait hommage à la civilisation française: notre patriotisme se contentait de cette victoire de l'esprit. . . . Son rationalisme (that of an eighteenth-century Frenchman) lui interdisait les préjugés de couleur et de race.

81

L'homme digne de ce nom est celui qui n'obéit qu'à la raison: mais cet homme n'est pas Français plutôt qu'Allemand: il est Européen, il est Chinois, il est partout où il y a des hommes; et toutes les verites que concoit la raison humaine sont faites pour cet homme universel.'[8]

From the writings of the Greek intellectuals I have already quoted passages testifying to a fully developed cosmopolitanism and a brave contempt for patriotic limitations: you remember how Democritus of Abdera said that 'every country is accessible to a wise man, and that a good soul's fatherland is the whole earth.' The Renaissance follows suit, for as soon as men begin to think freely the grip of patriotism is loosened; so one is not surprised to find Codrus Urceus, to pick a name at random, writing somewhere about the year 1500, that 'wherever a learned man fixes his seat, there is home.' and obviously an Englishman who cares for beauty, truth, or knowledge, may find himself more in sympathy with a Frenchman, German, or Chinaman who shares his tastes than with a compatriot who shares those of *Punch* and *John Bull*.

Patriotism, however, is a prejudice which will hardly be eradicated from a state or society. Cosmopolitanism, the logical consequence of Individualism, is naturally an attribute of an individual rather than of a community. The Athenians were certainly patriotic; but their patriotism is cleared of some of its ugliness by the fact that they do genuinely seem to have loved Athens for what she was, not simply and brutally because she was *their* city. Their emotion was felt intelligently for definite and lovable qualities, not stupidly for a flag or a name. Also the Athenians had this excuse: their state was surrounded by hostile and menacing states; they felt inevitably that they were on the defensive. By the middle of the fifteenth century the patriotic fervour of the Italian cities had cooled considerably. The tyrants hired armies of mercenaries for their own political purposes; the citizens took little or no part in the dynastic wars. Had the Italians realized that Italian civilization as a whole was menaced, as it was, by German and Spanish barbarians, and had they armed themselves in defence, certainly they would have lowered the level of their civility, but they would have had the same justification as the Athenians. Almost all the wars of the eighteenth century were contests between highly specialized armies of professional soldiers: the absence of patriotic passion and hate amongst the better-educated civilians is notorious.

All civilized people have a sense of values, which is not the same as saying that they have a system of ethics. In ethics they may be completely sceptical, they may accept some standard *a priori* theory, or one based on personal intuition, or they may adopt the utilitarian doctrine and profess to seek the greatest happiness of the greatest number; but one morality no thoroughly civilized person will ever accept, and that is the morality which aims at the greatest happiness of the majority of an arbitrarily and indiscriminately chosen group. A highly civilized person can never unquestioningly accept the ethics of patriotism. Indeed, the civilized person will tend to think less and less in terms of groups; the conception of 'his country' as an entity with interests distinct from those of the rest of the world will gradually lose precision in his eyes; until, at last, recognizing the individual as one entity with distinct interests and the planet as another, he begins to feel that the boundaries and frontiers of all other reputed entities are vague and arbitrary. There are individuals and there is the human race: where powerful and well-trained

83

minds are speculating freely, the belief in the existence of trustworthy stepping-stones between these two solid realities tends to collapse. For convenience — *e.g.* for administrative or biological purposes — individuals may be considered in groups: men, women, and children, people with only one leg or lung, short people, tall people, red-haired people, educated people, dipsomaniacs, railway-porters, hairdressers, Germans, English, Turks: but such groups can never possess the reality, the unmistakable character and incontrovertible existence, the individuality, in fact, of individuals. What is more, no groups appear to the civilized consideration to have less reality or fewer or vaguer common characteristics than those which are based on geographical position or ethnological hypotheses.

Cosmopolitanism is a weapon with which civilization is apt to defend itself when nationalism becomes menacing. For nationalism is a terrible enemy to civility, a disease which undermined at last the constitution of Athens and threatened more than once the serene health of the eighteenth century. It may be doubted whether religion itself has been so fruitful a mother of barbarous woes as this modern manifestation of the herd instinct. How many millions of human lives have been broken or impoverished by this survival from a pre-human age? What possibilities of general good have been sacrificed to this irritable appendix? And yet nationalism is a bogey: none can tell you precisely what a nation is. Germany and England exist as two football clubs exist. The executive committees can put up two elevens to fight each other; while their respective backers cheer and hoot. Yet no one seriously doubts that a railwayman from Crewe has more in common with a railwayman from Sheffield than with the chairman of the Crewe Chamber of Commerce who happens also to be chairman of the football club. All men are capable of taking sides, and most are capable of taking any side: that is why the spirit of nationalism is so easily kept alive. But if there be any real meaning in the classification of men under national headings, there must surely be certain characteristics common and peculiar to all those of one class. What are they? What common and peculiar characteristics have Milton, Mr. Bottomley, Shelley, Mr. Lloyd George, Darwin, Sir Oliver Lodge, the Duke of Wellington, Vesta Tilley, the Bishop of London, Bishop Berkeley, Blake, Coleridge, and Sir William Joynson-Hicks? If it comes to that, what peculiar characteristics have you or I in common with the man who won the war for us? He speaks English; so did President Wilson, so does the Kaiser: Mr. George speaks Welsh also which I, at least, do not. There are, however, other ancient and modern languages in which I believe we have the advantage of him; so that language, instead of bringing us together, suggests rather a classification which might keep us apart. We were all three born in the British Isles; so perhaps were Karl Scheidnitz, Marius Pierrefitte, Demetri Protopopoff, Socrate Konrioulos, Haggi Baba, Abdul Latif, Po Chi Ling, Ernst Rothschild and Chiozza Money. Am I to suppose that nationality, that thing for which so many evils have been endured, so many blessings foregone, is just the thing that these gentlemen have in common with each other, with Mr. Lloyd George, and with me? If so, you can easily understand why civilized people see a certain unreality in the grouping of men by nations.

One of the qualities that most clearly distinguish a civilized man from a savage is a sense of humour; and the sense of humour is in the last analysis nothing but a highly developed sense of values. By a sense of humour I do not mean a taste for buffoonery and romps; for aught I know the Veddahs of Ceylon set thorns in each other's mats, and the Yorubas of West Africa regale each other with breezy anecdotes. I mean the power of perceiving the ludicrousness of taking things too seriously and giving them an undue importance; and this power is enjoyed only by those who can tell ends from means. To attach to a means the importance due to an end is ridiculous; and because all human achievement falls something short of the ideal, to a thoroughly civilized person all human endeavour will appear at moments slightly comic. Nevertheless, the passionate pursuit of love, beauty, and truth will be laughed at loudly and for long only by fools who cannot understand the passion or appreciate its object. The state of mind of a lover, of one who is creating or contemplating beauty, or of one who is lost in a speculative 'O Altitudo' is good in itself, and however laborious and unlovely the means employed in attaining to it we ought not to judge them inappropriate—though in fact we often do. Because they are good as ends such things can hardly be taken too seriously. But quit this sanctuary of ends and enter the world of means: begin to consider people busying themselves about politics, trade, dignity, comfort, reputation, honour, and the like; and soon you will catch them treating these means with the intense, inflexible earnestness due only to ends. They are taking these things much too seriously; your sense of values will tell you that, and your sense of humour will reward it with a glow of peculiar, civilized pleasure.

This pleasure which the savage, with his rudimentary sense of values, his inability to distinguish ends from means, cannot know, is enjoyed by all civilized people in a greater or less degree. A sense of humour is a character-istic of the highly civilized individual; but, for reasons that I hope presently to make clear, it does not follow that the most highly civilized individuals have lived in the most highly civilized ages. On the contrary, it seems that the most highly civilized people in any century at all civil-ized should be more highly civilized than their counter-parts in the preceding one, always provided that they have easy access to, and the means of enjoying, the leg-acies of the past. Because the middle ages could draw hardly at all on antiquity or make much use of the little they got, the most civilized man of the thirteenth century was infinitely less civilized than a cultivated Athenian or Roman even. Even in the fifteenth and sixteenth centu-ries there was way to be-made up, and I do not imagine that the most accomplished gentleman of the Renaissance would have cut a very good figure in the circle of Aspasia. But if the Renaissance was still making up leeway, it is certain, I think, that by the middle of the eighteenth cen-tury there were men and women who outwent any of their predecessors in civility, chiefly, no doubt, because they had learnt so much from them. Nevertheless the highly civilized men and women of the eighteenth century, per-haps because they were a smaller proportion of the popu-lation, did not colour their age so richly and profoundly as did the civilized Athenians. Eighteenth-century civili-zation was inferior to Periclean; yet I dare say no Athen-ian was as highly civilized as Voltaire. In his sense of humour, at any rate, the perfectly civilized man of the eighteenth century was distinctly subtler than the Athen-ian. Aristophanes, himself, was never so *fin* as Lafontaine (to begin at the beginning), as Gresset, Montesquieu, Marivaux, Voltaire, and Beaumarchais, or, for that matter, as Congreve, Pope, Goldsmith, Sterne, and Gibbon. What is more, in this matter of humour, in appreciation at any rate, the most civilized people of this present age perhaps outgo all others in subtlety: if this be so, I need not labour my point that one swallow does not make a summer.

In these last paragraphs, I perceive, I have been wandering by a back way into a subject which ought to be approached later and with ceremony. A sense of humour, and cosmopolitanism too, are characteristics of a civilized person rather than of a civilized society; and though I mean to prove that a civilized society is nothing but a society that has been coloured by a group of civilized people, I have not proved it yet. My immediate business is not to describe civilized men and women, but to discover characteristics common and peculiar to those three societies which I have taken as paragons. And as, for the moment, I have done with those characteristics which spring from a sense of values, I must turn now to those which can be traced to the enthronement of reason.

V

THEIR CHARACTERISTICS:
REASON ENTHRONED

THE very heart of Athenian civilization — so think the historians — is to be found in that oration wherewith Pericles consoled his bereaved fellow-citizens by giving them an account of their own virtues. Historians, however, think wrong sometimes. The speech of Pericles is a fine performance suggesting a fine atmosphere: it could have been made only by a great man to men far above the modern average of thought and feeling. It would be equally out of place in the House of Commons or at a Trade Union Congress. But it is not to any speech or to any politician that I should go for a thing so subtle as the heart of civility. Of civilization, political speeches may be manifestations, as may be laws, hats, and cookery, but of its essence they cannot be: to discover the secret of Athens it would be wiser to explore the writings of Aristophanes, Euripides, and Plato, and the tradition of the Sophists, than the speeches of Pericles, Isocrates, and Phocion. In the poets, philosophers, and historians, if anywhere, is to be found that saffron which at once flavours and colours Hellenic culture. I do not say that in them alone it existed or even that they were its chief propagators. On the contrary, I hope presently to show that the stream of civility springs from nameless wells and reservoirs — from a class in fact — though it flows down famous conduits; that the disseminators of culture are a group of men and women of whom most create no tangible work and leave no eximious monument, though they diffuse the influence which manifests itself in the spirit of the age. At any rate, it is absurd to make of a politician the representative of a spiritual or intellectual movement. No one would judge Utilitarianism, that product of the minds of Adam Smith and Ricardo, of Bentham and the Mills, by the speeches of Mr. Hobhouse and Mr. Roebuck, of Mr. Cobden and Mr. Bright. Turgot and Necker even, great though they were, would give a miserably inadequate notion of the *philosophical* movement. The revival of learning and free thought in Northern Europe was something very different from Luther's bawling propaganda and the opportunism of Frederick of Saxony and Henry VIII. Politicians, for their hour, loom as large as actors and jockeys and then, like them, fade from the public mind, and are known to curious erudition only.

'Alive ridiculous, and dead forgot.'

If the last part of the quotation be true, so must be the first: for what could be more ridiculous than one, doomed to speedy oblivion, giving himself the airs cabinet ministers are apt to assume? And, tell me, how many of your friends could tell you who was Prime Minister of England at the time of Waterloo, who was at the War Office, who was First Lord of the Admiralty. Of how many politicians alive and active in the year 1815 are the names familiar to the reading public? Of Canning perhaps, and Castlereagh (chiefly because he was the object of Byron's satire and Shelley's), and possibly of Grey. Does anyone but an avowed student of military history know the names of more than two of Wellington's generals? And who was in command of the British fleet when Napoleon came on board the *Bellerophon*? But if well-educated English men and women do not know the name of the Prime Minister who presumably 'won' the Napoleonic War, nor the names of his cabinet colleagues, nor of more than two of his soldiers, nor of a single one of his admirals, every second-class undergraduate can tell you that Shelley, Byron, Keats, Wordsworth, Coleridge, Southey, Lamb, Hazlitt, Scott, Moore, Rogers, and Jane Austen were writing at that time. And the explanation is simple: these are remembered because they have had, and have still, a real and direct effect on the minds of men; because they are still creating, still stimulating new thoughts and feelings, still suggesting new points of view or changing old ones; because they are even adding now to the world's store of good. Politicians, at best, do but manipulate and distribute the good things others have produced: never do they create. When they are remembered it is chiefly for the great and dramatic events with which their names are associated but of which they were not the cause; and, as we have seen, great events even will not save them always. They belong, as a rule, to that third or fourth order which, though it may play a conspicuous, can never play a leading part in the history of the race. Politicians leave scars and scratches on the disk, but they do not make the tune: they neither originate nor conclude nor greatly modify those more conscious impulses of the human mind which give shape to human history. It is a mistake, therefore, to expect them to be of those who create civilizations, though often they will be found significant manifestations of the civilizations of which they are parts.

So I shall not go to Pericles for the secret of Athenian civility, though I gladly accept him as a type of what

CIVILIZATION

Athenian civility could produce. And there is one passage
in that speech of his on which I would dwell because it
seems to express exactly what the Athenians felt about the
first and most important of those civilized characteristics
that spring from the enthronement of reason — Tolerance
I mean. 'The spirit of freedom,' says Pericles, 'prevails
alike in our public and private affairs. Without a scrap of
jealousy we tolerate peculiarities of all sorts in each other's daily lives: we have no objection to our neighbour
following the bent of his humour: nor do we put on black
looks, innocuous maybe, but annoying.'9 That kind of
tolerance, one of the surest indications of a high state of
civilization, comes only of a belief in reason: good taste is
not enough. A sense of values may lead by winding paths
to a sense of the necessity for personal freedom; but the
one sure basis of toleration is a clear intellectual perception that reason alone has the right to constrain liberty.
Only reason can convince us of those three fundamental
truths without a recognition of which there can be no
effective liberty: that what we believe is not necessarily
true; that what we like is not necessarily good; and that
all questions are open. Our sense of values ought to show
us that to prevent anyone fully expressing himself is to
impoverish life; but only reason is strong enough to keep
in hand that insatiable desire that lurks in us all to compel others to be like ourselves. Reason must be the sole
judge: and reason will suffer us to limit other people's
self-expression only in so far as it can be shown, *reasonably,* that such self-expression destroys more good than it
creates.

The maximum of self-expression for all is what our
sense of values makes us feel to be desirable. Wherefore,
we must learn to tolerate not only other people's ideas but

their ways of life too. It may be impossible for society to bear with the man who can find complete satisfaction only in homicide and arson, but there can be no excuse for imprisoning people who merely hurt our feelings. Let me take an extreme case. To most normal men and women the idea of incest is disgusting and absurd. I share the popular prejudice. But there is something that shocks me far more than incest, and that is sending people to prison for it. Last night perhaps you were sitting in a club, playing bridge, smoking a cigar, and drinking whiskey: observe that you were doing simultaneously three things which many excellent people consider extremely wrong. Does it not make you horribly uncomfortable to reflect that perhaps, a mile away, two lunatics were committing incest, and that you, as a citizen and voter, were invoking the whole power of the state to prevent and punish them? What they were about in no way interfered with your complete self-expression, or with that of anyone else. They were expressing themselves in what seems to you a disgusting and ridiculous manner, and you were expressing yourself in a way that seems disgusting and ridiculous to many high-minded people. But if you do not admit the right of those high-minded philanthropists, sitting in the cosy corners of their garden cities and enjoying a glass of barley-water and a sense of moral superiority, to tear you away from the bridge table and cast you into prison, with what conscience can you pay policeman and judges to interfere with the self-regarding activities of those unfortunate, and probably feeble-minded, lovers.

Let me say, at once, that the quarrel of the eugenists with these eccentrics, when not disingenuous, is perfectly respectable. To justify their interference, the eugenists invoke, not their prejudices, but the health of the community; and I make no doubt they are clever enough to manœuvre statistics and history into helping them to get round the fact that inbreeding has been employed before now as a means of preserving the purity of a race.[10] But until they have succeeded in making illegal the begetting of children by drunkards, idiots, and consumptive and syphilitic persons, eugenists may as will leave in peace a handful of oddities who find happiness in what seems to us perversity.

The laws against incest are typical examples of gross intolerance.[11] Most of us feel a sharp physical reaction — something like a shudder — at the idea of connections of this sort; and these reactions we are apt to mistake for profound ethical judgments. I know all about this feeling of disgust and disapprobation because I feel it, not only for incest and things of that sort, but for cheese. To me the sight of cheese is offensive, the smell shocking, the mere thought disturbing and vexatious: to see people eating it revolts my whole being to its depths and undermines my sense of human dignity. Yet reason tells me that the eating of cheese is no sin. Reason forbids me to mistake a physical reaction for a moral judgment, which is what every other part of my nature longs to do. Reason overrides prejudice. The essence of intolerance is the exalting of prejudices into principles, and the imposing of them on other people. The old gentleman, sitting to cards and whisky, and interfering, through the police, with the harmless eccentricities of his neighbours, the friend of humanity, nibbling his nuts, and devising schemes of interference with the pleasures of that old gentleman, are alike the formidable and funest expression of man's ineradicable barbarism. Let us

set up against them, as the motto of civility, the splendid
boast of Athens:

> 'And not only in politics are we open-minded: without a
> scrap of jealousy we tolerate peculiarities of all sorts in each
> other's daily lives; we have no objection to our neighbour
> following the bent of his humour; nor do we put on black
> looks, innocuous maybe, but annoying.'

No good purpose can be served by telling me that the
Athenians put Socrates to death. I am already aware of the
fact. But if one swallow does not make a summer, neither
do three dark days constitute winter. By the freedom of
their thought and criticism, by their open-mindedness,
curiosity, and taste for experiment, the Athenians set an
example which the best of later ages have tried in vain to
emulate. Towards Athens the finest Western minds turn
ever for inspiration and encouragement. Athens alone
gives a semblance of possibility to their dreams of the
ideal, for from Athens alone the heroic desire for truth
and beauty did receive some sort of practical expression.
The Athenians cared instinctively for Beauty and believed in Truth. And this belief gave them something
better than a taste for freedom: it gave them a conviction
of its absolute necessity. The Athenians had a State religion, not much encumbered with dogma, nor, after the
middle of the fifth century, much believed in by the intelligent. It was a religion which seems to have hindered
no one except Socrates and, for a moment, Anaxagoras
from speculating freely. A formal respect for one or two
ancient taboos they did require; but the only morality of
which law and public opinion took much account was
practical morality. A citizen was required not to commit

grossly anti-social acts. But by an anti-social act the Athenians did not mean anything the majority misliked or misunderstood: they had no objection to a neighbour following the bent of his humour. They tried to be tolerant.

When I say that the enthronement of reason is typical of a highly civilized society, you will not imagine that I suppose every Athenian to have taken a strictly rational view of every question that came his way. You do not imagine that when Julius Caesar said that the Belgians were a brave race, he supposed that each individual Belgian was as bold as a lion. The French eighteenth century, to be sure, which was even more enamoured of Reason than the Hellenic fifth, does seem to have believed that it needed only a few constitutional changes to make all men happy and rational; but we, of the twentieth, who have enjoyed the blessings of so many great reforms and glorious revolutions, are inevitably less sanguine. The Italians of the Renaissance did their best to break down the hideous intolerance of the middle ages: the measure of their success is the barbarity of the reaction. Remember, it was the considered opinion of the judicious Burckhardt that between the middle of the fifteenth century and the Spanish terror which brought in the counter-reformation such questions as that of the immortality of the soul were treated by all educated Italians as open. Of course, highly civilized ages have not all been equally tolerant; only, all have struggled towards the light, feeling that the attempt to impose by force ways of thinking, feeling, and living was ugly. They have realized, more or less clearly, that dogma is death. In so far as they have been superstitious, they have tended to keep their nonsense to themselves; they have not much tried to impose it by force or by the

threat of a moral sanction. Superstitious, with its stars
and philtres, the Renaissance undoubtedly was, but
much less so than the middle ages. Of Athenian citizens a
great number were not superstitious at all, however it
may have been with the mystery-mongering mob — the
majority of whom were slaves. The French eighteenth
century was not only sceptical, it recognized superstition
for what it is — the inveterate enemy of what makes life
precious. *Ecrasez l'infâme*.

For superstition is a thing which comes between a man
and his sense of reality, robbing him of that most intense
and thrilling experience, which is the apprehension of
reality. To realize truth, to see the thing in itself, these
are experiences comparable with love and aesthetic ecstasy. But how is the watcher of the skies to get that thrill
which comes of a new planet swimming into his ken when
superstition compels him to believe that the sky is an in-
verted bowl, the stars chinks through which peeps God,
and that there are no such things as planets? As the lover
who sees the beloved always through a cloud of romance
will never know that supreme joy which comes from the
complete realization of another human being, of another
existence as real as his own, so he who contemplates the
universe through the spectacles of superstition can never
know the thrill that answers the recognition and passionate acceptance of the naked truth. Superstition cheats
emotion of one of its finest stimulants; and, not content
with that, by imposing bounds on the discursive intellect
deprives us of our most delicate and subtle amusements.
For the intellect, though it die not, grows fat and clumsy
in captivity. All that makes conversation amusing and society brilliant — wit, irony, paradox, repartee, intellectual
fooling, the intellect can give, provided the intellect be

free. There must be no taboos, no closed subjects; for from the shackled intellect you will get nothing better than pompous disquisitions and practical jokes. The intellect must be free to handle, not only in earnest but in fun, all things in heaven and earth. It can range gloriously as an eagle; but, like an eagle, once maimed, mopes. All things that are, or have been, or may be, are its appropriate toys. Superstition would put it to play with counters. And with these playing, within the precincts of dogma, the intellect grows blear-eyed and childish. There is an end of thrilling speculation and an end of intellectual refinement. Superstition robs life of half its glory and a good part of its fun. And because the eighteenth century knew this, the eighteenth century declared war on superstition.

People who are tolerant and not superstitious are unlikely to be very cruel, unless they happen to take that sadistic pleasure in cruelty for its own sake which is, at any rate, not more common amongst civilized than amongst savage people. Useless cruelty they are sure to dislike, and they will see that most cruelty is useless. Torture was forbidden by the laws and was repugnant to the spirit of the Athenian people who, when, as a body, they acted with unusual ferocity, had the grace, as a body, to be ashamed of themselves: such humility is, however, too rare to be reckoned a characteristic of civilization. The strident individualism of the Renaissance produced a gallery of supermen, few of whom quite escaped a smear of that peculiar disgustingness which distinguishes the sect. They have left a record of some outrageous and purposeless brutalities over which the pale historian never fails to gloat; but most of their crimes were severely practical. And if you remember — and I have invited you to remember—that these private crimes were often substitutes for war, you may begin to wonder whether it is for this age to throw the first stone at Renaissance politicians. The humanity of the French eighteenth century was such that the public was positively shocked when it discovered that Calas had been unjustly executed: also Voltaire did not die mysteriously in prison as he might have done in the twentieth. In the age of faith people would simply have been at a loss to understand what he was making so much fuss about: they would have burnt him none the less. Superstitious ages are inevitably cruel; one of their superstitions being, invariably, that pain is good as a means, a doctrine which commends itself especially to those who are ashamed to confess that they deem it good as an end. After all, the sadism of civilized eccentrics may be nothing more than a relic of barbarism.

Reason will be tending ever to scrutinize those barbarous instincts and memories which are at once the wells and shrines of prejudice. For prejudices spring either from physical reactions, as my prejudice against cheese does, or from the forgotten taboos of savage ancestors. To this day in Central Africa there are young ladies whose lives are made bitter by the recurring danger of seeing the moon over their left shoulders; while others slink through the jungle in constant terror of coming on their aunt's second cousin unawares. It is as easy for a girl to lose her character in the Congo as in a cathedral town. We owe more than we think to our remote grandmothers. Sir Edmund Gosse has told us how grievously some years of his childhood were burdened with the conviction that he had committed the sin against the Holy Ghost; and Mr. James Joyce, in that strange half-baked study of his, showed us, only the other day, that a mind still saturated in superstition can be tortured to madness almost by the recollection of having done what most boys do and thought what most boys think. There is no remedy, I admit, for that remorse which all sensitive people feel for the wanton unkindnesses they have done and the pleasures they have forgone: but that sense of sin, from which so many well-meaning people still suffer, and for which they make so many others suffer, is, as a rule, nothing more than a remnant of barbarism which will yield to treatment. Curiosity, which grows stronger and stronger as men become more civilized, is the antidote.

Savages have their curiosity; but it is a cramped and cabined thing. There are a certain number of facts only that they dare examine, and these they dare examine only in a certain way. It is not truth they want, but safety. Their curiosity is instinctive, not rational, and their fear-ridden brains cannot convert it to knowledge. But as no one denies that ignorance, in the common acceptation of the word, is a characteristic of barbarism, I need no more labour this point than I need demonstrate by instances the vivid curiosity of Periclean Athens, fifteenth-century Florence, or eighteenth-century France. Only on one consequence of this civilized curiosity must I insist: civilized people can talk about anything. For them no subject will be taboo so long as there is anything to say about it which seems interesting or gay. In civilized societies there will be no intellectual bogeys at sight of which great grown-up babies are expected to hide their eyes. I shall have so much to say presently about the *Symposium* that here I will do no more than observe that from that inimitable picture of an ideal after-dinner conversation we can see that, in a company of educated Athenians, there were no closed subjects. Students of the *Decameron* — and the

Decameron was for two centuries the favourite reading of
men and women throughout the length and breadth of
Italy—know that, in the ages of Petrarch, Cosimo dei
Medici, and.Michael Angelo, neither what are called 'the
great facts of life' nor the most dignified institutions and
sacred persons were considered unsuitable objects of bold
and lively criticism. And to anyone who cares to know
with what freedom ladies and gentlemen of the eighteenth century ranged over the universe of facts and ideas
I will recommend Diderot's *Rêve de d'Alembert,* the second, and frankest, part of which is presented in the form
of a monologue uttered by d'Alembert in his sleep, and
written down by Mlle Lespinasse, while the third, and
most startling, consists of an imaginary, but clearly not
impossible, conversation between Mlle Lespinasse and
M. Bordeu.

If it be a civilized society you want, the intellect must
be free to deal as it pleases with whatever comes its way, it
must be free to choose its own terms, phrases, and images, and to play with all things what tricks it will. There
must be not one Bluebeard's chamber; for to bar the intellect from one room in the house is to hobble it in all
the rest. That is why prudery is a dangerous enemy; and
it is not less dangerous because its pretentions are grotesque. What is seemly or unseemly in sentiment or expression is clearly a matter of taste. To my taste the sentiment
of most of those songs which touch the heart of the people—'*Good-by-e-e*' or '*The heart stood still*'—is disgusting, and the expression vulgar. I would not, however, on
that account have them suppressed by force. I recognize
that my taste is different from that of my fellows: but I
could never suppose that my distaste for what they like
could be a reason for depriving them of their pleasures. I

am reasonable enough to be tolerant; and I would not wish to see vulgarity punished by law. In the reign of Queen Victoria the taste of the middle classes was offended by what had seemed interesting and amusing and beautiful to most of the great poets, artists, thinkers, and critics of other ages. You might have thought that in what is admittedly a matter of taste the opinions of such people would have counted for something, would have given pause even to those curates and tradesmen who had discovered so suddenly and so exactly what was delicate and what was not. All I can say is, the curates and tradesmen were made of stouter stuff: they had no sort of doubt that Plato and Aristophanes and Sappho and Catullus and Lucretius and Dante and Boccaccio and Rabelais and Shakespeare and Milton and Lafontaine and Voltaire and Diderot and Pope and Swift and Fielding were rough and insensitive in those matters where they themselves could judge unerringly. What is more, the curates and tradesmen hold the field. No living author could print, in England, such things as were written by Plato, Dante, or Shakespeare. The law takes cognizance of breaches of good taste. Certainly it suffers what would have seemed insufferably vulgar to those great men whose works now need our apology; for it suffers what Victorian gentility esteemed and the great public still loves. It suffers literature, plastic art, and music, freely displayed on bookstalls, in public galleries and in music-halls, which is an incessant humiliation to any man or woman of taste; it suffers the ideas of popular journalists and the emotions of popular playwrights; it suffers even our public monuments, and puts up with Nurse Cavell; in a word, it tolerates and patronizes an attitude towards life and art which Milton, with his smutty jokes, and Shakespeare, with his

deplorable sonnets, would have supposed too shameful to
be avowed by the lowest wretch. Let us not complain:
everyone, even Sir Hall Caine and Mr. Ivor Novello,
should be allowed to express himself as completely as
possible. But let us hope that should good taste and power
ever be united, that happy combination of forces will be
too highly civilized to commend *The Doctor* and *The
Rosary* and *Keep the home fires burning* to the flames.

All that can be hoped for, and all that is to be desired,
in matters of taste is absolute toleration. Let us not complain of the Lord Chamberlain's preference for *Chu Chin
Chow* to *Six Characters*, but only of his interfering with
our enjoyment of the latter. It seems odd, I admit, that in
questions so subtle and delicate as those of taste, any
common police-court magistrate, county councillor, or
bishop should be allowed to know better than the finest
artist or the most fastidious critic; but, in my judgment,
it would be as undesirable for the intelligent and sensitive
to control the pleasures of the stupid and vulgar, as it is
deplorable that the stupid and vulgar should control the
pleasures of the sensitive and intelligent. Those admirable enthusiasts who bestir themselves from time to time
to get questions asked in Parliament about the censorship
of books and plays, and even complain when they find
that politicians care not a rap for the interests of culture,
go the wrong way to work. They should not insist on the
aesthetic superiority of what they like, but on the general
principle of toleration. They are up against a kind of vanity which is particularly virulent in this country and in
America; and if they are to circumvent it they must try,
for once, to be as clever as they are good. The fact is, to
make a judgment in a matter of taste requires a degree of
sensibility higher than that with which the normal voter

has been blessed. But repeatedly to be told this gives the normal voter no pleasure at all. It is quite true that the intellectual force and honesty required to judge any question whatever on its merits is such as to put all judgment beyond his reach. Yet on judging he is bent: and that is why he accepts and enjoins mechanical standards. These standards are not, of course, standards of taste: for to taste mechanical standards cannot apply, taste being a matter of personal reaction and sensibility. But to people who have never known a first-hand, personal reaction, much less formed a judgment on one, they are serviceable. Also, a good mechanical standard, in the steady hand of stupidity and insensibility, has this immense advantage — it can be applied to anything. Relevancy ceases to exist; once you have got into the habit of judging peaches by their weight you will find it delightfully easy to go on to books and pictures. The normal man loves a ready-made standard that is always ready and can be applied to anything. Just as he cannot know whether a work of art is beautiful, but can understand the evidence for thinking that it was not made by Raphael, so he cannot know whether a thing is vulgar — vulgarity being a matter of sentiment and expression — but can know whether certain definite words have been used and certain definite subjects mentioned. He has his standard, and he can apply it every morning and evening in his third- or first-class railway carriage. Prudery is mechanical taste just as sanctimoniousness is mechanical religion. And just as no truly religious person is troubled by profanity, so no man of real taste objects to indecency. But these are not the arguments with which you will persuade the electors.

The way of Reason is not always smooth, but he who follows it honestly may be sure of overtaking one reward:

he will lose the unreasonable fear of enjoying the good things of life. Reason may be trusted to hunt down those sport-spoiling, inhibitory bogeys that haunt the brains of barbarians. The frank enjoyment of all life has to offer is the privilege of the completely civilized. To enjoy perfectly a man must have cleansed himself from taboos; he must be free from prudery, superstition, false shame, and the sense of sin. This reason alone can do for him: and his moral code must repose on that other pillar of civility—a sense of values. His sense of values will tell him that the pleasures offered by the senses, or by an alliance between sense and emotion, or by an alliance between sense and intellect, are not bad in themselves. It will tell him, rather, that pleasure, so far as it goes, is always good: it is for civilized intelligence never to allow it to become a means to bad by hampering and making impossible greater good. For instance, no truly civilized person will think it wrong to get drunk; but all civilized people despise a sot. A sot soon makes himself incapable of good states of mind, and a public nuisance to boot: but a gay supper-party is one of those things that no civilized person will refuse so long as he is in good health. Why, austere Plato himself held that it was a citizen's duty to get drunk at the Dionysia.[12] And a civilized man is not to be scared from pleasures by hearing them called bad names—corrupt, vicious, or shameful. As a rule, such epithets mean no more than that most people are frightened by the unexplored or ill-explored parts of human nature. Since pleasure is not bad in itself, there can be no reason for being ashamed of any pleasure: and if there are pleasures in which a civilized man decides not to indulge, it is not because they are bad, but because their consequences are. Assuredly, it is shameful to be such a slave to appetite that, reason dethroned, one loses the power of weighing the consequences. It is shameful to suffer an addiction to crude sensualities to benumb a capacity for subtler enjoyments and more thrilling experiences. A civilized man will be ashamed of unfitting himself for civilized enjoyments, of lowering his capacity for clear thought and fine feeling; he will be ashamed of indulging any passion which cannot be indulged without violating his sense of values and dethroning reason; and he will be ashamed of nothing else. Savages will call him shameless.

Since the study of Greek became part of a gentleman's education it has been to the majority of those who were paid to teach it a source of constant and painful surprise that no people were ever more fearless in enjoyment of life than the Athenians. Certainly they knew what shame was, seeing that they invented it. They invented it by bringing their sensibilities to a sharpness hitherto unknown. But the Athenians were not ashamed of their pleasures: also, they indulged in them pretty freely. They were ashamed of losing all self-control and making brutes or fools of themselves; and they seem to have been haunted by remorse for acts of cruelty and violence. But so far were they from despising pleasure that Greek philosophy reckoned it an essential ingredient of the good life. Only, as no schoolmaster fails to tell his class when he feels — as feel sometimes he must — the sharpness of clash between Greek and Hebrew ethics, the Athenians, above all pleasures, and indeed above all things, set the moderator, the harmonizer, Reason. It is a pity that the Italians of the Renaissance, who borrowed so much, could not have borrowed from Athens a little more of this *sōphrosunē*, this sweet reasonableness. It is a pity that from their superb endowment the gift of temperance was somehow omitted. It is a pity that they could not better control their passion to enjoy—a pity, but nothing to my immediate purpose. Assuredly the men and women of the Renaissance were not afraid of the good things of life. They might dabble in astrology and black magic; they made short work of those superstitions that came between them and their fun. They were shameless: if you don't believe me, read Benvenuto Cellini's autobiography. 'Since God has given us the Papacy let us enjoy it,' said Leo x., and he meant precisely what he said. His pleasures were those of a highly civilized man (a typical man of a typical age); they included an appreciation of art and letters, music and scholarship; song was there, and so were women and wine. And His Holiness was not ashamed.

That adorable eighteenth century got nearer again to the Greek ideal. Indeed, the charm of that charming age comes, more than of anything else perhaps, of its extreme reasonableness having been sweetened by an extraordinary sense of values. And that is the mixture, I am sure, which gives us high civility. The Italian Renaissance, because its instinctive aesthetic sense was tempered and fortified by a belief in reason more serious far than that which inspired the scholastic philosophers, achieved a civilization superior to anything which the middle ages could have conceived. And what gives the second part of the eighteenth century its peculiar deliciousness is that, while men, and women too, thought as vigorously and boldly on all subjects as men have ever thought, while they not only speculated but were prepared to see their ideas growing into actions, a sense of values enabled them to conduct their critical propaganda and subversive activities with the exquisite urbanity of an earlier generation. They believed so sincerely in pleasure that they thought even politics should be made agreeable. Economists were expected to present their theories in a form acceptable to fine ladies; but, remember, to be fine, a lady was almost obliged to take an interest in theories. The serious discussion of fundamental questions, thought these amiable and courageous people, was not incompatible with good temper and humanity. And the century which produced Voltaire, Gibbon, Hume, and two philosophical popes, had not only the intellectual honesty of radicals, but the indulgence of sceptics and the manners of ladies and gentlemen. Such a combination will always appear attractive; and particularly so to an age unfortunate enough to suffer from revolutionaries who have neither wits nor manners and reactionaries who have neither manners nor wits.

In the eighteenth century it was Reason that was expected to keep things sweet by purging the passions of grossness and savagery. Pleasure, reasonable pleasure, was the end of an honest man's desire. It was the eighteenth century that made it the touchstone in political discussions, trying systems and projects of government by the extent to which they might be expected to increase happiness. It was the eighteenth century which found the romantic past sadly to lack in this commodity, and was more impressed by the abject misery of the eleventh century than by the glamour of the first crusade. And, in the eighteenth century, for the first time since the end of the ancient world, was elaborated and expounded in able if not very learned tomes a philosophy of pleasure, a philosophy of which the essence may be culled most agreeably from the stories and miscellaneous writings of Voltaire. For example:

REASON ENTHRONED

' . . . tout le monde avouait que les dieux n'avaient établi
les rois que pour donner tous les jours des fêtes, pourvu
qu'elles fussent diversifiées; que la vie est trop courte pour
en user autrement; que les procès, les intrigues, la guerre,
les disputes des prêtres, qui consument la vie humaine, sont
des choses absurdes et horribles; que l'homme n'est né que
pour la joie; qu'il n'aimerait pas les plaisirs passionnément
et continuellement, s'il n'était pas formé pour eux; que
l'essence de la nature humaine est de se réjouir, et que tout
le reste est folie. Cette excellente morale n'a jamais été
démentie que par les faits.'

And you must not suppose that the eighteenth century
elaborated a philosophy for the benefit of one class only.
On the contrary, its conception of progress consisted in
the gradual extension to all of the means of enjoyment, of
the means, let us say, of fulfilling their natures, since
'l'essence de la nature humaine est de se réjouir.' In the
eighteenth century this philosophy of pleasure, under its
old-world name of Philanthropy, was extremely popular.
Today it is disdained as deficient in idealism, since it aims
at the satisfaction of the individual rather than at the
glorification of a race, a creed, or a class. It is as much
detested by patriots as despised by communists, and only
a few old-fashioned people still believe that there may be
something to be said for it.

Seeing that it has for long been the opinion of those
whose opinions are generally taken seriously that Athens
towards the end of the fifth century brought civilization
to a pitch of intensity which has never been equalled, it
would not be amiss, I think, to wind up this chapter with

an examination of what is allowed to be the best picture of Athenian society at its best. If Plato's *Symposium* has been held, not only by poets, scholars, and artists, but by bishops, judges, and cultivated tradesmen, not only by pagan philosophers but by the Fathers of the Church, to have been one of the most beautiful and moving compositions that ever issued from the mind of man, that is not more on account of the radiant ideas that shine clearly through the web of Socrates's rather over-sophistic speech than of the exquisite picture given of an exquisite way of life. In this lovely dialogue we catch a glimpse, and something more, of a civilization which seems to come nearer the heart's desire than anything less favoured ages have conceived possible. Still about this picture of a way of life hangs the air of an instant in the ideal caught by an artist and immortalized. And, remember, the picture is not the ecstatic vision of a rapt saint, no plan of some celestial paradigm, inaccessible to imperfection, but the record of a life that once was lived by mortal men and might by men be lived again.

The story is told by one Apollodorus who had it from Aristodemus, an atheist, Xenophon says, a little fellow who always went about without sandals, a rather insignificant member of that set of which Socrates, Agathon, Phaedrus, Pausanias, Eryximachus, Aristophanes, and Alcibiades were the stars. Here we have them all collected at an intimate dinner-party given by Agathon to celebrate his success in the contest of tragic poets. The previous day had been devoted to public congratulations and 'a crush'; pretty good evidence, it seems, of the seriousness with which the arts were taken at Athens. On his way to this party Socrates, dressed up uncommonly fine, is met by Aristodemus, who naturally seeks the cause of this

unwonted grandeur. 'Why I am off to dinner with Agathon,' says he (adding, what is probably a distortion of
the Euripidean line, *kalōs ioimi para kalon kaloumenos*'),
and 'I am handsome that I may go handsomely to a handsome man' — *'tauta dē ekallōpisamēn, hina kalos para
kalon io.'* Socrates, who by common consent was the
ugliest and shabbiest fellow in Athens, suggests that
Aristodemus should come along with him. Aristodemus
demurs, as being unbidden; but Socrates insists, knowing
that hospitality and good-fellowship are virtues not peculiar to savages. Having insisted successfully, he (Socrates) lags behind in meditation, so that his embarrassed
companion arrives alone, and has to be put at his ease by
Agathon, who says that he has been looking for him all
day long, anxious to have him but unable to find him.

The guests arrive. Agathon, who, besides being a
tragic poet, was reputed as charming as he was gifted,
and as beautiful as he was either, declines to play the host
and, turning to the servants, says — 'Pray, consider us all
your guests and treat us accordingly.' Late and last in
comes Socrates, refusing to sit, or rather lie, till he has
enjoyed a bout of what I can only describe as 'flirtatious
irony' with Agathon — irony which, I need hardly say, is
taken in excellent part — after which the whole company
dines. Let us glance at it for a moment. Here, amongst
others, are two poets, Agathon and Aristophanes, a doctor Eryximachus, that hard-up, out-at-elbows, street-
corner preacher, Socrates, and, later, Alcibiades, a well-
bred, popular politician, a dandy, and the richest man in
Athens. Here were Phaedrus and Pausanias; and here
were others of whom Aristodemus makes no mention, for
he does not profess to give a complete list of names or a
record of all the speeches. And amongst these others may

have been craftsmen and casual labourers and sophists, who were little better than vagabonds, but amongst them, we may be sure, was no one who devoted the best part of his life to making money. Time, which, according to modern business men, is money, was, according to Socrates, made for slaves. It never occurred to an Athenian that anyone could voluntarily subject himself to that discipline which is the life of the money-maker, of those who live to work. To be completely civilized, thought the Athenians, a man must be free from material cares. And as he must have ample leisure in which to enjoy whatever good things the intellect, the emotions or the senses put before him, there must be slaves. And because these lived to produce rather than to enjoy, because, lacking culture and leisure, they were incapable of thinking freely and feeling finely, they were inferiors. Between citizens equality was absolute. Differences of intelligence and education which are, unfortunately no doubt, real bars to pleasant and easy intercourse were the only differences recognized at Athens. Amongst citizens there were no class distinctions. In Athens there were no snobs.

Dinner over, the question is raised by Pausanias, shall they have a carouse, get drunk, and keep the flute-player, or shall they have conversation and send her away 'to play to herself or, if she will, to the servants within?' We are on the threshold of what is admittedly one of the most sublime arguments in human record: mark well the attitude of those about to hold it. Reason makes them unafraid of the good things of life; they are not ashamed of enjoying, even to what is called excess, such pleasures as wine and flute-girls can afford: but they are neither sots nor lechers; and a sense of values, strengthened somewhat by the recollection of an overnight carouse, induces them to choose, on this occasion, the more exquisite pleasure of serious discussion. Not so serious, though, but what they can take it playfully. There is plenty of intellectual and some physical ragging, there are little disputes as to who is to sit next whom, there is personal banter, there is fun, there is downright teasing. Very early in the argument, it being the turn of Aristophanes to speak, he complains of the hiccups and claims that Eryximachus, the doctor, shall either take his turn or cure his disease. Eryximachus immediately offers to do both, and prescribes a ridiculous but most effective remedy. Highly civilized people are rarely solemn.

Everyone knows what was the theme of this most famous argument: Love. Not everyone realizes that, not to invalidate their conclusions by limiting their premises, the disputants excluded from discussion no aspect of the subject. They spoke of love in its most admired and respectable forms; also they had much to say in praise of a form for which in England people are sent to prison. To this form my instinctive reaction resembles that of the bulk of my fellows; it is one of amazement and slight disgust. But I am not such a conceited fool as to trust my reactions blindly against the sentiment and considered opinion of some of the wisest and best of mankind. I think of those misguided and shocking people who eat cheese, and I try not to be silly. Whether my taste or that of Socrates and his friends be the better I cannot pretend to decide; but I can listen respectfully to the arguments of my awe-inspiring opponents, I can refrain from passing off my physical reactions as moral indignation, and I can protest with all my heart against treating what has seemed good to many great men as a crime. No one has a right to call himself civilized who cannot listen to both sides of an argument; and he is no better than a brute who cannot tolerate many things which to him, personally, are distasteful.

It is not my intention to discuss the *Symposium* save in so far as it throws light on my subject. I may note the genuine desire for truth underlying all the speeches, and the sense of values which causes each speaker to present his case as beautifully as he can. Not even Socrates argues for victory: no one is unwilling to surrender an untenable position. Phaedrus speaks earnestly; Pausanius is a trifle sententious; Eryximachus is professional. The doctor, however, unlike the majority of his confrères, is not afraid of facing the inferences of his science, and points out, with admirable sense, that we should submit ourselves to the Pandemian Venus (Lust), 'only so far as to derive pleasure from it without indulging to excess, in the same manner as, according to our art, we are instructed to seek the pleasures of the table, only so far as we can enjoy them without the consequences of disease' (Shelley's translation). And then there is the speech of Aristophanes, which is, I suppose, about as brilliant as a speech can be. With a delicious air of intellectual fooling it leads by unexpected and exquisitely comic ways to a serious conclusion, indicated rather than established, and smothered at birth — it is the moment to take risks with metaphors — in motley swaddling clothes. I take note of an irreverent tumbling of the gods which proves pretty clearly that these civilized people had run through the current superstitions. I regret to say the speech is not free from smutty jokes; but then we agreed that a willingness to talk and laugh about everything is a characteristic of civilized people. And I fancy few lovers, even the most ethereal and the most genteel, will take exception to this

account of their state. 'These (those who have discovered
their lost halves) are they who devote their whole lives to
each other, with a vain and inexpressible longing to obtain from each other something they know not what; for
it is not merely the sensual delights of their intercourse for
the sake of which they dedicate themselves to each other
with such serious affection, but the soul of each manifestly thirsts for, from the other, something which there
are no words to describe, and divines that which it seeks,
and traces obscurely the footsteps of its obscure desire'
(Shelley).[13] To be sure, in the very next paragraph he falls
back into ribaldry, arguing that if we are not extremely
attentive to the gods, it is to be feared that Zeus will chop
us in two again (his theory of love being that we have
once already been so divided, and that the halves are ever
seeking to reunite), and then, says he, we shall have to go
about, like the figures that artists paint on columns, with
our noses split down the middle, to say nothing of having
to hop on one leg. This civilized habit of not being solemn
when one is serious is very perplexing.

Agathon's speech is lyrical, lovely, and eloquent. He
begins by saying that it is one thing to address the multitude in the theatre and quite another to appeal to a really
critical audience. 'Surely, Socrates,' he says, 'you don't
suppose me so blown up with my theatrical triumphs as
not to know that to a person of any sense a few competent
critics are more formidable than all the men in the
street.' To me this remark seems to indicate a sense of
values. To Socrates it gave an opening for a little sophistry
and flirtation, to which, however, Phaedrus puts a stop
by saying—'My dear Agathon, if once you get into an
argument with Socrates there will be no end to it, for he
will go on wrangling for ever about anything with any-

one — or, at any rate, with anyone who is sufficiently good looking. To be sure, it is always a pleasure to hear him talk, but tonight I must see to it that Love (our chosen topic) is not defrauded.' So Agathon proceeds; and asserts, amongst other things, that Love can make a poet of any man, citing, in support, some part of a distich of his own which betrays the influence of Euripides:

pas goun poietēs gignetai 'kan amousos ē to prin' hou an Erōs hapsetai.
No matter how prosaic formerly a man is touched to poetry by Love.

This gives Socrates, a little later, the chance of poking fun at Agathon's master, whom he did not love. After all the fine things Agathon has said, protests Socrates, it will be impossible for him to keep his promise. 'Such praise I do not understand; and in ignorance I agreed to compose a panegyric:'

But my tongue only promised, not my mind
(*he glossa oun upeskheto, he de phren ou*),

exclaims he, in the high Euripidean fashion. And then, just raising an eyebrow at Agathon's coloured style, he begins his famous discourse on the nature of love. The speech is marvellous, though a little sophistic for my taste: perhaps it is worth noting, as a symptom of civility, that, at its most intense moment, the speaker gets in a gay gibe at the fopperies of the professional sophists, his enemies. As he ends, in bursts Alcibiades, extremely drunk, followed by flute-players. He comes to crown Agathon, which done, he will stay if they are for drinking, and go if

they are not. They keep him, of course. True philosophers make the best of both worlds.

So they set to drinking, chaffing each other very clev-
erly about their love-affairs, and showing an exquisite
superiority to that hardest dying of all barbarous passions — jealousy. And now, says Eryximachus, is this fair?
Is it just that Alcibiades should drink with us without con-
tributing to our entertainment? Let him, too, speak in
praise of Love. It is as much as my skin is worth, says
Alcibiades, to praise anything in the presence of Socrates
but Socrates. Very well then, is the reply, Socrates you
shall praise. And here comes the speech that so profoundly troubled Dr. Jowett. Alcibiades recounts, with
some particularity, the story of his fruitless passion for
Socrates, while Socrates sits by, smiling blandly one
imagines. Alcibiades was certainly not ashamed of his
feelings; and as he does not fail to see that they will appear slightly comic to his friends, as he does not make the
mistake of taking himself too seriously, nothing in his
confession seems to the company shocking or unpleasant.
He is frank, amusing, and shameless. Not quite shameless, though; he feels shame enough when Socrates con-
victs him of pursuing popular applause rather than truth
and beauty. Here, at last, we have something that does
appear disgraceful to a civilized man. Alcibiades concludes his tale of woe by imploring Agathon not to fall in
love with Socrates lest he should suffer a like fate; but
here Socrates is waiting for him and declares that from
the first he foresaw that this eulogy was nothing but a
cunning device for putting him wrong with Agathon. In
putting it right, the three,[14] who are sitting together, get
up a pretty scrimmage as to who is now to praise whom,
and who is to sit next whom, which is interrupted by the

influx of a crowd of uninvited revellers, 'and the whole place being thrown into an uproar, order went by the board, and everyone felt bound to drink furiously.' (*kai thorubou mesta panta einai, kai ouketi en kosmō oudeni anagkazesthai pinein pampolun oinon.*)

That feast of reason which has been the wonder and admiration of twenty-three centuries ended, I am sorry to say, in what a London police-court magistrate would call 'a disgraceful orgy.' The professional Eryximachus and the earnest Phaedrus were the first to totter home: Aristodemus, for his part, fell asleep where he was. He slept a good while; it was winter and the nights were long. At daybreak he awoke: most of the quests were asleep — it seemed quite natural to eminent Athenians to curl up in their cloaks and sleep on the dining-room floor floor — but he noticed that Agathon, Aristophanes, and Socrates were still awake, drinking out of a great bowl, and talking. So far as Aristodemus could make out, Socrates was compelling the others to admit that tragedy and comedy are essentially identical; but being drowsy and still rather drunk he was none too sure how the argument went. Only he was certain that Aristophanes first began to doze and then dropped off, and that when it was full day Agathon followed suit: 'having tucked them both up, Socrates (followed by Aristodemus) walked to the Lyceum, where, as usual, he took his bath; the day he spent at work, and in the evening he went home to bed.'

VI

CIVILIZATION AND ITS DISSEMINATORS

I HAVE not yet defined civilization; but perhaps I have made definition superfluous. Anyone, I fancy, who has done me the honour of reading so far will by now understand pretty well what I mean. Civilization is a characteristic of societies. In its crudest form it is the characteristic which differentiates what anthropologists call 'advanced' from what they call 'low' or 'backward' societies. So soon as savages begin to apply reason to instinct, so soon as they acquire a rudimentary sense of values — so soon, that is, as they begin to distinguish between ends and means, or between direct means to good and remote — they have taken the first step upward. The first step towards civilization is the correcting of instinct by reason: the second, the deliberate rejection of immediate satisfactions with a view to obtaining subtler. The hungry savage, when he catches a rabbit, eats it there and then, or instinctively takes it home, as a fox might, to be eaten raw by his cubs; the first who, all hungry though he was, took it home and cooked it was on the road to Athens. He was a pioneer, who with equal justice may be described as the first decadent. The fact is significant. Civilization is something artificial and unnatural. Progress and Decadence are interchangeable terms. All who have added to human knowledge and sensibility, and most of those even who have merely increased material comfort, have been hailed by contemporaries capable of profiting by their discoveries as benefactors, and denounced by all

119

whom age, stupidity, or jealousy rendered incapable, as degenerates. It is silly to quarrel about words: let us agree that the habit of cooking one's victuals may with equal propriety be considered a step towards civilization or a falling away from the primitive perfection of the up-standing ape.

From these primary qualities, Reasonableness and a Sense of Values, may spring a host of secondaries: a taste for truth and beauty, tolerance, intellectual honesty, fastidiousness, a sense of humour, good manners, curios-ity, a dislike of vulgarity, brutality, and over-emphasis, freedom from superstition and prudery, a fearless ac-ceptance of the good things of life, a desire for complete self-expression and for a liberal education, a contempt for utilitarianism and philistinism, in two words—sweet-ness and light. Not all societies that struggle out of bar-barism grasp all or even most of these, and fewer still grasp any of them firmly. That is why we find a consider-able number of civilized societies and very few highly civ-ilized, for only by grasping a good handful of civilized qualities and holding them tight does a society become that.

But can an entity so vague as a society be said to have or to hold qualities so subtle? Only in the vaguest sense. Societies express themselves in certain more or less perm-anent and more or less legible forms which become for anthropologists and historians monuments of their civil-ity. They express themselves in manners, customs and conventions, in laws and in social and economic organiza-tion, above all, in the literature, science and art they have appreciated and encouraged: less surely they tell us something about themselves through the literature, sci-ence and art, which they may or may not have appreciated, but which was created by artists and thinkers whom they produced. All these taken together may be reckoned — none too confidently — to compose a legible symbol of a prevailing attitude to life. And it is this attitude, made manifest in these more or less public and permanent forms, which we call civilization.

Civilization, if I may risk a not easily defensible metaphor, is the flavour given to the self-expression of an age or society by a mental attitude: it is the colour given to social manifestations by a peculiar and prevailing point of view. Whence comes this colouring view of life, this flavouring attitude? From individuals of course; since, as far as we know, individuals alone have minds to strike attitudes or select viewpoints. Past question the individual mind is the fount and origin of civility; but one human mind is a drop of sweetness in the ocean, a speck of cochineal on the shore. One civilized human being will not make a civilization. Possibly, during the last three thousand years the world has never been without civilized inhabitants: in the darkest ages, though not, of course, amongst utterly barbarous and primitive tribes, it is likely enough that one or two existed. In Western Europe of the tenth century — and one can hardly go lower without falling amongst Veddahs and Bushmen — we come across Gerbert looking oddly like a civilized man; and the emperor Otho III., who may have been merely a prig, may on the contrary have been another. We cannot be sure that in the eighth century even there did not lurk unknown in quiet monasteries men who would not have been out of place at the court of Lorenzo the Magnificent. One swallow does not, and cannot, make a summer. It is only when there come together enough civilized individuals to form a nucleus from which light can radiate, and sweetness ooze, that a civilization becomes possible. The disseminators of civilization are therefore highly civilized men and women forming groups sufficiently influential to affect larger groups, and ultimately whole communities. A group of the civilized becomes civilizing when, and only when, it can so influence the community in which it exists that this community, tinted with its peculiar graces, begins to manifest them in ways of thinking and feeling. A civilized nucleus becomes civilizing when it is sufficiently numerous and powerful to colour the mass. And 'a civilized nucleus' is merely a definite looking name for an indefinite number of highly civilized men and women. These men and women are the creators and disseminators, the *sine qua non*, of civility.

It is in the mind of man that we must seek the cause and origin of civilization. Not laws nor customs nor morals nor institutions nor mechanical contrivances, as we discovered from a glance at savage communities and the British colonies, can create it: such things cannot make because they are made by men. It is the mind, the individual mind, which conceives, creates, and carries out. It is the influence of a number of minds, thinking and feeling sympathetically, which fashions, unconsciously and unintentionally as a rule, societies and ages. And so, at last, we are come to something precise—the civilized human being. Him or her we shall expect to find endowed in a finer, subtler, surer way with those qualities we noted as characteristic of civilized societies. The thoroughly civilized person will be willing at any moment to follow intellect into the oddest holes and corners, while his instinctive reaction to life will be ever conditioned by taste. Life for him or her will not be altogether a matter of necessity; to some extent it will be a matter of choice. His rabbit caught, he will have the self-restraint to decide how, where and when it shall be eaten. Essentially the civilized man is artificial. It is artificial to clean one's teeth and say 'please' and 'thank you.' It is unnatural not to knock down a weaker person with whom one is angry. But do not suspect me of trying to prove that the civilized man is the good man. The best man — if good mean anything — will be he who is capable of the best states of mind and enjoys them longest. It is amongst artists, philosophers, and mystics, with their intense and interminable ecstasies of contemplation and creation, that we must look for our saints. Reason will assure the civilized that here is the best, though a perverted taste may whisper that the best lacks variety. There are so many good things falling just short of it to be enjoyed. But perfection admits of no inferior ingredient. The ideal is an instant of perfection made infinite — the best of the best for ever. It is always high noon in Heaven. Yet a man may be exquisitely civilized notwithstanding that he loves the evening shades and starlit nights, to say nothing of the rain and snow that make his fire burn brighter. The ideal is something permanent and unique; and in the unmitigated beatitude of Heaven I do not know but that a very highly civilized person might find himself occasionally ill at ease.

Mind, I am not saying that an artist, a philosopher, or a mystic cannot be highly civilized, I am saying that a completely civilized person will not be of the single-eyed sort. Neither St. Francis, nor Dante, nor Blake, nor Cézanne, nor Dostoievsky was completely civilized, nor, given his work and all its implications, could he have been. Even Plato, once he gets on his high horse, as he does in the *Republic*, takes leave of his sense of values. A highly civilized man is too widely appreciative — and notoriously many-sidedness has its defects as well as its graces — to lose often or for long in an 'O Altitudo' his sense of everything but the moment. He is an appreciator above all things. He gains in breadth and diversity but loses in intensity, and intensity according to the philosophers is best. Should he happen to be an artist it will be, I suppose, that part of him which is not feverishly intent on self-expression — self-expression which comes perilously near self-assertion — which will be most highly civilized. (And yet, precisely this civilized appreciativeness, this cultivated habit of self-criticism, what works of art have they not given us, from Horace, Pope, Mérimée, Milton even, Mantegna, Poussin, Wren, etc., etc., etc.) Anyhow, the civilized man will be highly susceptible to aesthetic impressions, and to aesthetic impressions not of one sort only. He will be eclectic. He will be discriminatingly appreciative and ever open to new aesthetic experiences. And yet, all regardful of beauty, truth, and knowledge, as he must be, filled with gratitude and a natural respect for the triumphant expressions of the spirit, he will inevitably feel more acutely than professional artists, thinkers, and savants are apt to feel, that there are other things in life meriting a perhaps not less eager pursuit.

If his intellectuality is not passionate enough to make of him a devoted philosopher or savant, it will make him aware at any rate of the importance of thought and knowledge as means to desirable states of mind and to self-development. Wherefore the highly civilized man will prize above most things education. For him its unassayable virtue lies in this: education unlocks the door to the world of his desires. Education and sensibility are the most precious implements of the intelligent pleasure-seeker. The man of sensibility but of no education, the man who therefore cannot relate his personal experience to the past, the future, or the forces of nature, who cannot investigate the causes and consequences of his own ideas and feelings or dally with their analogies, is as one who has swilled choice wine all his life without ever lingering over the flavour, relishing the bouquet or smiling at the colour. Without education, be he never so sensitive, a man must stay in the forecourt of experience; he wants the key to the inner palace of pleasures. Every thought and every feeling has overtones inaudible to the uneducated ear: to toy with each as it arises, to recognize the most unexpected implications in the most unlikely places, to see every question from a dozen different angles, to see oneself in other circumstances, to feel oneself at once heir of all the ages and a poor player who struts and frets his hour, to understand why Dr. Johnson is a credit to the race and a ridiculous old donkey to boot, such are the pleasures which education, and education alone, can procure: believe me, they are the champagne and caviare of the spiritual life, and more delicious even than their material counterparts.

Education is our sixth sense. As for that technical instruction which is sometimes called education, it has nothing to do with what we are talking about. It has its importance; it is well that boys should be taught how to get the greatest possible amount of milk out of six cows, and that girls should learn book-keeping. Such knowledge is a means to good, and a means to civilization as well. It is a remote means, however. For the rest, it is confusing to honour the inculcation of what is merely a means to 'getting on' with the name of 'education' which is a 'drawing out'—the drawing out of our subtlest and most delicate powers. It is wrong philosophically, I know, to describe this liberal education as the pursuit of knowledge as an end. Knowledge, as we have seen, is sought, not as an end, but as a means to valuable states of mind: knowledge in itself is worthless. Yet the common saying that the purpose of a liberal education is the stimulation of disinterested curiosity is not amiss; for by it is understood to be meant that a liberal education will not help anyone to 'get on' or 'make good' — in precise English, to make money — but to understand life and enjoy its finer pleasures.

At this time of day a civilized person, male or female, should be unshockable. Barbarism dies hard; and if History, with its record of what the best and wisest have thought and felt, of the tyranny, the imbecility, of the taboo, and Science, with its picture of man as a tangle of sub-conscious reactions, have not enabled us in this twentieth century to distinguish between an ethical judgment and a physical jib, blame not Reason. Against stupidity the very gods are said to fight in vain. Being shocked means that reason has been dethroned. Prudery, like fear, comes between a man and his impartial judgment, pulls this way and that, and perplexes the issue. Artillery officers have told me that the moment an observer loses his nerve (textually 'gets rattled'), he is powerless to direct accurately his gun, or to judge of its effect on the enemy. Fear takes charge, and plays what tricks it will, perverting judgment to its own uses. Prudery has a like effect. Had anatomists been so disgusted by the sight of a dead human body that, averting their eyes, they had refused to proceed with their dissections, we should to this day be in a state of complete biological ignorance. And how should those who refuse to consider and, if possible, understand

disagreeable, that is unfamiliar, tastes, habits, and tendencies, physical and emotional extravagances — how
should they, starting away, screaming, 'I am shocked, I
am shocked,' ever come to know anything of psychology
or ethics? The causes and consequences of what distresses
them they will not examine. They never see, steadily and
whole, the thing itself, because some physical qualm or
hard-dying taboo — which they are pleased to call 'moral
indignation' or a 'sense of decency' — surges up and blinds
them. They cannot touch a snake, it gives them the
creeps. So it may; so much the worse for them: but do
not let them make a virtue of a physical disability, or
condemn snakes and snake-students on that account. But
they are quite 'upset.' Indeed they are; the word is well
chosen since reason is overthrown. And they know that
snakes are 'horrid,' though zoologists assure them that
they are beautiful and interesting. This prudery, unlike
fear, which is often a means to self-preservation, and may
well be founded on reason, springs wholly from superstition when it is not a mere physical qualm. It is a curse
without compensation. We cannot wish entirely to eliminate fear: but if we could rid ourselves of prudery we
should be better off in a thousand ways and worse off in
none.

The completely civilized man is above prudery: also,
because he desires to come at truth he will try to put himself above rage and prejudice, which have the same inhibitory effect. A civilized man will be tolerant and liberal, which is not to say he will never show temper or stick
his toes in. Only, just as he discovered that by putting
the padlock of prejudice on any door of the mind inevitably he turned away some of its most charming visitors, so
he will learn that there are very very few cases of anger

127

which will not yield to intelligent treatment. As surely as a meek answer turneth away wrath does a sense of humour deflate tantrums. A civilized man will be liberal and tolerant.

Surely no one imagines that when I say 'liberal' I am thinking of politics. There is no knowing what the political opinions of a civilized man will be. This alone is certain, they will be the logical consequence of some clear notion of what he really wants. What he wants may be absolute good, or merely to secure so far as possible his own comfort. Either is an intelligible object, and either, clearly perceived and genuinely desired, will prevent him attaching the least importance to those stunning phrases with which professional politicians make play. Liberty, Justice, Equality, Fraternity, Sanctities, Rights, Duties, Honour, all these expensive vocables may mean anything or nothing. To say that you are in favour of the Trade Union Bill because it is just is as senseless as to say that you are in favour of it because it is unjust. Justice is not an end in itself: a world that was entirely just and nothing else would be as insignificant as a world that was entirely unjust and nothing else. To be in favour of the Bill because it is a remote means to absolute good is a bold saying but a respectable position (the conclusion stands on valid premises and has only to be shown to have been logically drawn); similarly, to oppose the Bill because you think that in the long run it will diminish your wages is a perfectly good reason for opposing: but to support it because it is just, or oppose it because it is iniquitous, is to support or oppose it for no valid reason, or for no reason at all. The only question a civilized man will ask about a political measure is, 'Is it a means to what I want, or does it make against what I want?' No one wants justice or

equity in the void; these things, if desired at all, are desired as means, and the civilized man will ask himself —
means to what? Of course it may happen that you and I,
both desiring the same end, differ as to whether a particular Act of Parliament will be a means to that end. Here
will be room for argument and explanation. Still more
probably what is a means to what a man with four pounds
a week wants will not be a means to what is desired by a
man with ten thousand a year. Here, since the measure
proposed is judged by different criteria, ultimate agree-
ment is out of the question and compromise is the best
that can be hoped for. But in such a case for either side to
invoke such catchwords as 'rights' and 'duties,' or to ac-
cuse the other of immorality is about as sensible as it
would be for an Oxford batsman to denounce the Cambridge bowler who got him out. The aims of the two parties are reasonable but different, and there is no occasion
for hard names. That occasion arises when people desiring the end that we desire employ means manifestly destined in the long run to defeat it: them we call stupid not
wicked. Moral censure would be admissible in political
controversy only if we could get everyone agreed as to
what is good as an end, which might be possible, and
further, as to what political measures are means to that
end, which will not be easy. Is my having an additional
fifty pounds a year likely, in the very longest run, to produce more absolute good — more valuable states of
mind — that the provision of sand-heaps and waste-paper
bins in the playgrounds of St. Pancras? It is a nice question; and one on which, as you will see if you read to the
end of my book, I have a quite definite opinion. But, as
you will also see, I have not much hope of getting everyone to agree with me. Mindful of all these things, a thor-

oughly civilized person, though deeply concerned about politics, will neither appeal to those grand old principles which are nothing to the purpose, nor deem his natural desire to hold what he has more meritorious than the desire of his opponent to get it for himself. He will not deceive himself with words and phrases. A civilized millionaire will not really believe that his objection to the present Russian government is that it has made strikes illegal; and Mr. Lansbury, were he civilized, would not in his heart believe that his constituents have any more 'right' to a living wage that the Duke of Northumberland has to his fortune. Incidentally, this inability to suppose that any man's private hopes or fears are identical with absolute good makes it unlikely that a highly civilized man will often find his way into a popularly elected assembly.

Tolerant and unwilling to interfere, a civilized man will have manners. His sense of values would convince him of their importance as amenities even were reason not there to tell him that they are essential to knowledge. If to understand all be to pardon all, to pardon all is half-way to understanding. Put a man at his ease by good manners and address, and you are on the road to establishing sympathetic relations, you have made it easy for him to give his best; put up those barriers which manners were made to throw down, thrust between yourself and him suspicion, irritability, combativeness and self-assertion, and be sure that you will get nothing better than you give. Never to the overbearing and underbred are we tempted to betray our dearest secrets. That is why the cad, the bounder, the bully, the mistrustful wiseacre, and the self-assertive superman shove or slink through life without tasting it; all their contacts are one-sided. When they are very strong they can sometimes seize life and shake it: a man with hooks at the end of his arms can sometimes catch you by the ankle and bring you down, but never can he know the thousand curious thrills of giving a caress or taking the pressure of a hand. Doubtless there are good things in life at which mere force of intellect and character can come; there are better, subtler at all events, which nothing less than manners can buy. Of these the best is conversation — real conversation — the exchange of sentiments and ideas between people completely disarmed and at their ease, people without fear or suspicion, having no axes to grind, seeking neither to impose nor display themselves, seeking truth by way of pleasure. Conversation is a delight known to the civilized alone.

Of course he will be a man of taste, the highly civilized man, of taste in life. He will discriminate. He will have peculiar wants and particular desires. Civilization, that elaborate protest of individual intelligence and sensibility against the flock instinct, will never accept reach-me-down standards or bow to the authority of shop-walkers. The savage rams and silly sheep are slaves to the gentleman in a frock-coat. Shop-walkers dictate what should be their most intimate and personal decisions. Messrs. Harrod and Selfridge choose their wines and cigars, frocks, shoes, hats, and chemises; Messrs. Hatchard and Mudie decide what books they shall read; the Bond street dealers provide pictures; Sir Thomas Beecham and Sir Henry Wood music and pills; Sir Oswald Stoll and Hollywood wit, beauty, and a sense of romance. 'Here, ladies and gentlemen of the British Empire,' shout the emporium kings, 'here is the best.' And the ladies and gentlemen of the British Empire take their places obediently in the queue. Only a few highly civilized venture to inform these decorated purveyors that what they offer happens not to be what they want.

131

CIVILIZATION

To be civilized a man must have the taste to choose and appreciate, but — let me say it once again — he need not have the power to create. If create he does his creations will bear marks of his civility. But these marks, since they are entirely adventitious and affect in no way the intrinsic significance of his work, will, though of the greatest importance to historians attempting to discover the character of the age in which they were made or of the artist who made them, be irrelevant to the pure aesthete. If the *Odyssey* be superior to the *Chanson de Roland*, that is not because one has been coloured by a dawning civilization and the other by the twilight of barbarism. Though a civilized artist will make manifest his civility in his art, this manifestation will be no essential part of it. Creativeness is no more an attribute of the civilized man than of the savage; but discriminating, conscious appreciation is. A man or woman entirely insensitive to all the arts can hardly be deemed civilized.

At any rate, without frequent and violent aesthetic emotions the civilized life runs a risk of becoming empty. The pleasures of that life are mainly contemplative, and of contemplative experiences the aesthetic are perhaps the the most important, for, though less intense than the emotions derived from personal relations, they are more certain and more durable. This preference for contemplation (I use the term in its widest sense), which is one of the most endearing characteristics that civilized people derive from their sense of values, accounts for their dislike of that state of perpetual interference which partial biographers call 'a life of action.' Obviously there are activities which may be means to good, and these a civilized person must always approve and sometimes practise. But since already his life is full of immediate means to good, since there are personal relations to be enjoyed, beauty to be contemplated or created, truth to be sought, he will be generally disinclined to sacrifice this substance to what may prove a shadow. Work for a living he will—if he must; life is a necessary means to good. But existence secured, his dealings with life will be mainly receptive. At its best, the life of action may be an agitated pursuit of what may turn out to be a means to good—good for the actor or more probably for others; but action in itself is worthless, and the state of mind it engenders rarely valuable: at its commonest, action is a stimulant of bad states of mind in the doer, and to everyone else an unmitigated nuisance.

I have admitted that the life of action (and I do not call a life devoted simply to earning one's living 'a life of action'—the agricultural labourer is not 'a man of action') may be a means to good—especially to the good of others. Real men and women of action, however, do not as a rule make wars and massacres, do not domineer over the weak and provoke the strong, meddle with their neighbours and turn the world upside down from altruistic motives. These things they do because only in doing can they assert themselves. What is called a man or woman of action is almost always a deformed and deficient artist who yearns to express himself or herself but, unable to express by creating, must assert by interfering. Such people are our misfortune, and there are a good many of them. They cannot find satisfaction in love, friendship, conversation, the creation or contemplation of beauty, the pursuit of truth and knowledge, the gratification of their senses, or in quietly earning their daily bread: they must have power, they must impose themselves, they must interfere. They are the makers of nations and empires, and the troublers of peace. They are the saviours of mankind from its better self. They are the pillars of barbarism or, still to follow the biographers, of society. Themselves inapt for civilized pleasures, they will not suffer their more fortunately endowed neighbours to enjoy them. They must impose their standards and ways of life. Worst of all, they drive the less clear-sighted of the potentially civilized into self-defensive action — into semibarbarism that is to say.[15] From these pests comes that precious doctrine, the gospel of work: as if work could ever be good in itself. From them come wars, persecution, the inquisition and police regulations. By force they fancy they can impose on others beliefs and sentiments; and the others are fools enough to believe them. They can and do impose external uniformity and discipline. They organize hostility to whatever is unusual and unpopular — to whatever is distinguished and rare that is to say. They are a small minority no doubt; but as they have nothing better to do than seek power, and as the majority is stupid and docile, they generally get it.

Let us turn back to the civilized. The civilized man is made not born: he is artificial; he is unnatural. Consciously and deliberately he forms himself with a view to possessing and enjoying the best and subtlest; and yet in another sense, all sophisticated though he be, he is the least distorted of human beings. He is the least distorted because his reactions are the least biassed. To understand this seeming paradox we must fix our minds on two images: on life, or experience, as an ever-flowing stream, and on that strange conduit through which we make it flow, which is personality. The odd thing about personality is that it at once conditions and is conditioned by experience. No two personalities in their original shape are identical; but during the first years of every human being's existence his personality — the thing I mean through which the stream of experience passes — is twisted and modified by circumstance and education. Here it is bunged up and given a bulge by the *débris* of superstition or the accumulations of habit, there bent and dent by traditional prejudices; and sometimes by culture it is deliberately refashioned. That it may appreciate the exact force, temperature, and quality of the stream passing over it, that it may register the eddies and react to the backwash, that it may distinguish surely between drought and spate even, this delicate instrument must be kept scrupulously clean. Incessantly our experience-conductor needs scouring; and only reason can perform that radical operation. For ever challenging accepted beliefs and instinctive reactions, reason alone keeps personality clear of fixed ideas and foregone responses. The personality of a savage is foul with superstitious prejudices and terrors; that of a civilized man is not assuredly the personality with which he was born, since it has been battered by fate and shaped by education, but it is clean. No hard-dying taboos, baseless conventions or useless fears come between him and life. Wherefore he stands a chance of one day experiencing something directly, completely, and personally, not as a Christian or a Devil-worshipper, not as an English gentleman or a newspaper-reading proletarian, but as himself.

Not for love of conformity, nor yet for intellectual and emotional security — the great objects of the herd — does a civilized man tamper with his native characteristics. Only when they stand between him and the understanding and enjoyment of life will he try to mend them. He will try to cure himself of a violent temper as of a stutter; he will fight against jealous tendencies as he would against incipient consumption. Barbarous passions bring with them no gift of lasting joy. They are as destructive of happiness as hollow teeth. They make us suffer as the sick and behave as the insane. Intruders between consciousness and reality, twisters of judgment, clouders of vision, them a civilized man will do what he can to be rid of. He will try to expel nature with the pitchfork, education, and so trying will become artificial. Thus, though he will never refuse a pleasure on principle, his habit of analysis and sense of values will often convince him that by following his natural bent he would be sacrificing a superior to an inferior. The taste for inferior pleasures he will eliminate or curtail. Should common greed seem to be blunting his sensibility to thought and feeling, he will control his appetite: a savage will eat and drink till he is sick, a half-civilized man till he is stupid. A civilized man will be trying always to improve on nature, and probably he will succeed. He will stimulate here and eradicate there. He will not accept nature as she is, and I see no reason why he should. Those who do, those who disapprove of any tampering with the goddess, those who have set their hearts on eliminating all that is unnatural, I advise to get back to the inter-tidal scum as fast as fins, flappers or plain prehensile bellies will carry them.

Such is my picture of the civilized man. Does it strike you as slightly unsympathetic? It was none of my business to make it otherwise. Whether you like it or not, whether leniently you describe my picture as 'sketchy' or curtly dismiss it as 'feeble,' I believe you will agree that the sort of person it is intended to portray is, in fact, the sort of person one calls civilized. He is not the good man nor the natural; he is not the artist, the hero, the saint, nor the philosopher; but he appreciates art, respects truth, and knows how to behave himself. To enjoy life to the full is his end, to enjoy it as a whole and in its subtlest and most recondite details; and to this end his chief means are the powers of thinking and feeling, intensely cultivated. He is a man of taste in all things. His intellectual curiosity is boundless, fearless, and disinterested. He is tolerant, liberal, and unshockable; and if not always affable and urbane, at least never truculent, suspicious, or over-bearing. He chooses his pleasures deliberately, and his choice is limited neither by prejudice nor fear. Because he can distinguish between ends and means he values things for their emotional significance rather than their practical utility. All cant about 'rights,' 'duties' and 'sanctities' blow past him like grit and chaff, annoying without injuring. His sense of values, intelligently handled, is a needle to prick the frothy bubbles of moral indignation. He is critical, self-conscious and, to some extent at any rate, analytical. Inevitably he will be egregious. Conscious of himself as an individual, he will have little sympathy with the unanimities of the flock: but educating his mind, his emotions and his senses, he will elaborate a way of life which he will clear, so far as possible, of obstructive habits and passions. No, he will not be natural.

A single specimen of the civilized human being may exist, I suppose, rather drearily alone, sufficient unto himself, and in himself valuable. But only when a number of civilized human beings come together does the civilized man become civilizing. It is a group of civilized human beings that is the nucleus of civilization. 'Enfin,' said Voltaire, 'partout la bonne société règle tout.' But it takes

137

more than one to make a society, good or bad. When it exists, *la bonne société,* the civilizing nucleus, reigns, if it can be called reigning, only by faintly colouring its surroundings. Those surroundings—the city, state or age—may be said to have become highly civilized (for surroundings) when an appreciable part of the mass, though barbarous enough when tried by such searching tests as I have been applying to individuals, has yet absorbed a tincture of the precious dye. In lucky ages and in favoured spots it has happened that a considerable part of the population has displayed a liking for fine sights and sounds, has given signs of a stirring of intellectual curiosity, and has manifested impatience with those savage limitations on thought and feeling which keep the majority normally on the confines of bestiality. Cities have been embellished by great artists whose work appears to have been deliberately and consciously preferred to that of bad ones. We assert with confidence that the statue of Miss Cavell could not have been displayed in Periclean Athens or Florence of the Medici. Times have been when many people began to feel a dislike, at once rational and aesthetic, for lies and ignorance. In the eighteenth century Voltaire laughed right out of public consideration publicists more plausible than Mr. Belloc and Sir Arthur Conan Doyle; and in that age Mr. Valentino himself would have been given a less impressive funeral than Sir Isaac Newton. The Athenians made art the first charge on the exchequer. By the Italians of the Renaissance Raphael was reckoned the greatest of national glories. From such straws one divines the direction of the wind; and closer examination confirms the impression that there have indeed been communities in which existed a vague but fairly widespread respect for the supreme values and the more comely things of life, and, what is more, a will to ensue them even at the expense of more obvious satisfactions. This was the doing of a group of intensely civilized individuals. The group, acting on the mass, unintentionally and indirectly for the most part, coloured its age. Groups of highly civilized men and women are the disseminators of civility.[16]

VII

HOW TO MAKE A CIVILIZATION

TWO questions remain. Do we want civilization? Could we have it if we did?

Do we want it? Well, besides the word of allied statesmen, there are reasons for thinking that civilization is desirable. We have the deep-seated conviction of every decent man and woman; for in his heart or hers, every decent person feels that those golden ages, the characters of which I attempted to adumbrate, were golden indeed. We all feel that they are a credit to history. Not but what there are cleverish people who delight in hymning the beauties of barbarism; while even the intelligent are aware of the diseases of civilization and the attractions of savagery. Amongst the most highly civilized you will notice a tendency from time to time to react against their own refinement, and very often you will find a little cult of innocence and animality. Back to the inter-tidal scum, via arts and crafts, gardening and abuse of Voltaire, is a paradox generally acceptable to civilized people in need of a pill. Nothing more natural than that such should contrive small coteries to regret ingeniously and melodiously even the lost pleasures of ignorance and the beatitude of unattainable imbecility. Nothing less surprising than that these coteries should get a good deal of sympathy, and some financial support, from people who have remained barbarous because they are incapable of becoming anything better. It is desirable, however, that the clever ones, the accredited exponents of palaeolithic home-sickness, should be clever enough to recognize that there is all the difference in the world between a pet theory and what one really believes. Sculpture and war-dances, friendliness, brown breasts and bananas notwith-standing, every intelligent person knows in his heart that the life of the savage is what Hobbes said it was. With its imminent supernatural terrors, its material insecurity and lack of variety, to us it would be intolerable. We may be thrilled by romanesque architecture and moved by a revelation of passionate faith, but in our hearts we know that the dark ages were dark. We know that, with their appalling terrors, necessary and unnecessary pain, lack of fresh ideas, emotional and intellectual inhibitions, and perpetual menace of utter disaster, those dream-like days would have been nightmares to live through. And after the handsome sample of savagery offered us between August 1914 and November 1918, we, nostalgic intellec-tuals, know that we have returned to the artificial pleas-ures of a fashionable dinner-party, where we can sit and rail in security against the unheroic quietude of civilized life, with a secret but profound sense of relief.

This unquenchable, though often concealed and some-times disguised, conviction that civilization is a thing im-mensely to be desired, is the best reason we can possibly have for supposing that it is desirable. But anyone who requires the sanction of philosophy can have that too. The ethical philosophers will tell him that he ought to desire civilization; for philosophers seem to be pretty well agreed that the only things good in themselves are certain states of mind amongst which conspicuous stand the states of creation, contemplation, speculation, and being in love. Now assuredly civilization will do nothing to check artistic creation: artists crop up in civilized soci-

eties as often as in savage; and a highly sophisticated atmosphere, though it may be asphyxiation to one artist,
may be the breath of another's life. A glance at history
satisfies anyone capable of reading it that between the
quantity and quality (though not the superficial character) of an age's artistic output and the degree of its civility
no certain relation can be maintained. If civilization is
less favourable to the ecstasies of unreasoning faith at
least it will not actively discourage them; it will neither
forbid nor persecute; while those other raptures, the raptures of the saints of science, speculative philosophers,
mathematicians, researchers, all sorts of students and
thinkers, it promotes — nay, very often, alone makes possible. As for the states of appreciation and contemplation, they are of its essence — as are personal relations. Indeed, it is not denied that the civilized man in search of
exquisite pleasure is, and must be, an amateur of exquisite states of mind. Wherefore let the professors of ethics give him their blessing.

But ethical systems are dull at best, and the tendency
of professors to confound ethics with conventional morality too often renders them downright disgusting. Flinging
out in a rage, we hotly maintain that Sardanapalus was in
the right when, in Anchiale, he set us that inscription
which caught the eye of Aristobulus *ESTHIE PINE
PAIZE* — 'Eat, Drink, and . . . Play' (though that is not
what *paize* means in the context), 'the rest's not worth a
fillip.' Sardanapalus was wrong, however, and the life he
recommended would soon become as tedious as the ideal
existence of a professional moralist. Intelligent human
beings will never long be satisfied with animal pleasures.
For them the pleasures of the intellect and emotions come
first; those of the senses, a little in the rear, from a

charming background. And that is just the place civilization assigns them.

Why people desire civilization is another question, and one which I am hardly called upon to answer. What impulse draws a certain number of savages from their natural state of superstition and sheepishness towards reflection and individualism, let those say who know that an impulse it must be. I should not be surprised if one day they were to discover that this singular impulse was nothing better than our notorious and discreditable taste for pleasure. At any rate it is possible to see civilization as a consequence of this common desire. For, whether or no you share the opinion of Hobbes that the life of the natural man is nasty, brutish, and short, you will hardly deny that the noblest savage is debarred by fear and ignorance from many of our delights. None of those that derive from the free play of intellect are for him, and few that are born of taste. From his sculpture and textiles he gets pleasure no doubt; and he has music of sorts: all of which we appreciate too. But try your noble savage with a play by Aristophanes or Shakespeare or Racine, with a Byzantine mosaic or a Poussin, a fugue or a symphony, a subtle argument, a witty conversation or an elaborate flirtation, and you will have to admit, I suppose, that lack of culture does bar him out from pleasures we have acquired the taste to enjoy. According to Mr. MacQueedy, 'the savage never laughs.' I believe Mr. MacQueedy to be wrong; but I fancy the savage rarely smiles; he grins. He never raises a shoulder or an eyebrow; intellectual graces are as meaningless as subtle shades of sentiment to him. His pleasures are limited and monotonous. And think for one moment of the necessary and unnecessary pain he endures. For the grand promoters of pain, the most redoubtable enemies of pleasure, are superstition, ignorance, and uncontrolled passion — the essential characteristics of savagery. It is all very well for some obese and esurient neo-catholic, swelling with beef and beer and hate, to gurgle that he is as happy as he is credulous. He is not genuinely superstitious: he is not superstitious as the savage is. If happy he be, he is happy because he believes genuinely in very little except the efficiency of his own digestion: also, without the security and science of which civilization makes him a present, he would not believe in that long. He does not believe passionately enough to know what superstitious terror is. But the mediaeval peasant who was convinced that by following his bent he would walk straight into the everlasting bonfire, and the savage living fearfully under the shadow of the taboo — these know terror and pass great parts of their lives in agony and agitation of spirit. Civilization can rescue them by showing that life is a thing to be enjoyed, and then by showing how to enjoy it; by putting them — if they have any propensity to the finer pleasures — out of conceit with the beatitude of repletion and the satisfaction of hating in comfort; by showing them a glorious world of ideas to be explored and emotions to be cultivated. Like Satan, civilization will show a man all the kingdoms of the world — the world of the spirit — in a moment of time, and bid him possess them. Perhaps, after all, that mysterious impulse for which we were in search is the devil — in other lands and ages known by the name of Prometheus.

Be that as it may, I am pretty sure that if anyone capable of understanding the term will put himself on his honour to answer the question — Do I desire civilization? he will have to admit that he does (but then how many are capable of understanding?). Also, I know that philosophers will tell him that he ought to desire it. But that the majority ever has desired civilization or ever will desire it, is more than I know. The majority desires pleasure, but the majority cannot take long views; and civilization is not the obvious road. That was an exceptional savage who took the rabbit home and cooked it. Happily it is none of my business to persuade the majority or forecast the future. But since I have attempted to explain what I take civilization to be; and since it is an end I do desire; I shall permit myself to adumbrate the means. I shall sketch machinery by which people might create civilization if civilization happened to be what people wanted.

A civilized population, as distinct from that nucleus which gives it civility, will consist of men and women a fair proportion of whom adopt a slightly critical attitude to life and possess a rudimentary taste for excellence. Clumsily but consciously it will try to train itself to make the most of such powers of thinking and feeling as it possesses. The Spartans discovered that a whole community, or rather the free part of it, could train itself for war: the Athenians were, so far as we know, the first to train themselves, deliberately, for the appreciation of life. This deliberate and self-conscious training is a peculiarity of civilization; the ensuing enjoyment, the good states of mind that come of it, is the end to which civilization is a means. 'A means,' I say: for though civilization is the most fecund that we know of, it is not the only means to good. And this most likely means to good that human wit has yet devised is, as we have seen, nothing but the colour given to a community by a small but potent core of highly civilized individuals. If, therefore, society would civilize itself, it must first discover, then establish, conditions favourable to the production of civilizers.

No one can become highly civilized — and henceforth I use the term 'highly civilized' to distinguish the civilizers from the simply 'civilized' who take colour from them — no one, I say, can become highly civilized without a fair measure of material security. In fact, the *civitas*, or state, came into existence in consequence of a desire for material security. Do not run away, however, with the idea that material security alone can give the least tincture of civilization — think of the well-organized communities of the modern world. But to live a highly civilized life a man must be free from material cares: he must have food, warmth, shelter, elbow-room, leisure, and liberty. So here, at the outset, the eager philanthropist who, touched by my eloquence, has decided to devote his political abilities to the promotion of civilization, will be confronted by an urgent and awkward question: How are the civilizing few to be supplied with the necessary security and leisure save at the expense of the many?

The answer is that nohow else can they be supplied: their fellows must support them as they have always done. Civilization requires the existence of a leisured class, and a leisured class requires the existence of slaves — of people, I mean, who give some part of their surplus time and energy to the support of others. If you feel that such inequality is intolerable, have the courage to admit that you can dispense with civilization and that equality, not good, is what you want. Complete human equality is compatible only with complete savagery. But before plumping for barbarism let the philanthropist remember that there are such things as willing servants or, if he pleases, people content to make sacrifices for an ideal.

HOW TO MAKE A CIVILIZATION

At any rate, to be completely civilized, to experience the most intense and exquisite states of mind, manifestly a man must have security and leisure. He must have enough to eat and drink, and the assurance of it, he must have warmth, shelter, and some elbow-room, all the necessaries and some of the superfluities of life. Also leisure is essential. He must have leisure to educate himself for the enjoyment of the best, and leisure to pursue it. Again he must have liberty: economic liberty which will put him above the soul-destroying dominion of circumstance and permit him to live how and where he will, and spiritual liberty—liberty to think, to feel, to express and to experiment. He must be free to cultivate his receptivity, and to be putting it always in the way of adventure. To get the best a man must live for the best.

Unluckily, material security, leisure, and liberty all cost money; and ultimately money is to be obtained only by productive labour. Now almost all kinds of money-making are detrimental to the subtler and more intense states of mind, because almost all tire the body and blunt the intellect. The case of artists, of whom the majority would cease altogether to create were they compelled to break stones or add up figures for six or seven hours a day, will serve to illustrate this truism. Further, a man who is to be educated to make a living cannot well be educated to make the most of life. To put a youth in the way of experiencing the best a liberal and elaborate education to the age of twenty-four or twenty-five is essential; at the end of which the need for leisure remains as great as ever, seeing that only in free and spacious circumstances can delicate and highly-trained sensibilities survive. How many thousands of barristers, civil servants, and men of business, who left Oxford or Cambridge equipped to relish the best, have become, after thirty years of steady success, incapable of enjoying anything better than a little tipsy lust or sentimental friendship, cheap novels, cheaper pictures, vulgar music, the movies, golf, smoking-room stories, and laying down the law. As for physical labour; if anyone pretends that after a good day's digging or plumbing, hunting or shooting, he is in a mood to savour the subtler manifestations of the spirit, he is talking nonsense.

And there is more to be said. A combination of security, leisure, and liberty alone can give that sense of ease and that magnanimity lacking which life never attains its finest and fullest development. Generally speaking, those only who never had to earn money know how to spend it; they alone take it simply for what it is — a means to what they want. If freedom from wearing labour alone can preserve the fine edge of the mind, only independence will give a man courage to use it. Those who have never been obliged to please a master or conciliate a colleague alone retain the power of thinking and feeling with absolute honesty on all subjects. Only they know how to be perfectly disinterested and detached; how to pursue an idea without constantly looking to right and left for its practical implications; how to be remorseless in logic and in passion uncompromising. Will the most intellectual captain of industry be quite abstract in discussing political economy? Will the sublimest Platonist, should he happen also to be a paid teacher of Greek, judge the case for classical education wholly on its merits? even socialists, when they happen also to be ill-paid wage-earners, fail to bring open minds to the very question we are discussing — Is economic equality compatible with the greatest good? Whereas socialism itself is the invention of leisured-class thinkers by whom mainly it was brought into practical politics.

As a means to good and a means to civility a leisured class is essential; that is to say, the men and women who are to compose that nucleus from which radiates civilization must have security, leisure, economic freedom, and liberty to think, feel, and experiment. If the community wants civilization it must pay for it. It must support a leisured class as it supports schools and universities, museums and picture-galleries. This implies inequality — inequality as a means to good. On inequality all civilizations have stood. The Athenians had their slaves: the class that gave Florence her culture was maintained by a voteless proletariat: only the Esquimaux and their like enjoy the blessings of social justice. Because few are born with ability to discover for themselves that world of thought and feeling whence come our choicest pleasures; because the abilities of these rot untended and run to seed in the open; because to be civilized society must be permeated and, what is more, continually nourished by the unconscious influence of this civilizing élite; a leisured class is indispensable. The majority must be told that the world of thought and feeling exists; must be shown, lying just behind the drab world of practical utility, a world of emotional significance. To point the road is the task of the few. Neither guides nor lecturers these, the highly civilized, will merely live their lives; and living will be seen to have pleasures and desires, standards and values, an attitude to life, a point of view, different from those of the busy multitude. By living passively they become the active promoters of good. For when it begins to appear that the few have discovered intense and satisfying delights which have escaped the notice of less inquisitive

149

and less gifted pleasure-seekers, the many will begin to wonder. They will wonder whether there may not be pleasures better than their own. Can art and thought, the play of wit and fancy, and the subtler personal relations really mean more to these odd people than racing, yachting, hunting, football, cinemas, and whisky? One memorable day it will become unmistakably clear that they do; that there are people who could afford the latter and yet pursue the former. That makes one think. Here and there a barbarian grows inquisitive, grows suspicious of those easy, obvious pleasures the superiority of which he had always taken for granted. What if the more hardly won were the better worth having? As on a hot evening in late June the scent of hay will sometimes blow into a sub-urban slum, the faint fragrance of civility floats across his path. Dimly he surmises that here is good — better at any rate. As he passes across the public square that he has crossed a thousand times he is surprised by an inexplicable sense of well-being, and catches himself to his shameful amazement staring at a handsome fountain. Anything may happen. A sudden feeling of satisfaction may overcome him when he detects a contradiction in the newspaper which hitherto he had read with uncritical awe. The passionate decunciation, at a street corner, of some foreign government for doing what his own has failed to do may strike him as amusing rather than right-eous. The fact that a bishop or a magistrate has declared something or other to be untrue or immoral may, on a sudden, be seen to prove nothing. One day, to his shock-ed delight, our barbarian will find himself laughing with Boccaccio at the monks.

That only a leisured class will produce a highly civilized and civilizing élite is an opinion supported by what seem to me incontrovertible arguments and borne out by history. In Athens, Florence, and eighteenth-century France the dirty work was done by a proletariat. Philanthropists seem to forget that Athenian culture was slave-supported: but he who would discover the conditions necessary to civilization must have a better memory, must remember that two-thirds — if not three-fourths — of the inhabitants of Attica were slaves, without forgetting that Alcibiades was an exception. In Athens there were very few rich men. Civilization is not incompatible with socialism: a socialist state that wished to be civilized would support an idle class as a means to good just as it would support schools and laboratories. The only question would be how that class should be chosen. At present it is chosen by inheritance, a grossly extravagant system. There is no reason for supposing that the children of rich parents will be exceptionally intelligent and sensitive; and, in effect, the proportion of the existing leisured class which could be described as 'highly civilized' is absurdly small. Modern England maintains a multitude of idlers amongst whom are not enough highly civilized men and women to constitute a civilizing nucleus. Such a system is clearly uneconomical; and without undue optimism we may suppose that the future could devise some method which would exclude from the leisured class at least two-thirds of those whose names now swell the peerage and whose portraits enliven 'the weeklies.' Without sacrificing anything more precious than Ascot and Cowes I think we might reduce considerably the cost of maintaining a leaven of idlers. Here it is none of my business to contrive the means: projects will be in the minds of all. There is something to be said for competitive examination. Each year the top boys and girls in the state schools might be promoted to the state-supported leisured class. Or, if you think it important — as I do rather — to begin the career of optimate at birth, choose by lot. Take every two-thousandth baby and make him or her a member, and you will get almost certainly a better result than you get from the present system. Remember, too, it is not necessary that all your idlers should be of the élite; it is necessary only that an adequate proportion should be. Some wasters you will get by any method. That does not matter. You will keep the number as low as you can without jeopardizing the essential, which is that there should be a class of men and women of whom nothing is required — not even to justify their existence; for, in the eyes of most of their contemporaries, many of the greatest benefactors of humanity, most of the great artists and thinkers, most, no doubt, of the nameless civilizers, have not justified theirs. Generally, their age could not appreciate their services; and only the existence of a leisured class, to which they belonged or in which they found patrons, made it possible for them to exist. Wherefore the existence of a leisured class, absolutely independent and without obligations, is the prime condition, not of civilization only, but of any sort of decent society. Not under compulsion, nor yet from a sense of duty, will the most valuable and difficult things be done. But create a class of which you ask nothing, and be sure that from it will come those who give most.

Do not mistake a crowd of big wage-earners for a leisured class. Men who earn several thousand pounds a year by their trade, profession, or calling are generally nothing better than overpaid helots. Of course there are exceptions; but by the nature of their lives these as a rule

are rendered as incapable of becoming completely civilized as is any manual labourer by the nature of his: indeed, when he happens to be what is called 'a captain of
industry,' or 'a great employer of labour,' the master is
worse placed than the man. For the employer of labour,
the great industrial, and the small, too, for that matter,
tends to acquire a taste for power, a belief in success as
the criterion of value, and a sense of the importance of his
own undertakings, which unfits him peculiarly for clear
thinking and fine feeling. It is a pretty comment on
modern political thought that taxation should discriminate between earned and unearned income in favour of
the former. The man who makes his money uses it generally as a means to more, as a means to power, consideration, ostentation, animal pleasures and barbarous
amusements; it is amongst the receivers of unearned income that you must seek that leisured class which uses
money as a means to good. The man who earns tends to
grow hard, unsympathetic, narrow, impenetrable; he
holds ferociously what he has and seeks ever to increase
his store: it is from men of leisure have come most of our
liberal, socialistic, and anarchical theories, to say nothing
of that scepticism as to any individual's right to property
or power which is nowadays a characteristic of culture
almost. Seldom is earned income of much use to anyone
but its owner — as mere capital it would be just as useful
in the hands of the State; but of unearned income a fair
part has ever been devoted to supporting those who by
their unremunerative labours confer the highest benefits
on mankind. That the basic principle of taxation should
be the squeezing out of the leisured class for the benefit of
great and small wage-earners is typical of a half-civilized
age.

CIVILIZATION

In a famous essay Renan points out with his usual persuasive reasonableness that the proper function of a leisured class is to stand aside from affairs and devote itself to maintaining standards by sacrificing the useful to the comely, and preserving in honour the fine and difficult things of life. A leisured class, bred to a tradition of independence, is in his opinion the *sine qua non* of civility. So far, naturally, I agree: where he seems to me to be on less sure ground is in his deduction, implied rather than stated, that the leisured class, if it is to exist, must rule. I see no necessity. On the contrary, it seems to me difficult, if not impossible, for anyone immediately and deeply concerned with the exercise of power to be completely civilized. Is not a ruling leisured class a contradiction in terms? What Renan had in mind was, I suspect, an aristocracy divided into two parts: a leisured class and a ruling, brought up in the same traditions and intermingling at every point. Certainly this is a possible way to civilization, providing as it does for a leisured class and a ruling class in sympathy with it; and on this system France was organized during the hundred and thirty years of her supreme civility — albeit Louis XIV drew the bulk of his administrators from a class that was not technically noble. An aristocracy may easily be divided into an active class (the *cracy*) and a contemplative. The latter will provide civilization; the former government; but it has yet to be proved — I express no opinion one way or the other — that active aristocrats make the best rulers. Clearly it is desirable that the civilizing élite should have no say whatever in the government, since the exercise of power, as we have seen, is likely to play havoc with a man's finer abilities. On the other hand, there is a danger, which Renan foresaw, that, unless the rulers have traditions, beliefs, sympathies, and material interests in common with the civilizers, human jealousy and stupidity, inflamed by a public and expensive recognition of human inequality, will, by refusing to maintain the leisured class, allow society to slip back into pantisocratic savagery. The question does arise therefore — What form of government will be most favourable to civilization? It is a question almost impossible to answer.

Any form of government may be favourable provided it supply a sufficiency of children with the most thorough and liberal education wit can devise or money buy, provided it support these throughout life with an income adequate to their cultivated wants, provided above all it ask nothing of them. The notion that what are called 'free institutions' are necessary to civilization is contradicted by reason and history. To say nothing of the East — of China and Persia, of which we agreed to say nothing — we know that the civilization of the Renaissance was fostered and brought to flower in the age of the tyrants. For, as Burckhardt, writing of the Italian tyrants, sensibly observes, 'political impotence does not hinder the different tendencies and manifestations of private life from thriving in fullest vigour and variety.'[17] But even after the government — whatever it may be — has decided to maintain a leisured class, still it will have to count and distribute the cost. On precisely what sum a man or woman can support his or her civility it is impossible to say, because the figure will vary with varying conditions. In present circumstances I do not think one could do with less than seven or eight hundred a year, the State, of course, making itself responsible for children. Likewise, it is impossible to say what proportion of the population must be highly civilized to civilize moderately the rest. All one knows is that in England the proportion is inadequate. This seems to require explanation: the amount of unearned income in the country is vast, and the number of recipients considerable. One reason may be that a great many of those who draw unearned income and should therefore belong to the civilizing, leisured class prefer to increase their incomes by producing, and thus remain half-civilized at best; another, that too much unearned income is stuffed into a few pockets. Two obvious and practical measures for the promotion of British culture would be: a law to compel the rich to be idle; another to abolish that barbarous anomaly, the individual with more than three thousand a year.

This may be good political advice, it does not I fear bring us much nearer an answer to our question — What form of government would be most favourable to civilization? To answer that confidently we should have first to ask another, a psychological, question: Human envy and suspicion being what they are, is it conceivable that men should ever support freely, with eyes wide open, for their own spiritual good, but to their material detriment, a priviliged group of apparently idle, happy, highly civilized people? Only politicians and police-court magistrates can tell for certain of what human nature is or is not capable; and to them I gladly leave the task. Only this I know: unless men are capable of such enlightened generosity, democracy and civilization are incompatible.

There never has been a civilized democracy, but then until the twentieth century there never was a democracy. In the so-called democracies of Greece and Italy it was a small priviliged class that exercised power. Nevertheless, because throughout the nineteenth century there was a steady movement towards democracy — though not till

the twentieth did the whole adult population of any country obtain so much political power as a vote may be supposed to confer — had I written this essay immediately after it was sketched — twenty years ago — I should have said
that to discuss the prospects of civilization under any
form of government other than democracy was an academic, though perhaps not unprofitable, exercise. The
war has changed all that. The war, with its attendant ca-
tastrophes, has revealed the, to my generation, startling,
fact that military despotism is not only a still possible,
but, during the next fifty years, a probable form of government. The war has reminded us that the true source of
power remains what it ever has been: not the will of the
people, but a perfectly armed and disciplined body of
men which can be trusted to execute unquestioningly the
orders of its officers. Of this fact, in comfortable periods,
such as the later nineteenth century, one tends to lose
sight, because in such periods a situation rarely arises in
which men are determined to have their way, and all
their way, at any price. Between what A wants and B
would prefer there is in quiet times room for an infinitude
of adjustments and compromises. But the beauty of the
great war, as expounded by allied statesmen, was that
compromise was out of the question. Wherefore I think
allied statesmen should be less surprised than they appear
to be when they find that a good many people have come
to perceive that, if you want to impose your will — your
whole will — on others, the way to do it is to make those
others realize that the only alternative to unconditional
obedience is torture and death. The war brought home to
everyone what to political philosophers has been known
always, that the last arguments are fear and force. Those
who command most force and can most thoroughly
frighten the rest can always, if they wish to, rule.

CIVILIZATION

Under the Military Service Acts we saw men in thousands taken from their homes, their work, their amusements, and driven to a life they detested to be followed shortly by a death they feared. They entered the Army for precisely the same reason that sheep enter the slaughterhouse. They obeyed because they were afraid to disobey. It was the same in all belligerent countries where conscription obtained. Never have I met a man compelled to join the army during the last two years of the war who would not admit that his sole reason for fighting was that he was afraid not to fight. By 1917, at any rate, the issues at stake meant nothing to the ordinary conscript. If, instead of being told to march against the enemy, he had been told to march into the flames of Moloch's sacred furnace, it had been all one to him. If in their years and categories these terrorized victims had been called up for the service of the god — as indeed they were — they would have done their bit. Now when a central government, depending frankly on a controlled press courts-martial, and the peculiar horror inspired by the process of trial and execution, has the power to make men do this, it has power to make them do anything — as a number of alert people in Russia, Italy, and elsewhere have been quick to discover.

Not its best friends claim that Bolshevism is based on public opinion and sentiment; and the popularity of Fascicm is an open question. Yet the Russian and Italian governments can prohibit strikes and compel recalcitrant operatives to produce, which is more than any democratic government can do. They can do it because MM. Lenin and Mussolini had the audacity to organize pretorian guards and the constancy to make logical use of them. The success with which a few able and resolute men have established, and continue to exercise, despotic power in Russia and Italy must provoke the envy and catch the imagination of less fortunate rulers elsewhere. In one way or another their example may well be followed all the world over. And I do not know that civilization stands in the long run to lose by the change. In its first stages a revolution is likely to be disastrous, for the small, leisured, civilizing class is generally the first to perish. Naturally such stragglers as survive, acutely conscious of two facts — that they were civilized and that they are ruined — complain bitterly of the barbarism of the new régime. However, in the long run, the experiment may turn out, in the short — for them that is to say — it has turned out lamentably. These broken and disinherited exiles cannot be expected to look at the matter philosophically; but we who remain more or less intact cannot, if civilized indeed we be, look at it otherwise. And, considering it philosophically, we shall have to admit that there are no good reasons for supposing that the Russian military despotism will develop along lines widely different from those along which other military despotisms have developed. In the long run, a reshuffling of the pack seems the most likely outcome of the revolution. To rule and administer, the head of a state — be he Augustus or Lenin, Mussolini or Napoleon — must gather round him a group of civil and military chiefs. These have power and desires; and what they desire will be pretty much what the exiles and executed enjoyed. And since they have power to gratify their desires, gratify them they will: a new class of possessors will arise, from which will arise a leisured class, from which may spring a civilization.

Likely enough the return journey will be made by a shorter route. Few things are more coveted by an upstart government than prestige; and, except military prowess, nothing confers that mysterious glamour more conspicuously than culture. (Be it noted, in passing, that the cost of running a first-rate culture is as nothing compared with that of half a dozen undistinguished campaigns.) Wherefore one of the earlier preoccupations of most usurped tyrannies is to patronize art and science and encourage the growth of cultivated society. The example of both Napoleons will be present to all minds, and in most there will be some recollection of the Augustan age and its eponymous chief. Such civilization as Rome did achieve, she achieved under the earlier emperors, of whom the most efficient, as a means, was that typical military despot Hadrian. The great conquerors, Cyrus, Alexander, Charlemagne, Timour, Akbar, appear all to have had a snobbish belief in culture; and it needed only a short period of gestation for the successors of the prophet and of Genghis Khan to become the Prince Consorts, if not the Medici, of their empires. Certain it is that sweetness and light have often radiated from the courts of tyrants and usurpers; for though for creative artists rulers can do little directly beyond giving them the benefits of order and security and leaving them alone, for civilization they can do much. They can endow and defend a civilizing class. That is why I think of sending copies of this essay to the Russian 'bosses,' to Signor Mussolini, and to Mr. Winston Churchill.

I have no love for despotism; in itself it is neither good nor beautiful. But I am surprised at the frivolity of those earnest people who, without a moment's reflection, assume that it cannot be good as a means. If despotism and its correlative slavery are, or at some moment happen to be, the means to the greatest good—to the maximum of good states of mind—I should suppose only bad men would be averse from employing them. In fact what these thoughtless philanthropists are prone to assert is that no state of affairs can be good, no civilization worthy of the name, which is not based on liberty, justice, democracy, etc. These they make ends in themselves, thereby making themselves ridiculous: for democracy, justice and all that, are valuable only as means. A world that was entirely free or entirely just and nothing more would be as insignificant as a world that was entirely pink or blue. To discredit a civilization it is not enough to show that it is based on slavery and injustice, you must show that liberty and justice would produce something better.

All else being equal, I should prefer a civilization based on liberty and justice: partly because it seems to me the existence of slaves may be damaging to that very élite from which civilization springs; partly because slaves too deeply degraded become incapable of receiving the least tincture of what the élite has to give. A sensitive and intelligent man cannot fail to be aware of the social conditions in which he lives, and the recognition of the fact that society depends for its existence on unwilling slavery will produce on him one of two effects: a sense of discomfort, or callousness. And it does seem to me that a state of mental malaise, inducing either a turning away from one important side of life or a hardening of heart, is bound eventually to lower the value of the civilized man as an end and impair his efficiency as a means. In this I know that the best theological opinion is against me. The beatitude of the saints would be incomplete without the felicity which springs from contemplating the sufferings of sinners; and St. Augustine held that it would be unspeakable wickedness in the elect to pity the damned. My stomach is weaker than the bishop's: indeed, it disturbs my peace of mind to have to scold my cook. Wherefore, to a despotism which secured the existence of a civilized class by organizing slavery, or to a plutocracy which, fearing to jeopardize its own interests, threw over its civilized fellow-shareholders the aegis of a police force, I should prefer a social democracy which maintained the means to civilization of its own accord. But such an enlightened democracy has yet to be heard of.

For all civilizations of which we have heard have been either imposed by the will of a tyrant or maintained by an oligarchy. What is erroneously called 'the Athenian democracy' was an oligarchy depending for its means to civilization on slaves. In Attica, the learned compute, out of a population of about half a million, there were not above twenty-two thousand possessing the right to vote or exercise power of any sort: add to these free-born women and children, and you may get as many as a hundred and fifty thousand free Athenians. Of the slaves, who were notoriously less miserable there than elsewhere, a great many were skilled artisans let out for hire by their owners, and many were domestic servants. These seeem to have been pretty well used and to have enjoyed some of the benefits of Athenian culture. They went to the theatre; and if they appreciated that privilige they must have been superior in taste, intelligence, and education to our board-school proletariat. Had the Peloponnesian war been avoided, even had it been ended at the Peace of Nicias, it is probable that these superior slaves would have become more and more like citizens: but we may be sure that slaves they would have remained, if by 'slave' we mean one who is denied political power and compelled to work for others. Below these skilled and educated servants we find a herd of mere human beasts of burden. These, in this twentieth century, might surely be replaced by machines.

You see how absurdly ignorant are those would-be cultivated politicians who cite Athens as an example of civilization based on liberty, justice, and democracy. What profitably they might insist on is that, between members of the civilized possessing class—between citizens in fact—existed complete social and political, and almost complete financial, equality. This citizen class has at first sight something the look of that civilized social-democracy of which for so long so many excellent people have been dreaming. Here, living largely on the earnings of others, you have a class a considerable proportion of which lives mainly—not entirely—for things of the mind and the more exquisite pleasures. Amongst them you will find easily your nucleus of disseminators, the high priests and priestesses of culture, and just below a block of citizens so thoroughly imbued with their spirit as to be only just below. It remained to unite in culture the higher slave with this lower citizen class; and to us of the twentieth century, fortified by the scientific discoveries and inventions of the last two hundred years, the junction seems to require no improbable leap. What, then, is there to prevent a modern society becoming civilized? The answer comes pat. Athens was possible because most Athenians wished to be civilized. Not only the leisured class, but artisans and operatives too, desired 'the good life.' In England we still have the unearned income to support a huge leisured class; the producers, guided by civilized thinkers, have conquered for themselves a fair measure of security and ease; but of what should be the civilizing minority the majority prefers to barbarize itself by lucra-

163

tive soul-destroying labour and coarse pleasures, while the artisans and operatives devote their newly acquired means to imitating them.

Always towards Athens the best minds are turning for a ray of hope. Wherefore it is well to remember that Athens was a large oligarchy; that all adult male citizens were politically and socially equal; that amongst citizens there were no paupers and very few rich men; and that women, though they did not vote, were by no means all slaves. The position of women, at Athens in particular, in civilization generally, cannot, when we are considering the means to civilization, go undiscussed: women being, in more ways than the obvious, means to civility. Truly, the ordinary Athenian housewife was treated very much as though she were a highly respected slave. Naturally, for a housewife is a slave. And in this, as in most matters, the Athenians tried to see things as they are. They faced facts and called upon intellect to deal with them, thus elaborating a civilization in advance of anything that went before or has come after. In contemporary life it is generally admitted that the position of women is not satisfactory. They have the vote; and they are beginning to discover just what that hard-won boon is worth. They remain at a disadvantage. And there they will remain until they have got the work of mother and housewife put on precisely the same footing as that of mechanic or barrister. For the housewife is a worker; and the Athenian housewife was recognized as such. She was treated with the respect due to every honest and capable worker; but she did not, because by the nature of her interests and occupations she could not, belong to the highly civilized and civilizing élite. The Athenians appreciated her importance; but they also appreciated the importance of the highly civilized woman — they appreciated her importance as a means to civilization. They knew that without an admixture of the feminine point of view and the feminine reaction, without feminine taste, perception, intuition, wit, subtlety, devotion, perversity, and scepticism, a civilization must be lop-sided and incomplete. And for this feminine ingredient they depended on the *hetairae*. That at least is how I see it. There is a prevalent superstition, diffused I surmise by dons, that life in Athens was something like life in a college or a cloister, that in it women played little or no part. All I can say to these old gentlemen is that they have read their classics partially; and I would commend to their attention, first the demoded Bekker, then the authorities of whom a list may be culled from his writings. To be sure most modern writers on ancient society do appear to have gone to him for a list, and to have gone no further. Let them pursue their researches; for these authorities will adumbrate at least the immense part played in the best Athenian society by exquisitely civilized *demi-mondaines*.

The Athenians, I conclude, perceived that, like highly civilized men, highly civilized women must belong to a leisured class. Wherefore they divided women into two groups: a large active group consisting of those excellent, normal creatures whose predominant passion is for child-rearing and house-management; and a small idle group composed of women with a taste for civilization. To the latter went, or tended to go, girls of exceptional intelligence and sensibility, born with a liking for independence and the things of the mind. To these the Athenians gave intimacy, adoration, and perhaps no excessive respect. The former, unfit for the highly civilized pleasures which they did not even desire, got what they wanted most — a home, children, authority. They were respected and obeyed; but they were not adored. Being normal, they had, and it was recognized that they had, interests and ambitions totally different from those of their husbands. They were the wives, mothers, housekeepers, of highly civilized men, but they were not their companions. The highly civilized Athenian gave his passion and intimacy only to highly civilized companions; and if he happened to have a taste for women there were female companions to whom he could give them. These were the *hetairae*.

For amongst the *hetairae*, though there was, of course, a vast majority of common prostitutes, there was also a minority of cultivated *demi-mondaines* ready to become the companions and mistresses of cultivated Athenians. And when a cultivated Athenian desired feminine society it was to these he turned. As the most intimate community of thought and feeling can hardly exist between a man and woman without love-making, the *hetaira*, as a matter of course, became his mistress. The Athenians were not likely to forget that the most exquisite of human relations is the *liaison*, that the subtlest and most impalpable things of the spirit float from one mind to another most easily on a mixed flood of sense and emotion. But it must not be supposed that, a *liaison* formed, the lover took his mistress out of society. The Athenians, with their taste for company and conversation, would never have tolerated Turkish manners. The *hetairae* were an essential part of life; and if strictly male dinner-parties were as common at Athens as in London, if the *Symposium* played an inestimable part in shaping and fostering Athenian culture, so, I presume, did the *souper fin*. Now a *souper* cannot be *fin* without ladies. In exquisite Athenian parties you were likely to find *hetairae*. In male society they mixed freely. How otherwise could they have played their part in flavouring civilization? Amongst them were all the most brilliant, accomplished and learned ladies of Greece: naturally, far from being ashamed of their company, the most eminent men were delighted to meet them.[18]

If the *hetairae* were able to hold their own with the pick of Athenian manhood that was because they were not workers, but lived for pleasure — pleasures of the mind, the emotions and the senses. They were not house-wives, and if by accident they became mothers they did not rear their children. Nowadays the most sensitive and intelligent women are between the horns of this dilemma: they must become either wives or old maids. Well-off even, a modern woman, blessed with elaborately educated gifts, once she is the mistress of a house and the mother of children, finds it difficult to keep her place in the first flight. Difficult, but not impossible: the thing can be done, for I have seen it done. But the loss of free-dom, time, and energy, the cares and schemings in which any modern woman must be involved who bears and rears children and orders a house, will tend generally to blunt the fine edge of her intelligence and sensibility, will indis-pose so delicate a creature for that prolonged study and serious application which to the highest culture are indis-pensable. Remark that the great ladies of the Renais-sance and the fine ladies of the eithteenth century never dreamed of rearing and educating their babies — Talley-rand never slept under the same roof as his parents: and who that has seen the enchanting promise of girlhood, after four or five years of happy prolific marriage, whit-tled down to drawing-room culture, but will admit the substantial truth of my melancholy thesis? What is the al-

ternative? Spinsterhood. With exceptional luck, aptitude, and physique, a married woman may retain her
civility. Can a maid? The peculiar intelligence and sensibility of youth fade not less surely than other youthful
charms. What is to take their place? If her intellect preserve its point and purity, her understanding shrinks:
only her erudition waxes. When I consider that tolerance,
receptivity, magnanimity, unshockableness, and taste
for, and sympathy with, pleasure, are prime characteristics of civilization, I sometimes wonder whether an old
maid is fit for anything less than the kingdom of heaven.

Now an *hetaira* could, if she chose, combine the leisure
and irresponsibility of a virgin with the sweetness, sympathy, and experience of a married woman. Had she the
gifts and inclination to become highly civilized, there was
nothing to prevent her living a life favourable to her ambition. She had a wide choice of delightful lovers, and
might be devoted to one or kind to many. She was, if not
a queen, at least a favourite, of the best society, enjoying
at once the advantages of a *demi-mondaine,* a *femme du
monde*, an art-student, and a Newnhamite. Grudgingly,
the virtuous Bekker concludes that many were 'distinguished for wit and vivacity,' and 'by their intellect and
powers of fascination, rather than by their beauty, exerted an extensive sway over their age.' They were as
much admired in public as adored in private. They
flirted with Socrates and his friends, and sat at the feet of
Plato and Epicurus. As was to be expected, they were not
free from blue-stocking affectations and seem to have
been a little too conscious of their superiority. But though
great wits and poets have never tired of laughing at 'the
blues,' it is to be remarked that they have generally been
found amongst their humble servants. Moreover, nearly

all the most famous *femmes d'amour* have been bluish.
Anyhow, I hope I have made it clear that the cultivated
hetairae counted, if only by reason of their influence on
their lovers and admirers, for something appreciable in
Athenian civilization, for in that case I have a fair excuse
for this rather long excursus.

If I were tyrant I would abdicate immediately. But had
I inherited along with power a taste for doing good, my
ambition would be to civilize. As a first step to that end I
would establish and endow a leisured class every member
of which should have enough and no more: also I would
make it impossible for anyone in that class by any means
to increase his or her income. To organize society so that
the lower class, the workers, should have leisure and well-
being enough to profit by the existence of the idlers
would be my next care. For my élite there would be an
elaborate education and all the approved means to culture; for the rest as good an education and as many opportunities of enjoying what education makes possible as
my treasury could afford. For means to popular leisure
and comfort I should look hopefully in two directions: I
should look to invention, which enables one man by
minding a machine to render the services of a hundred,
and I should look to depopulation. In the matter of labour-saving considerable progress has been made, but
the wealth so conquered has not for the most part been
taken out in leisure; mostly it has been devoted to the
accumulation of more wealth, to war and armaments, to
inferior pleasures (*e.g.* picture-palaces, golf, motor-cars,
greyhound-racing, football), and to child-rearing. People
will propagate. When science gives them a machine
whereby one can do the work of a hundred, the whole
hundred, without lowering their standard of living, could

afford to have more time to themselves. Instead they beget ninety-nine children to consume the surplus, and remain precisely where they were, in a state of laborious barbarism that is. I have heard experts assert — but experts will assert anything — that even today the wealth of the world, were production intelligently organized, could be produced by half the population, which means that by halving the population everyone could double his wages or income. In my state the surplus of potential wealth over reasonable necessities should be taken half in material well-being — amusements and commodities — and half in leisure: once reduced to the point at which production and leisure made a happy match the population should remain stationary. As it is, each new invention means merely increased production to provide for increased population and a few added comforts; and so long as invention is paced by procreation no one is going to be much the better for it: civilization, at any rate, will be as far off as ever.[19]

I should give my subjects complete freedom of thought and expression, and the right to make what experiments they chose in their own lives, but complete freedom of action I should not give — action having nothing to do with civilization, which is a matter of states of mind. This would come hard on those luckless barbarians who only in action can express themselves. They will have to be content with making speeches, sitting on committees, and trying to persuade, not compel, us to do as they wish; and of some of them I may be able to make policemen. But in my state born thieves, homicides, and meddlers, budding Napoleons, and hot-blooded exponents of the unwritten law will be taken into custody. Unqualified liberty of action is incompatible with civilization. There are in the world a number of interfering, fanatical, greedy, reckless, brutal people who, given the chance, will behave in such a way as to make life intolerable and civilization impossible. In my state they will not be given the chance. Tolstoy may have conceived a world in which everyone would be so good that he would not wish to interfere with anyone else, a world cleansed of greed and hatred, envy and ambition, in which even if he had them a man would never act on his evil passions. More probably, Tolstoy believed that there would always be violent, meddlesome, greedy, and envious brutes who would follow instinct down any dirty alley, but held their existence unimportant so long as the others preserved their saintliness unspotted. Saintliness, argued Tolstoy, can be preserved by submitting passively and with a good grace. And so it can, and enormously increased to boot; but civilization would perish. The tortured and over-driven slave of a savage can be a saint or a stoic, but a perfectly civilized human being never. He lacks the indispensable leisure, security, and opportunities. Wherefore, control of action, which means an efficient police force, will, it seems to me, be necessary everywhere except in a society of angels or of brutes — brutes so convincingly below hope of melioration that it matters not a straw how much they injure and impose on one another.

Now a policeman, I am sorry to say, cannot be a perfectly civilized human being. Those who use authority, like those who create wealth, can be civilized but not completely civilized. They must be of the second order. The mere exercise of power, the coercing of others, will tinge a man with barbarism. My praetorians, my policemen, my administrators and magistrates, and I myself — if I am to be an efficient ruler, which, however, I decline to be — must be content to be the imperfectly civilized

guardians of civility. Fortunately, there are in the world
a number of people who appear, not only to enjoy ruling
(an all too common taste), but to enjoy ruling well. These
also are the instruments of civilization. They had rather
rule well than ill; and if in fact they generally fail that is
the result not of malevolence but of stupidity. It should
not be impossible for a civilized élite by bringing intelligence and education into fashion partially to remedy
this; and if I were a highly civilized Hindoo that would be
my plan. Gladly I should leave to high-minded young
Englishmen the dirty work of governing; but I should try
by hook or by crook to make the high-minded young Englishmen a little brighter in their heads.

The perfectly civilized are essentially defenceless.
Whatever reason may say, their sensibility will make it for
them impossible to strike a blow in cold blood or deliberately to inflict a punishment. Unless their fellow-citizens,
or the ruling power whatever it may be, think it worth
while to support and defend them, they cannot exist; for
the moment they begin to defend themselves they lose
their perfection. No: I have not forgotten that every
Athenian was liable to be called upon for military service.
That was the prime cause of the instability of Athenian
culture, which deteriorated steadily during the war and
might at last have sunk to the Spartan level had not a
remnant been saved by the crowning mercy of Aegospot-
ami. And if organizing for defence works havoc on the
civility of a state, how much more devastating will be its
effects on a thing so sensitive as a highly civilized human
being. Socrates made a good soldier: Socrates was a philosopher, besides being Socrates. Horace threw away his
shield at Philippi. It is a truism, and is, or was, a popular
one, that universal military service destroyed the old Ger-

man culture. To my mind French civilization has suffered appreciably from the same cause. Does it not stand to reason that a perfectly trained and disciplined soldier cannot be a perfectly civilized human being? Bayonet practice is enough to blunt his finer edges; and the habit of giving and obeying orders is unlikely to stimulate the critical faculty. Whoever reads and dislikes this paragraph will be ready, I feel sure, with the name of some admired artist who was also a man of action. Let me remind him or her again of something I have called to mind too often already — not all, perhaps not most, great artists have been highly civilized. Homer was not, Dante was not, Michael Angelo was not, what more do you want? And, then, let me quote one who, destined for a life of action, though he never succeeded in eradicating the live stumps of barbarism, did succeed in civilizing himself to a surprising degree, and has left in his '*Vita dell' Autore*' a curious record of the process. 'Non mi potendo assolutamente adattare a quella catena di dipendenze gradate, che si chiama subordinazione; ed è veramente l'anima della disciplina militare: ma non poteva esser l'anima mai d'un futuro poeta tragico.' This was the opinion, based on personal experience, of the pugnacious and tragic poet, Alfieri. It remains for those who dislike to disprove it.

I shall need a police force to protect civilization, not to impose it. Civilization cannot be imposed by force. If it consisted in holding certain opinions it might indeed be rammed down unwilling throats; but since it consists in an attitude to life, in ways of thinking and feeling, it must be disseminated. He who would civilize his fellows must allow them to discover for themselves that he has got hold of a better way of life: thus have superior civilizations been transmitted almost always. How often have barbarous, pillaging nations set out convinced of their superiority in all respects to the unwarlike race they were about to subjugate and assimilate? How often has·history repeated itself?

> 'Graecia capta ferum victorem cepit et artes
> Intulit agresti Latio . . . .'

First, the conquering chiefs perceive that the conquered possess secrets unknown to them for converting what appears to be insignificant experience into intense delight. Soon, impressed and seduced by the prestige of a superior culture, the barbarian king begins to depend for amusement, and before long for counsel, on the women and men of the 'inferior' race. Presently to these, by reason of their superior understanding and knowledge, go places of trust, honour, and profit; till at last the king himself is half civilized, and along with him are converted the more intelligent of those who came with him as captains and vassals-in-chief. This is the moment for the less intelligent to begin to grumble, to grow seditious, to organize a reactionary opposition. But by this time, with luck, the king and those of his chiefs who have been influenced by their conquered betters will, in their turn, have educated a sufficiency of the horde that followed them to be a match for the fine old defenders of tradional beastliness. And thus the leaven works: conquering Mongols are partially civilized by conquered Chinese and Persians; a like good fate befell the Arab hosts in Persia, India, and Egypt; the earliest Median invaders were civilized in Mesopotamia; and throughout the first century we can watch the struggle at Rome between *simplicitas romana* and the refinements of the conquered East. There the Catos and Tiberiuses were never properly brought to book by the Ovids and Julias; yet in the second century we do find something more like a civilization than anything that could have been expected to emerge so soon from the dark barbarism of the appalling republic. The leaders of those peoples even who penetrated and finally populated the empire made their effort — too feeble and too late — to profit by the superior culture of the Roman provincials. They failed, chiefly because the provincials were neither civilized nor numerous enough for the task: wherefore the barbarians acquired only such gaudy tags of culture as bedeck the pathetic courts of Charlemagne and the Othos. Had they become truly civilized they might have spared Europe the dark ages.

Though the means to civilization be established, though a benevolent government maintain a leisured and cultivated class, guarantee security, grant liberty of self-expression in art, thought, and life, promote education and control action, one thing still is needful to call civilization into existence. There must be the will. This will to civilization may be nothing more than the desire for pleasure refined and intellectualized. To suppose that it is firmly planted and ever operative in human nature would be absurd; but not more absurd than to suppose that it has never existed. If the will to civilization never existed, how has civilization come to exist? By luck? Have men climbed out of savage anarchy into some sort of order by luck? Why climb? If states of quasi-civilization abound, if there have been high civilities, is it not a little absurd to attribute the whole process, the vast, the painful effort implied, to chance? On the other hand: seeing that in some places civilization has made no headway at

CIVILIZATION

all, that in others it has pushed its nose above the slough only to sink again, that in many after making some way it has lacked strength to maintain itself, and that very rarely has the impulse been strong and continuous enough to raise a society within measureable distance of a conceivable and modest ideal, it would be as absurd to suppose that this will to civilization was something uniform, permanent, and fundamental in human nature. There are numerous reasons for disbelieving in continuous progress; there are as many for thinking that the present level of what are popularly called civilized societies is well below high-water mark; there is none for supposing that society will or will not again touch that mark or surpass it. All we can be sure of is that men, desirous always of pleasure, sometimes go on to desire intelligently, that sometimes they conceive pleasures rarer, remoter, subtler than those to which instinct leads, and that sometimes they attain them. Obviously, civilization was not the goal of that savage who took the rabbit home and cooked it. Only he conceived and desired a pleasure subtler and less immediate than that of eating it raw. So conceiving and desiring men may come at last to civility.

A will to civilization has existed, has never ceased to exist perhaps. But certainly from place to place and time to time it has varied beyond measure in vigour and efficiency. Theoretically this will should go hand in hand with that will to good which, according to some philosophers, exists always and has existed everywhere. Unluckily it is so difficult to distinguish between ends and means that practical moralists are always mistaking indirect and obsolete means to good for good itself; and thus the will to good, not only does not aid always, but sometimes positively counters, the will to civilization. The virtuous will too often concentrates its energies on what was once a remote means, and in so doing combats the mediate and immediate. At a moment in the history of any society a form of government, a religion, or a moral code may be a means to good and to civilization; but long after it has served its purpose, long after it has become no better than an impediment, good people will still be devoting their lives to its maintenance. The Protestant Reformation, in so far as it was a means to clearing away a mass of superstition, was doubtless in Northern Europe a means to good: but this means, exalted to an end, at last became Puritanism—a concentration on certain theological and ethical fads—and in England has perhaps done more than anything else to hamper and sufflaminate the will to civilization. Puritans, for all their good intentions, are the enemies of good, because they make it more difficult than it need be for themselves and everyone else to enjoy good states of mind. They attach to what were once means to good an importance due only to the end, and on these obsolete means insist often to the detriment of means more hopeful because more appropriate. Thus continence, which in an age of extreme brutality and armed foraging, when to ride was to rape, may have been a virtue, is still in this twentieth century insisted on as a means to good, capable of outweighing the benefits of popular birth-control clinics. Not until they have acquired a sense of values, and then only in an atmosphere of mental detachment, can men hope to distinguish between ends and means or between direct means and remote. The indirect vary from age to age and from country to country, their value is limited and temporary, their applicability local. Until benevolent people have grasped this truth a considerable part of their moral energies must go to promoting means which are contrary to their ends. Their will to good will become ill-will to that more direct means which is civilization.

In England there is abundance of moral energy which I am willing to consider no worse than a perverted will to good. But is there a will to civilization? A sufficiency of unearned income supports numerous idlers, but the income is ill spent and the idlers are uneducated. Wherefore in contemporary England, though some thousands I doubt not are as highly civilized as any that ever lived, the group is too small to form that operative nucleus which converts a passive culture into a civilizing force. And the few grow less. The spirit of the age is against them, against them the gospel of work and the notion that men came into the world to make money, play games, go to picture-palaces and race-meetings, drive cars, and beget children. This is the creed of the producers. Those who hold it have no use for economically unproductive work and subtle, difficult pleasures. Those who hold it have no will to civilization. But they have power.

The government of England is based on a precarious alliance between great wage-earners and small. It is plutocracy tempered by trade-unionism. In politics the plutocrats have slightly the better of it at present; and in life they call the tune. What that tune is anyone who studies the daily and weekly illustrated papers knows only too well. It is what the people want; also, it is what they call civilization. It is what they fought for to please the plutocrats, and what they may fight for again to please themselves. For this jolly alliance of great and small moneymakers is precarious. The small will always be breaking the tenth commandment: hence this incessant talk of revolution. And the odd thing is there are always philanthropic optimists who of such a revolution expect some good. Positively they upbraid me, because I am disinclined to let go such good as I possess in the hope of getting what they think may be a means to better. 'If only,' they assure me, 'the people were to come by their own, all your dreams of civilization would come true in a moment. The people, you must know, have always loved the good and the beautiful — the highest when they see it : here lies the road you seek.'

If, so adjured, I have not yet abandoned the study for the tub, that is because I have not yet noticed that the soon-to-be sovran proletariat, the working men of old England, manifest any burning desire to avail themselves of such means to civilization as they already dispose of. Rather it appears to me their ambitions tend elsewhither. Far from discovering amongst them any will to civilization I am led to suspect that the British working man likes his barbarism well enough. Only he would like a little more of it. He has so little fault to find with the profiteer's paradise that he would like it for his own. His notion of a glorious revolution is not the reshaping of life to bring it nearer the ideal, but a slipping into some rich man's shoes. The fact is, wage-earners and capitalists agree very well on all questions save that of the division of spoils. The revolutionary coal-miner conceives no better life than that of the reactionary owner ; rum and milk before breakfast, and breakfast of four courses, a day spent in pursuing and killing, or in some bloodless pastime, champagne at dinner, and long cigars after, an evening at the movies or music-hall, with an occasional reading of Miss Corelli and Michael Arlen, *The Mirror, John Bull,* or *The Strand Magazine,* and all the time a firm theoretical belief in the sancity of the marriage-tie and a genuine detestation of foreigners, artists, and high-brows. That is a life that would suit Bill Jones just as well as it suits Lord Maidenhead. It is the life he admires and understands: which not unnaturally, therefore, he desires for himself. And that is why he is revolutionary. One appreciates his position; one quite sees that he would willingly change places with his lordship. Also, one sees no reason why he should not. Also, one sees no reason why he should. Above all, one sees no reason why he should expect sympathy and admiration from anyone who stands in for no share of the swag in what he loves to hear called his 'fight for freedom and justice.' The pull-devil-pull-baker between Jones and his master for the plums of barbarism is their affair entirely. No impersonal issue is at stake to agitate those who stand outside the ring. Who gets the cars and the cocktails is a matter of complete indifference to anyone who cares for civilization and things of that sort. The trade-unionist is as good as the profiteer; and the profiteer is as good as the trade-unionist. Both are silly, vulgar, good-natured, sentimental, greedy and insensitive; and as both are very well pleased to be what they are neither is likely to become anything better. A will to civilization may exist amongst the Veddahs of Ceylon or the Megé of the Gold Coast, but no sign of it appears on the Stock Exchange or in the Trade-Union Congress.

NOTES

[1]My friend, Mr. Raymond Mortimer, who left Oxford not so very long ago, assures me that this school exists no more. He may be right: I hope he is. To be sure, when I wrote I was thinking of an older generation and of a state of mind prevalent five-and-twenty years ago.

[2]*Adversus Astrologos,* lib. xii. See also Burckhardt.

[3]*History of Civilization,* i. 430.

[4]I have discussed this question at greater length in *Since Cézanne,* in an essay from which I quote freely.

[5]Pericles in the funeral speech makes a point of Athenian good manners: 'in private life politeness is our guarantee of harmony.' Thucydides, ii. 37.
For the importance attached by the Renaissance to good manners, see *Il Cortegiano, passim,* and remember that this was the handbook of the educated classes.

[6]Here again I am repeating what I have said already in an essay on Criticism.

[7]*The Outline of History.* Introduction.

[8]Lanson, *Histoire de la Littérature française.*

[9]Thucydides, ii. 37.

[10]It has been maintained — I know not with what authority — that it was to this end some of the great Renaissance families affected incestuous relations.

[11]In Athens the marriage of half-brothers and sisters was allowed; so Lord Byron, at any rate, would have been respectable there.

CIVILIZATION

[12]*Leg.,* vi. 775.

[13]Shelley's translation, or paraphrase rather, of the *Symposium* is very pretty so far as it goes. Unluckily it goes a very short way. For a good part of what he has written, even when it expresses most beautifully the spirit of the dialogue, no warrant is to be found in the text. More important is the complete omission of some of the most significant parts of the argument. It has been said that these lacunae are due, not to the poet, but to that odious and unscrupulous prude who became his second wife and unfortunately survived him; but on this point in literary history I want the erudition that would entitle me to express an opinion.

[14]The custom was that two only sat on one *klinē;* for three to do so was in itself a provocation.

[15]The more civilized of the citizens consistently opposed the policy of war and colonial expansion which demagogues forced upon Athens. This forward policy led directly to the deterioration of Athenian civility as well as to her political collapse. Had Alcibiades been content with a life of thought and feeling he would never have set his heart on that fatal Sicilian expedition.

[16]A classical instance of civilized people coming together to escape their barbarous surroundings, forming a nucleus and gradually civilizing their age — and at the same time an example of relevant matter which cannot well be incorporated in the text — is provided by the history of the hôtel Rambouillet. In the early years of the seventeenth century one sees the Rambouillet colouring matter at work. It spreads. The group begets larger groups — its direct descendants — ever increasing in size, importance, and civility, ever extending the stain, till the movement culminates in the high wide-spreading civility of the later eighteenth-century salons.

'C'est vers 1607 (I cite a good authority, Boulenger), que Catherine de Vivonne, marquise de Rambouillet, âgée d'une vingtaine d'années, se déclara décidément écœurée par les mœurs et les façons des courtisans du Vert-Galant et "ne voulut plus aller aux assemblées du Louvre. Elle se retira dans sa maison et, comme elle était aimable, fort cultivée, sachant l'espagnol et l'italien, comme elle était riche, comme elle avait tant d'ésprit qu'il suffisait, pour tomber épris d'elle, de passer une après-dîner dans sa ruelle, même sans la voir, assure Mlle. de Scudéry, et en un de ces jours d'été où les dames font une nuit artificielle dans leurs chambres pour éviter la grande chaleur": comme avec cela toutes ces passions étaient soumises à la raison; et qu'enfin elle avait. pour *recevoir,* la vocation de certaines personnes de son sexe, son hôtel devint en peu de temps le rendez-vous d'une société choisie de dames, de seigneurs et de gens de lettres.' . . . 'Et l'hôtel de Rambouillet eut d'autres effets excellents. Dans la chambre bleue, on ne demandait aux habitués que d'amuser et de plaire, et c'était là l'originalité. Naguère encore, un gentilhomme se targuait peu de charmer par sa conversation et par ses lettres; ce qu'il souhaitait, c'était de passer pour brave d'abord, ensuite pour puissant, magnifique et capable d'une grande dépense: l'esprit était le cadet de ses soucis. D'ailleurs, avant l'hôtel Rambouillet, on n'avait point idée que la conversation pût être un plaisir si grand qu'on se réunit à seule fin de la prendre. . .' But soon, by reason of the prestige of the Rambouillet group, 'parmi les nobles eux-mêmes, celui qui ne se montra pas suffisament "honête homme" ou homme du monde cessa d'être goûté.'

According to Lanson the effect of l'hôtel Rambouillet was 'l'organisation de la classe aristocratique en société mondaine.' But civilization soon makes nonsense of class-prejudices and the bewildered seventeenth century 'vit là (dans la chambre bleue) des duchesses et des bourgeoises et des gens de lettres' (Boulenger). And let no one imagine that the conversation was frivolous: 'L'hôtel de Rambouillet était avant tout un salon littéraire; on s'y communiquait des poésies, des lettres, . . . on y écoutait, on y discutait. . . Ce public d'honnêtes gens et de femmes, connoisseurs en beau français — car on discutait avec passion des problèmes de grammaire, et l'on raffinait sur le style dans la chambre bleue — exerça indubitablement une influence sur la littérature et sur la langue.' Nevertheless — 'Hormis son petit cercle (le cercle de l'incomparable Arthénice), ce ne fut que peu à peu, lentement, que la noblesse et la huate bourgeoisie française s'affinèrent.'

[17]Burckhardt, *Renaissance,* i. 184.

[18]I once asked a French sculptor why little Toulon was such a deliciously civilized town — incidentally it supports one of the best bookshops in the world — when vast Marseille was so coarse and barbarous. He replied that an important and influential part of the population of Toulon consisted of mistresses, permanent or *de circonstance*, of naval officers, and that French naval officers who — unlike the military — are generally cultivated demand of their mistresses — be they the mere companions of a short leave even — something better than mere physical satisfaction. It is the *hetairae* of Toulon who give that delectable little city its elegance.

[19]The Athenians, as usual, had the courage to face the facts. They dealt with them by the, to us distasteful, expedient of child-exposure. Thus, at Athens, a rise in the birth-rate was met by a rise in infant mortality. Science has made unnecessary such old-fashioned methods, or would have done so, were scientific knowledge brought within reach of those who need it most.

INDEX

Action, life of: as not fully civilized, 132-34, 154, 170-71, 173; and gospel of work, 78, 134, 178
Aeschylus, 63
Aesthetic emotion, 41, 66, 69, 72, 124, 132. *See also* Arts; Beauty
Alberti, Leon Battista, 58
Alcibiades, 28, 110, 116
Alexander the Great, 37, 38, 160
America, 24, 25, 26, 29, 33, 34, 46, 57, 103
Ariosto, 57
Aristophanes, 38, 55-56, 66, 87, 111, 113, 114, 118, 143
Aristotle, 27, 37, 38, 74, 89, 102
Arnold, Matthew, 68
Art (Bell), 10, 25
Arts, 15, 32, 37, 38, 39-40, 43, 46-47, 48, 49, 64, 120, 123, 138, 141, 143, 152, 160, 175; appreciation for in civilized societies, 55-67, 68; conservatism in, 63-65, 70; creation of not superior among civilized, 65-67, 123-24, 142, 173; disregard for in England, 67-69, 102-3; purpose of, 66, 72. *See also* Aesthetic emotion; Beauty
Athens, fifth and fourth centuries B.C., 27, 33, 35, 37-38, 42, 45, 47, 49, 51, 54-57, 74, 84, 87, 91, 98, 100, 145; cosmopolitanism of, 82; education in, 77-78; civilization of, epitomized in the *Symposium,* 110-18; government in, 156, 162-64; homosexuality in, 113, 117; love of art and beauty in, 55-56, 57, 60, 63, 95, 138; love of philosophy and truth in, 80, 89, 95; love of pleasure in, 106, 109-18; slavery in, 35, 59, 97, 112, 149, 151, 162-63, 172; status of women in, 164-69; tolerance in, 79, 92, 95-96. *See also* Greece

Augustine, Saint, 161-62
Austen, Jane, 66, 91

Barbarians. *See* Uncivilized peoples
Beauty, 17-18, 51, 73, 75, 86, 95, 117, 120, 124, 133. *See also* Aesthetic emotion; Arts
Beecham, Sir Thomas, 131
Bentley, Richard, 46
Berkeley, George, 85
Blake, William, 66, 85, 123
Boccaccio, Giovanni, 42, 57, 100-101, 150
Boiardo, Matteo Maria, 43
Borgia, Caesar, 57
Boswell, James, 28
Bottomley, Horatio, 14, 85
Brontë, Emily, 66
Browning, Robert, 75-76
Brunelleschi, Filippo, 57
Brutality, 39, 98-99, 106, 120, 177
Burckhardt, Jacob, 96, 155
Byron, Lord, 90, 91

Caesar, Julius, 29, 39, 96
Calvin, John, 45
Castiglione, Baldassare, 78
Catherine the Great, 61
Catullus, 40, 102
Cellini, Benvenuto, 107
Cézanne, Paul, 64, 123
Chanson de Roland, 132
Charlemagne, 160, 175
China, 29-30, 34, 37, 46, 155, 174; Sung dynasty of, 34, 37, 46-47, 49; Tang dynasty of, 37, 46-47
Churchill, Winston, 160
Civilization: appreciative more than creative, 59, 124, 132, 137, 142; artificiality of, 30, 119, 123, 134, 136-37; characterized broadly, 16-22; creation of, 145-80; defined,

CIVILIZATION

121, 173; elite individuals constituting the nucleus of, 19, 66, 88, 89-90, 121-23, 137-39, 145-80 passim; goodness of as mediate, 16-18; good states of mind as goal of, 17, 53, 72, 76-77, 79, 123, 124, 126, 141, 142, 143-44, 145, 160-61, 170; ideal, 169-75; leisured class required for, 146-48, 149-55; level of in Near and Far East, 46-49; mistaken notions of, 26-35; paragons of, 20-22, 35-52; and progress, 52, 109, 119, 176; quasi-civilized societies contrasted with, 21, 33-34, 38-42, 46, 52, 67-71, 156, 175, 179-80; security required for, 146-48, 149, 172-73, 175; uncivilized societies contrasted with, 14, 20-23, 26-35 passim, 42, 50, 51, 52-53, 56, 59, 65, 81, 86-87, 96-100, 119, 121, 122, 132-34, 135-36, 140-41, 174-75, 179-80; and war, 13-17, 20, 31, 43, 46, 55-56, 77, 79, 83, 90-91, 99, 133, 134, 145, 169, 172-74; will for, 175-78. *See also* Reason enthroned; Sense of values; *and names of individual cities and countries*

Civilized individual, 122-39; full characterization of, 137

Classes, social: leisured, 146-48, 149-56, 159, 169, 175; slaves, 35, 59, 97, 112, 146, 149, 151, 160, 161, 162-63, 164; upper, 15, 56, 59, 61, 74, 78, 151, 154; working and middle, 15, 27, 56, 78, 102, 135, 149, 151, 152-53, 162, 169, 179-80

Coleridge, Samuel Taylor, 85, 91

Confucius, 29

Congreve, William, 46, 88

Conversation, art of, 40-41, 97, 100, 110-18 passim, 131, 133, 143

Corneille, Pierre, 63

Cosmopolitanism, 30, 81-85, 88

Dante, 102, 123, 173

Darwin, Charles, 76, 85

Decameron (Boccaccio), 100-101

Democracy, 35, 156-57, 161, 162, 163

Democritus, 82

Diderot, Denis, 29, 101, 102

Dolet, Etienne, 45

Dostoievsky, Feodor, 123

Dryden, John, 46

Economics, 76, 108, 120, 148, 151-53

Education, 24, 30, 31, 51, 53, 54, 73-74, 76-78, 106, 120, 124-26, 135, 136, 147, 148, 155, 169, 175

Eliot, George, 29

England, 13-16, 19, 25, 26, 27, 31, 34, 79, 89, 113, 135, 172; state of civilization in, 40, 41, 46, 56, 57, 62, 67-69, 71, 82, 102-3, 113, 118, 131, 138, 147-48, 151, 156, 163-64, 177-80

Epictetus, 30

Eugenics, 93-94

Euripides, 42, 89, 111, 116

Fabianism, 34

Fascism, 158

Firdousi, school of, 48

Florence, 47, 57, 58, 138, 149. *See also* Italy, Renaissance

France
   modern: 14-15, 33-34, 46, 47, 62, 67, 68-71, 100, 107, 151, 167, 173
   seventeenth and eighteenth centuries: 35, 45-46, 49, 51, 57, 59, 80, 87; appreciation of arts in, 59, 63, 75; cosmopolitanism of, 81-82; craving for knowledge in, 60-61, 75; devotion to reason in, 96-97, 98; interest in math and geometry in, 76, 78; politics and government in, 76, 154

Francis, Saint, 123

Genghis Khan, 49, 160

George, Lloyd, 14, 85

Germany, 14-15, 33, 42, 79, 82, 83, 84, 172-73

Gibbon, Edward, 88, 108

Giotto, 63

Gluck, Christoph von, 63

Goldsmith, Oliver, 88

Greece, 27, 39, 40, 41, 54, 58, 71, 74, 77-78, 80, 156. *See also,* Athens, fifth and fourth centuries, B.C.

Guicciardini, Francesco, 44

Hadrian, 28, 41, 160

Helvetius, 29

Hetairae, 165-69

Hobbes, Thomas, 141

INDEX

Homer, 40, 42, 132, 173
Horace, 124, 172
Hugo, Victor, 64
Hume, David, 24, 60, 108

Individualism, 58-59, 67-69, 71-72,
78-81, 98, 143
Inquisition, 44, 96, 132
Italy
— modern, 158-59, 160
— Renaissance, 37, 42-45, 49, 67, 71,
85, 87, 99, 100, 107, 138, 167; appreciation for arts in, 57-59, 60, 63, 75,
138; cosmopolitanism of, 82; education in, 77-78; glorification of individual in, 58-59, 67, 71, 80, 98, 138;
government of, 155, 156; tolerance
in, 96. See also Florence

Japan, 34
Johnson, Samuel, 125
Joyce, James, 99-100
Julius II, Pope, 57, 108
Justice, 13, 30, 161, 180; not an end in
itself, 128-29, 161
Juvenal, 40

Keats, John, 91
Knowledge: quest for, 60-61, 76-78,
120; not valued for its own sake,
72-73, 124, 125-26, 137

Lafontaine, 87
Law enforcement, 31, 170-73
Leisured class, 146-48, 149-56, 159,
169, 175. See also Classes, social
Lenin, Vladimir, 158, 159
Leo x, Pope, 57, 107, 108
Liberty, 13, 128, 161, 170-71, 180. See
also Tolerance
Locke, John, 46
Lorenzo the Magnificent. See Medici,
the
Lucretius, 40, 44, 102
Luther, Martin, 90
Lysistrata (Aristophanes), 55-56

Mallarmé, Stéphane, 64
Manners, good, 65, 80, 108, 120, 130-31
Mantegna, Andrea, 57, 63, 124
Marcus Aurelius, 30, 39
Marivaux, Pierre de, 88

Masaccio, 63, 64
Mathematics and geometry, 74, 76, 78,
142
Medici, the, 28, 43, 57, 101, 121, 138,
160
Michael Angelo, 57, 58, 63, 101, 173
Middle Ages, 43, 66, 78, 87, 96, 107,
141, 144
Military, the, 13, 24, 31, 34, 46, 55-56,
90-91, 157, 160, 172-73. See also
War, civilization and; World War I
Mill, James, and John Stuart, 90
Milton, John, 46, 66, 102, 124
Molière, Jean, 66
Montesquieu, Charles, 24, 87
Morality, 14, 23, 26-33 passim, 43, 69,
71, 74, 105, 106; 113, 126-30, 137,
141, 142, 150, 171, 176-77, 178; and
the gospel of work, 78, 134, 178; and
the sense of sin, 99-100, 105; sexual,
28-29, 30, 93-94, 166-68, 177; and
utilitarianism, 83, 90, 120. See also
Prudery; Religion; Superstition
Mozart, Wolfgang Amadeus, 66, 74
Mussolini, Benito, 158, 159, 160

Napoleon Bonaparte, 29, 91, 159, 160,
170
Nationalism. See Patriotism
Nature, submission to the laws of,
30-33
New Renaissance, The (Bell), 9-11
Newton, Sir Isaac, 46, 61, 138
Nietzsche, Friedrich, 15

Odyssey (Homer), 132
Origin and Development of the Moral
Ideas (Westermarck), 23

Paragons of civilization, 20-22, 35-52.
See also Athens, fifth and fourth
centuries B.C.; France, seventeenth
and eighteenth centuries; Italy,
Renaissance
Patriotism, 13, 14, 18, 29, 30, 55-56,
82-85, 109
Pericles, 33, 37, 45, 80, 87, 89, 91, 92
Persia, 48-49, 155, 174
Petrarch, 44, 57, 101
Phidias, 63, 66
Philanthropism, 35, 45, 109, 146, 151,
161, 178-79

CIVILIZATION

Philistinism, 69, 72, 73, 74, 76, 77, 81, 120

Philosophy and speculative thought, 40, 41, 43-44, 55, 60, 72, 73, 74, 78, 80, 89, 90, 95, 107, 123, 141, 142, 172

Pico della Mirandola, 44

Plato, 28, 38, 74, 89, 102, 105, 110-18, 123, 168

Pleasure, 107-8, 125, 142, 175, 176; philosophy of, 29, 108-9, 142; sensual, 74, 105-6, 112-13, 125, 133, 137, 142, 168; uncivilized, 143, 148, 150, 163-64, 169, 178

Politics and government, 13-16, 18, 34, 35, 39, 41, 42-43, 47, 51, 69, 74, 76, 79, 80, 86, 89, 90-91, 99, 108, 120, 128-30, 148, 150, 178-80; forms of, favorable to civilization, 155-64, 169-75

Pope, Alexander, 46, 88, 102, 124

Population control, 169-70, 177

Poussin, Nicolas, 62, 66, 124, 143

Praxiteles, 38, 63

Progress and civilization, 52, 109, 119, 176

Prudery, 100-104, 105, 120, 126-27. *See also* Morality; Religion; Superstition

Quasi-civilized societies, 21, 33-34, 38-42, 46, 52, 67-71, 156, 175, 179-80. *See also* America; England; Germany; Roman Empire; Russia

Racine, Jean, 62, 63, 66, 143

Raphael, 29, 57, 58, 63, 66, 104, 138

Reason enthroned, 50-53, 54, 78, 88, 92, 119, 120; epitomized in the *Symposium*, 110-18; and pleasure, 105-6, 108-9, 112-13, 120, 168; prudery opposed by, 100-104, 105, 120, 126-27; superstition opposed by, 96-100, 120; tolerance valued by, 65, 79, 92-96, 98, 101-3, 113-14, 120, 127-28, 130, 142, 168; truth and knowledge valued by, 60, 72-74, 120, 124, 125-26, 133, 137. *See also* Sense of values

Religion, 14-16, 18, 26-27, 30, 41, 43, 44, 45, 51, 67, 84, 96, 97, 99-100, 104, 107, 110, 123, 135, 141, 142, 144, 150, 161-62, 171, 177. *See also* Morality; Prudery; Superstition

Rembrandt van Rijn, 66

Renaissance. *See* Italy, Renaissance

Renan, Ernest, 154

Reve de d'Alembert (Diderot), 101

Roman Empire, 27, 34, 37, 38-42, 43, 44, 87, 160, 174-75

Rosa, Salvator, 55

Rossetti, Dante Gabriel, 64

Russia, 15, 76, 158-59, 160

Sacchetti, Franco, 43, 44

Sappho, 55, 102

Savages. *See* Uncivilized peoples

Savonarola, Girolamo, 57

Scepticism, 44-45, 51, 83, 97, 108

Science, 17, 30-33, 43, 44, 51, 60, 61, 72, 73, 74, 76, 120, 126, 142, 160, 169-70

Scott, Sir Walter, 91

Self-expression, 40, 43, 77, 92, 120, 124, 175

Seneca, 30, 40

Sense of humour, 85-88, 114-15, 120, 128

Sense of values, 41, 44, 50-53, 54-88, 103-104, 105, 120, 124-25; and an appreciation for art and beauty, 55-60, 72, 73, 74, 75, 124, 132, 133, 137; and the contemplative life, 132-33, 154; and cosmopolitanism, 81-85; and definite standards, 61-65, 104, 131; and the desire for knowledge, 60, 72-74, 120, 133, 137; epitomized in the *Symposium*, 110-18; and freedom, 92, 170, 175; and good manners, 65, 80, 120, 130-31; and individualism, 78-81; and liberal education, 76-78, 120, 124-26, 147, 155, 169, 175; and a sense of humour, 85-88, 114-15, 120, 128; and sensual pleasure, 105-6, 112-13, 125, 133, 137; and tradition, 63-65, 68-71. *See also* Reason enthroned

Sexual mores, 28-29, 30, 93-94, 166-68, 177

Shakespeare, William, 29, 66, 102, 143

Shelley, Percy Bysshe, 85, 90, 91

Significant form, 66

188

INDEX

Sin, sense of, 99-100, 105. *See also* Morality; Prudery; Religion; Superstition

Slavery, 35, 59, 97, 112, 146, 149, 151, 160, 161, 162-63, 164

Smith, Adam, 90

Socialism, 16, 148-49, 151

Socrates, 29, 95, 110-18, 168, 172

Sophists, 89

Sophocles, 40, 63, 66

Sparta, 56, 145, 172

Sterne, Laurence, 88

Stoicism, 30, 41, 171

Sung dynasty, 34, 37, 46-47, 49

Superstition, 41, 44, 45, 53, 80, 96-100, 105, 107, 114, 120, 126-27, 135, 143-44, 177. *See also* Morality; Prudery; Religion

Sweetness and light, 120, 121-22

Swift, Jonathan, 46, 102

Symposium (Plato), 100, 110-18

Taboos. *See* Superstition

Tacitus, 40

Tang dynasty, 37, 46-47

Taste. *See* Sense of values

Tennyson, Alfred Lord, 62

Titian, 29, 57

Tolerance, 65, 79, 92-96, 98, 101-3, 113-14, 120, 127-28, 130, 137, 142, 168. *See also* Liberty

Tolstoy, Leo, 171

Tradition, regard for by the civilized, 63-65, 68-71

Turner, J. M. W., 62, 66

Uncivilized peoples, 14, 20-23, 26-30, 34, 35, 42, 50-56 passim, 59, 65, 68-69, 81, 86-87, 96-100, 119, 121, 132-34, 135-36, 174-75, 176; attraction of, 140-41; essence of, 144. *See also* Civilization; Quasi-civilized societies

Utilitarianism, 83, 90, 120

Victoria, Queen, 27, 102

Villani, Giovanni, 44

Villon, François, 66

Virgil, 40

Voltaire, 24, 29, 37, 39, 45, 61, 80, 87, 88, 99, 102, 108-9, 137, 138, 140

Wagner, Richard, 63, 64, 66, 67

Walpole, Horace, 60

War, civilization and, 13-17, 20, 31, 43, 46, 55-56, 77, 79, 83, 90-91, 99, 133, 134, 145, 169, 172-74. *See also* Military, the; World War I

Wellington, Duke of, 29, 85, 90

Wells, H. G., 16, 56, 78

Westermarck, Edward Alexander, 23, 26, 27, 28

Whitman, Walt, 66

Wilhelm II, Kaiser, 14

Wilson, Woodrow, 85

Women, status of, 27, 164; in Athens, 164-69

Woolf, Virginia, 9-11

Wordsworth, William, 66, 91

Work, gospel of, 78, 134, 178

World War I, 13-17, 20, 33, 69, 78, 141, 157-58

Wren, Sir Christopher, 66, 124

189

OLD FRIENDS

PERSONAL RECOLLECTIONS

ROGER FRY AND THE AUTHOR
A CARTOON BY MAX BEERBOHM

By kind permission of Mr. Ronald Searle

CONTENTS

ILLUSTRATIONS

I

INTRODUCTION

THIS is not a collection of magazine articles, though at first sight it may look like one. Some years ago a publishing house—not Chatto and Windus—suggested tactfully, through a friend, that 'though not clean past my youth' I 'had yet some smack of age in me, some relish of the saltness of time', and that, to speak like a publisher rather than Sir John Falstaff, I had better begin to think about writing my memoirs. The word 'memoirs', with its hint of Saint-Simon and the great autobiographers, frightened me: flattered, I declined. But later it occurred to me that even I might be able to amuse a small public by giving some account of the odd and eminent people I had known; that I might reasonably attempt some modest appreciations mingled with small talk even at the risk of hearing them called memoirs. Indeed, I suppose these are memoirs of a sort. Anyhow, the proposal put an idea into my head, and I sat down to describe Walter Sickert as I knew him. That was to be the first chapter of a volume, the middle and end of which I foresaw as clearly as authors are apt to foresee such things.

I reckoned without the proverbial vanity of my trade. No sooner was the thing written than I hankered after seeing it in print. I wondered whether my friend Mr. Peter Quennell would publish it in *The*

9

Cornhill. He did; and I take this opportunity of thanking the present editor and the house of Murray for permission to reprint not only this but two more essays: *Lytton Strachey* and *Roger Fry.* Once again, and only once, did I betray my resolution by making an article of what should have been a chapter; and that was in my opinion a pardonable lapse. Our favourite excuse for premature publication Pope has made ridiculous for ever; yet truly it was at the request of my friend Mr. Geoffrey Hudson that I gave 'Bloomsbury' to *The Twentieth Century.* To him and to the other editors and owners of that evergreen monthly I am in debt for leave to reprint the article. It goes without saying, I hope, that this and all the other reprints have been revised and in some cases extended.

The sole contribution, perhaps I should say intrusion, which breaks the premeditated tenor of the book is the short piece on T. S. Eliot. Some admirers, on the occasion of his sixtieth birthday, thought fit to deck the poet with a florilegium. Me they invited to add a daisy or dandelion to the nosegay, and this I have included because I like to remember that Tom Eliot is an old friend. I seldom see him now, alas! But I have known him these forty years, and at one time we met pretty often. He is become a planetary figure, much sought and hardly to be found, occupied incessantly with affairs of this world and the next; so that the nearest I have come to him of late was in the London Clinic, where we were patients simultaneously and I believe on the same floor. Of whom I should ask permission to reprint this piece I do not know. To be sure, since the contribution was gratuitous, I am advised that legally no permission is required. But I am concerned less with legality than urbanity, and so I should like to say 'thank you' to somebody. The collection of tributes and memories was made by Mr. Richard March and Mr. Tambimuttu, and published by 'Editions Poetry London' in 1948. The firm apparently no longer exists; Mr. John Hayward knows not where I can find either of the editors, and what Mr. Hayward does not know about matters pertaining even remotely to literature I take to be unknowable.

Those who do me the honour of reading this book will perceive that it falls into two parts. The distinction, however, is not between the published and unpublished but between appreciations of people I knew intimately, and gossip about people whom I have known long but not very well. Of Lytton Strachey, Roger Fry, Maynard Keynes and Virginia Woolf my account, fair or unfair, is certainly based on close association, for with each I must have spent months, all told, literally under the same roof. They come first, or almost first, in the short list of people with whom I have lived on terms of perfect familiarity. We have talked about everything. We have quarrelled and made it up. With two of them, Lytton and Virginia, I carried on for thirty years and more an irregular correspondence. Of all four I could have told a hundred tales though in fact I have told only a few which seemed to illustrate the points I was trying to make. If I have misrepresented them I cannot exculpate myself on the plea of insufficient data.

With those other eminent contemporaries—Matisse, Picasso and Cocteau for instance—my relations were different. These are or were my friends, but I have not known them intimately. All I have to offer amounts to little more than tittle-tattle and random recollections; and the reader doubtless will observe that in recording these my approach is more distant, my manner less confident, than when I speak of those with whom I was familiar. To be frank, whereas I have the vanity to consider the five first chapters of this book genuine though incomplete appreciations, the two last I reckon no more than a collection of sketches and anecdotes to amuse the present generation and perhaps to instruct some future historian.

A further difference that an attentive reader will not fail to remark is a difference in the treatment of the living and the dead. 'On doit les égards aux vivants', said Voltaire, 'On ne doit aux morts que la verité'. May I add that besides 'les égards' an author writing of 'les vivants' does well to bear in mind the English law of libel?

This short introduction suffices, I hope, to explain the nature of the book to which it stands preface: there remains only the pleasant duty of thanking Mrs. Bagenal for letting me see the long, characteristic letter from Virginia Woolf, and Mr. Leonard Woolf for allowing me to print it.

Clive Bell

Charleston. August 1955

II

WALTER SICKERT

AT my preparatory school we learnt by heart a little poem called *The Chameleon*, the moral of which was, as you might guess, 'Remember others see as well as you.' Those who write or talk about Sickert would do well to bear this poem in mind; for those who knew him intimately, or at any rate saw him frequently and talked with him during thirty years or more, could never feel sure that their Sickert was Sickert's Sickert, or that Sickert's Sickert corresponded with any ultimate reality. Only the pictures were there to prove that a temperament, with an eye and a hand, called Sickert or Walter Sickert or Richard Sickert or Walter Richard Sickert existed and throughout a long development from Whistlerian days to the last could be recognised. If only the excellent Dr. Emmons had understood this, his not very good book *The Life and Opinions of Walter Richard Sickert* might have been better; but I doubt Dr. Emmons is of those who never so much as surmise that chameleons change colour. 'The opinions of Walter Richard Sickert', what were they? They boxed the compass between a first and a third glass of wine. Sickert was a chameleon, and the most I hope to suggest is some plausible explanation of the fact.

Sickert was a *poseur*: he belonged to an age of *poseurs*, the age of Wilde and Huysmans and Whistler.

13

If, to be an artist, it was not absolutely necessary to *épater les bourgeois*, it was necessary to do so in order to be reckoned one in the best circles. And it was in the best artistic and intellectual circles that Sickert was admired. In London, at the beginning of the century, his position was remarkable and, I think, enviable. He was not a popular artist but he was esteemed. English people of intelligence and culture, whose culture was mildly cosmopolitan and more or less up to date, had to have an English painter to admire, and whom could they have but Sickert? That he was their best may have counted for something: more to the purpose was the fact that he was neither Victorian nor precisely Edwardian, neither stodgy nor stupid nor quite respectable. Also, at that time, he was not provincial. He was a good European, a man of the great world, and well enough mannered to have taken a minor part in a novel by Henry James. He was extremely good and interesting looking: he was thoroughly presentable: and he was an actor. Never forget—Sickert never let one forget—that his earliest passion and profession was the stage.

Possibly it is significant that I met Sickert first, not in a studio, but in Bedford Square, lunching with Lady Prothero. That must have been about the year 1907; but already I had heard a great deal about him and had seen his pictures, not in London, but in Paris. I met him often during the first Fitzroy period, the period of Saturday afternoon tea-parties and discreet advertisements in *The Westminster Gazette*; and came to know him, or so it seemed, at the time of the first Post-Impressionist exhibition (1911–12). His behaviour in that affair was characteristic. Naturally the art of Cézanne, still more the art of Matisse and Picasso, was to him unsympathetic. It was, or seemed at the moment to be, a challenge to his own and to that of his masters; for in 1911, I am ashamed to say, to many of us post-impressionist meant anti-impressionist. Though Sickert never understood Cézanne, he was much too intelligent not to perceive that the Post-Impressionists were far superior to the pets of their enemies. Characteristically, he made the best, or worst, of both worlds. He jeered at Roger Fry (Rouchaud recalls having once asked him why he kept a peculiarly idiotic German picture on his mantelpiece and having received for answer 'pour emmerder Fry') and at the same time poked fun at the self-appointed defenders of orthodoxy, for instance at Mr. Henry Halliday and Sir Philip Burne-Jones. I seem to remember a letter by him in reply to one of the latter's intemperate outbursts beginning—'Let us see if Philip can be a little gentleman'. Sickert was fond of cracking jokes, some of them not bad, at my expense, which did not prevent him, when I published my first book—largely inspired by the exhibition of which he disapproved and to some extent a paean in praise of Cézanne—from publishing a long and flattering account of it in *The New Age*. Needless to say this friendly article by a friend was studded with disobliging quips. That is the sort of thing good Dr. Emmons cannot quite understand; but understood it must be if we are to get a notion of Sickert.

He was a *poseur* by choice; he was naughty by nature and he never ceased to be an actor. In order

not to be disconcerted and misled one had to know
what part at any given moment he had cast himself
for. One day he would be John Bull and the next
Voltaire; occasionally he was the Archbishop of Can-
terbury and quite often the Pope. He was an actor
in all companies and sometimes a buffoon. He would
dress up as a cook, a raffish dandy, a Seven Dials
swell, a book-maker, a solicitor, or an artist even.
And the disguise generally worked—*épaté-d* I mean:
only—so the story goes—when he went over to Paris
to see the Manet exhibition in the Orangerie dressed
up as one of the gentlemen in that master's *Musique
aux jardins des Tuileeries* did the performance fall flat.
That was a Parisian experience to which he never
referred. Also he was a rake amongst the scholars
and a scholar amongst the rakes; or rather, though
a rake he was in so far as a hardworking man who
takes his job seriously can be a rake, he was a man
of deep learning in Fitzroy Street and at Cambridge
little better than a dunce. Partly, I suppose, through
his first wife, née Cobden, he had rubbed shoulders
with what are called 'the Intellectuals', and so quick
a man had soon picked up from them a smattering
of history, politics and science. Unlike most painters
he was not wholly unfamiliar with ideas. 'Le pein-
tre', said Degas, 'en général est bête', and he might
have added 'ignorant'. Sickert would have been a
clever man in any company, clever enough to appear
to know a great deal more than he did. He had
attended lectures at King's College, and, I believe,
passed the London University matriculation examination; so we may credit him with all the erudition
these facts imply. But he was not what people in

studios and cafés believed him to be: he was not a
scholar. He was fond of quoting, and misquoting,
Latin tags in and out of season, and was not unwilling that his hearers should conclude that he was in
the habit of reading Horace with his feet on the
fender. I fancy he had dipped into a good many
books in different languages; but it was noticeable
that those which lay about in his studios remained
where they lay for months and years. French and
French slang he knew remarkably well. He could
read Goldoni's Venetian plays in the original, but I
am not sure that he ever did—all through. I dare say
he could speak German before he could read English. Certainly I remember how, one evening during
the first war, when he was dining in the Café Royal
with a lady, Sir Max Beerbohm and me, he burst
into such a torrent of German jokes and German
songs that the author of *Zuleika Dobson*—at least so
it seemed—grew slightly uneasy. It was that evening, after Sir Max had gone home, that he insisted
on showing us his 'studios'—'my drawing studio',
'my etching studio', etc. The operation involved
chartering a cab and visiting a series of small rooms
in different parts of London. These, as even in those
days there was a 'black out' of sorts, had to be visited
by match-light—the windows of course being blind-
less—and by match-light the works of art were in-
spected. Of one of them—a drawing of a woman with
long hair hanging in a plait to the waist—I happened
to say that I had known and admired the model,
whereupon Sickert insisted on my taking it, as a gift,
there and then, observing 'when a man's had a lech
on a girl he has a right to her picture'. Next day,

17   B

when we were more ourselves, I persuaded him to accept half the price he would normally have asked, and for five pounds became possessor of a little masterpiece.

Sickert was not a scholar, neither do I think he was a very good writer. Nevertheless, reading Dr. Emmon's book I discovered that his serious criticism and advice are far more interesting and better expressed than I had supposed. It would be well if these serious pieces could be collected and published in a single volume.[1] But if it is on his letters to the papers that his fame as a writer and a wit is to rest, then it will hardly survive the shock of these letters being re-read. For, to be frank, those famous letters, especially the later ones, while flaunting an air of profundity combined with scintillating snappiness, are as often as not silly, incoherent, beside the point and ungrammatical. Obviously he modelled his controversial style on Whistler's: a dangerous model, for Whistler was a born and reckless writer. As he grew older his communications to the editor of *The Times* became more incoherent and more frequent and at last suffered the crushing humiliation of being relegated to small print.

In no sense was Sickert a scholar; for, if his acquaintance with books was scrappy, his acquaintance with pictures was not much better. By his own account he used to visit the National Gallery as a boy, and as a young man we must suppose he went sometimes to the Louvre. For my part, I never met

[1]This has been done by Sir Osbert Sitwell. 'A Free House' (Macmillan, 1947).

him in either; but once I went with him to the National Gallery—for a moment, after lunch—and it
was clear he did not know his way about the rooms.
Almost always it is instructive to look at old masters
in the company of a good painter. The only picture
that seemed to hold Sickert's attention was a Cana-
letto, and what impressed him was the ingenious
way in which the master had managed a transition
from the tone of a chimney-pot to that of the circum-
ambient atmosphere. Sickert was the last of the great
Impressionists. But even in the Impressionists he
took only a limited interest. He took an interest in
them in so far as their art unmistakably impinged on
his own. Artistically, he belonged to a small clique—
a clique determined by topography rather than the
bounds of the spirit. Nothing that happened within
five hundred yards of Mornington Crescent or Fitzroy Square, as the case might be, was indifferent to
him. A rumour that Robinson of Rathbone Place
had invented a new method of rendering rime on
park palings filled him with excitement not un-
mingled with dismay. What had been done in Florence in the fifteenth century and what was doing in
Paris in the twentieth left him cold, though, in the
case of Florence, deferent. He had no standards. He
acquired a mass of junk from a little place round the
corner and persuaded himself that it consisted mainly
of paintings by Tintoretto. 'Whom else can it be by?'
he would query with an impressively knowing air.
Whom, indeed? always supposing that it was Venetian work of the period. For if it was not by Gior-
gione or Titian or Veronese only by Tintoretto could
it be, since Sickert would hardly have recalled the

names of other Venetian painters of the sixteenth
century. But 'the work of such imaginative painters
as Veronese, or, in our own time and country Leighton, Watts or Poynter . . .' (*The Times*, 3 July, 1913)
may suffice to give the measure of his connoisseurship.

My admiration for Sickert's painting is, I hope,
fairly well known. I have expressed it in many places
at different times; and if Sickert did me the honour
of treating me as a friend it was, I surmise, because
he was well aware of it. I consider him the greatest
British painter since Constable and almost as much
above Whistler as below Degas. But I do not think
he had genius; though I know that good judges hold
that his extraordinarily sure sense of tone amounted
to that. He had a great deal of talent, and yet perhaps less natural gift than some of his inferiors. What
he had besides talent was intellect, perseverance and
a grand training. For, when all insignificant niceties
have been brushed aside, it is clear that Sickert acquired his technique and his discipline in the France
of the 'eighties, and to find a time and place in which
the art of painting was pursued and studied with at
once such ardour, integrity and intelligence we must
go back to the Florence of the fifteenth century. He
learnt a good deal from Whistler and had the courage to forget the greater part of it; but he never forgot what he learnt from Degas. Foreign blood may
have made it easier for him than it appears to be for
most British painters to take his art seriously: hereditary also may have been his power of application.
It was because he was both intelligent and disciplined that he never attempted to stray beyond his

limits: and Sickert was limited. 'One's pictures are like one's toenails', he once said to me, 'they're one's own whether they're on or off.' I do not find the observation extraordinarily profound: it is characteristic in having a specious air of profundity and memorable as showing that he was at any rate willing to have it believed that to him his pictures were part of himself: also I doubt whether he felt as possessively and affectionately about anything which was not part of himself. His art he took seriously. Not quite seriously towards the end maybe, when he took to making those comic transcripts of Victorian illustrations. That was Sickert playing the fool. And he played it so heartily and with so good a grace outside his art that one cannot but regret he should ever have played it within. However, those facetiæ found their billets: they pleased certain ladies of fashion and amateurs who had taken to Sickert late in life; so now they hang in appropriate places, *dulce et decorum est*, as Sickert himself might have put it, *desipere in loco*.

Anyhow, let us agree that Sickert was a great painter and completely sincere. Outside his art he was an actor, a buffoon sometimes, and a delightful companion. His buffoonery, a little trying perhaps in the funny titles he gave his pictures, became in his later public utterances distressing. That famous speech at Sadler's Wells is not a thing of which his more fastidious admirers will wish to be reminded. He liked 'showing off'. About half of what he said and wrote and nothing of what he painted—except some of those 'Echos'—was meant to startle. His feebler jokes and many of his judgments were to show how unlike he was to other men. For similar reasons he was in the habit of lighting that end of a cheroot which most people put in their mouths, and of shaving or not shaving. His extravagances and oddities, his practice of breakfasting at railway stations or of keeping a taxi ticking at one of his front doors the best part of the day, his unpaid tradesmen and overpaid waiters were all means to the same end. So, to some extent, may have been that trick of sending for a dealer and giving him a corded bale of unexamined and sometimes unfinished canvasses in return for a handful of notes. But I am far from being convinced that Sickert was a bad man of business. Like Mr. Hutton, he believed in low prices and a big turn-over. He would have argued, with elaborate and affected cynicism, that, if an artist has a studio full of pictures, it is better for him to sell fifty a year at twenty pounds apiece than two at two hundred. 'Affected', I say, because I am certain that the deep and unavowed motive was not financial. Sickert sold his pictures cheap, and gave them away too, because he liked to think of Sickerts being looked at by as many people as possible. The more Sickerts in circulation the better, he thought: and so do I.

The biographer who one day will attempt a full-length portrait of Sickert, of Sickert with all his gifts and his absurdities, his contradictions and his charm, will have to realise—I repeat and am sorry to repeat it—that Sickert was a *poseur* besides being a great painter. Also he may discover, perhaps with mild surprise, when he has to explain so many inexplicable sayings and doings and give shape to a mass of refractory data, that at bottom Sickert was a solid,

WALTER SICKERT WITH THE AUTHOR
AT NEWINGTON

middle-class Englishman. There—he may say—there, but for the grace of God, or the wonders of science, went a Victorian paterfamilias. It is true that Sickert felt most of the respectable feelings though he generally succeeded in hiding them. When he called Albert the good he meant it. He was genuinely shocked when a married picture-dealer of his acquaintance eloped with his secretary, and vexed with me because I was not. 'It isn't done', he said—I can swear to his very words: but there he was wrong. When some young painters and students, mainly out of a sense of inferiority I surmise, took to pilfering in Fitzroy and Charlotte Street, he warned the shop-keepers, and warned the young thieves that he would tell the police; for he felt the sacredness of the rights of property instinctively as a citizen should. In fact, he was a sound conservative—or liberal—and would have endorsed most of his eminent ex-father-in-law's opinions had he been familiar with them. One need not take very seriously his pronouncements in favour of the Fascist or Nazi systems; so far as I know he came out with them only when someone was about likely to rise to that bait. But it is on printed record that he felt no pity at all for the blameless Ethiopians and no moral indignation against Mussolini. Sickert frequented men and women of all kinds, not only pimps and prostitutes, fish-wives and scavengers, but the less picturesque classes too—shop-keepers, officers of the merchant marine, solicitors, county-court judges and politicians. He was amused by all sorts and conditions of men and in his way took an interest in them: but he did not love them. If he was not a Fascist, he, like everyone who has anything to do that requires fine thought, great skill and continuous effort, detested disorder. Yet, being an artist, he was necessarily something of an anarchist and a bit of an aristocrat: at all events, he was an anti-panisocrat, and I think he would have liked the word. Better than most he knew that all men are not equal; and I can imagine few things he would have cared for less than a class-less society. Uniformity is not a dish to set before an artist: Sickert loved variety—variety in all things, in men, and women too, clothes, food, manners, ways of life. For that Καλὸς Κἀγαθός of popular philosophers, the common man, he had no respect whatever, he regarded him as a means; and, mocking our Radio Platos, he would, as likely as not, have referred them and their idol to that Authority which recommends us to learn and labour truly to get our own living and to do our duty in that state of life unto which it shall please God to call us.

III

LYTTON STRACHEY

'ANYONE can see you're a freshman, sir,' said the head porter at the Great Gate of Trinity. He was telling me, as tactfully as he deemed necessary, that to carry an umbrella when wearing a gown was contrary to custom. To soften the snub he made a little conversation designed to show that no one need feel the worse for a bit of advice from so knowing a man, and, indicating another gowned freshman who happened to be crossing the court, observed—'You'd never think he was a general's son.' The general's son was Lytton Strachey. Though unbearded, already he had encouraged a weak brown moustache, which, with his lank dark hair, pincer eye-glasses, and long chin, added somehow to that air of flexible endlessness which was his prevailing physical characteristic. No: Lytton Strachey, at the age of twenty, did not look a head-porter's notion of a general's son.

Whether I made his acquaintance in Sydney-Turner's rooms or Leonard Woolf's or Thoby Stephen's I cannot say, only I feel sure it was within a month of our going up. Also I think it was in our first term that we founded the Midnight Society. The date can be of interest only to those indefatigable searchers after truth who concern themselves with the small beginnings of things; but of them one or two may be glad to know that probably in the late

25

autumn of 1899 was laid the foundation of Bloomsbury. For the six members of the Midnight Society
were Saxon Sydney-Turner, Leonard Woolf, Lytton
Strachey, Thoby Stephen, A. J. Robertson and myself. Robertson, after he went down, disappeared
into the wilds of Liverpool and was never heard of
again—by me.[1] But the remaining five composed,
when they came to London, and when the band had
been reinforced and embellished by the addition of
Thoby's two sisters, Vanessa and Virginia Stephen,
the nucleus of that group to which the place of meeting—the Stephens' house in Gordon Square—was
later to give a name. But this is to anticipate by five
or six years. The Midnight Society, which met at
midnight because another—the X—of which some
of us were members, met earlier on Saturday evenings, assembled in my rooms in the New Court, and,
having strengthened itself with whisky or punch and
one of those gloomy beef-steak pies which it was the
fashion to order for Sunday lunch, proceeded to read
aloud some such trifle as *Prometheus Unbound*, *The
Cenci*, *The Return of the Druses*, *Bartholomew Fair* or
Comus. As often as not it was dawn by the time we
had done; and sometimes we would issue forth to
perambulate the courts and cloisters, halting on Hall
steps to spout passages of familiar verse, each following his fancy as memory served.

Lytton read well; and seemed to have those
squeaky notes, to which his voice rose sometimes but
by no means generally in conversation, under con-

[1] I am happy to say that, as a result of this writing, I have
heard of him again, and from him.

trol. In Restoration comedy, at unexpected but suitable moments, they would emerge, but never in high poetical drama. He was not however the best reader of the company; that honour goes to Sydney-Turner, who was also the most learned of the set. Leonard Woolf was the most passionate and poetical; Lytton the most grown-up; Thoby Stephen and I were deemed worldly because we smoked cigars and talked about hunting. Lytton, however, liked us the better for that.

What with sitting for a fellowship, which, by the way, he never obtained, what with one thing and another, Lytton must have lived in Cambridge, on and off, the best part of ten years. I was up for four, and a good part of my last year was spent in London. Thus it comes about that when I tell stories of Lytton at Cambridge men a little junior to me look amazed and incredulous. They think they knew him well, and so they did; only it was in the second—the King's period—that they knew him. In the years after I went down—after 1903, that is to say—Lytton when he was at Cambridge, more or less lived in King's; so much so, that when, at the time of the second Post-Impressionist Exhibition (1912), a University paper published a reproduction of Henry Lamb's portrait (not the big portrait in the Tate, but a head) and below it printed 'Lytton Strachey (King's)' few seemed aware of the error. In this second period two Kingsmen, Sheppard and Keynes, were, I suppose, his closest friends, though Norton of Trinity may have been almost as intimate: students will recall that *Eminent Victorians* is dedicated to H. T. J. N. But in my time his friends were mostly in his own college: there were, beside his cronies of the Midnight Society, McLaren (the mathematician), Hawtrey and George Trevelyan (a young and ardent don, violently radical, already marked out as a future Master); and of an older generation Verrall, Duff, MacTaggart. Also, of course, there was G. E. Moore, the philosopher, who at that time, and, as some maintain, ever after, was the dominant influence in all our lives. From London, with commendable regularity and a faint air of mystery, would come on Saturdays Bertrand Russell, E. M. Forster and Desmond MacCarthy: these also were friends, and I suspect they were the death of the Midnight.

The influence of Lytton while I was at Cambridge was appreciable but not great; it was after I had gone down that it became so impressive as to leave a mark on at least three generations of undergraduates. In my time it was mainly literary. As I have said, Lytton, who had not suffered the disadvantage of a public school education, was more grown-up than the rest of us—it should be remembered that in the Midnight Society were no Etonians—and his literary taste was more adult. To be sure, he had read less English—to say nothing of Latin and Greek of which, I surmise, he knew about as much as Shakespeare—than Turner or Woolf; but amongst newly fledged undergraduates, late sixth-form boys, he seemed to stand for culture or something like it. He had read a little French. He had admired Joachim. He had attended private views, and doted on Melville. He and I were, I believe, singular in our set, if not in the University, in that we took some interest in the visual arts. I am still surprised, and disconcerted maybe, on going into a modern don's rooms to find there a nice collection of contemporary paintings. It is so unlike the dear old days when an Arundel print or two represented the *ne plus ultra* of academic æstheticism. But Lytton and I, while still in *statu pupillari* if you please, once met by chance in the National Gallery and more than once in the Fitzwilliam. There he would bid me admire Veronese's *Semele* which he admired inordinately—for literary reasons—and about the authenticity of which I now have the gravest doubts. Also one of my earliest excursions in æsthetics must have been provoked by his query, as he contemplated the reproduction of a Degas pinned to my door—'I wonder what the uninitiated really think about it'.

Certainly Lytton helped to stimulate that enthusiasm for the lesser Elizabethans, and for Sir Thomas Browne, which came to boiling point about the time I was leaving Cambridge; and when at the beginning of our second year he developed a slightly affected passion for Pope he took us by surprise but he took us with him. He was a great figure, and in a world of very young men a great figure is, I suppose, bound to be a considerable influence. In public, at meetings of clubs and societies that is to say, and at Dons' evenings, his appearances were impressive and his comments noted. I recall a meeting of the Sunday Essay Society at which Bray—one, and the most sympathetic, of the Christian intellectuals and a judge's son to boot—anxious to be fair and reasonable in a teleological argument, put it to Lytton—'I expect, Strachey, you would maintain that self-realisation was the end of existence'. To which Strachey replied: 'My dear Bray, that would certainly be the *end*'. That struck us as worthy of Voltaire. And it is perhaps significant that when I had the good fortune to meet in my first year Desmond MacCarthy, travelling by train from King's Cross to Cambridge, and persuade him to lunch with me next day, it was Lytton whom I at once invited as the most suitable of my friends to entertain this charming and distinguished stranger. Of course it turned out they had already met.

But mainly Lytton's influence was literary; and in those early days it could hardly have been anything else. Philosophically we were dominated by Moore, and politics we despised. Let politicians disport themselves at the Union, where such small fry looked big; we liked some of them well enough in a patronising way. Nevertheless, the outside world— by which I mean the University—must have been dimly aware of Lytton's existence, must have heard something of him and disliked what it heard, for *The Granta* devoted one of a series of humorous pieces entitled *People I have not met* to 'the Strache'—the interviewer discovering him, robed in an embroidered silk dressing-gown, reclining on a sofa, smoking scented cigarettes and sipping *crème de menthe*. The Strache, if I remember rightly, was made to close the colloquy with the cryptic utterance—'Oh virtue, virtue, life is a squiggle,' from which it would appear that his reputation was not purely literary after all. Readers of *The Granta*, I dare say, called him a 'decadent'.

Be that as it may, it was not till after I had left Cambridge and Paris and returned to London that

I realised Lytton's influence was beginning to touch life at various points and at points not far from the centre. I have a few letters from this first period; mostly they are dated, and they could be placed were they not. All begin 'Dear Bell' or 'My dear Bell'; the first beginning 'Dear Clive' is of November 25th, 1906. This is a date in the history of Bloomsbury. It was at the time of my engagement to Vanessa Stephen that we took to Christian names, and it was entirely Lytton's doing. No question here of drifting into a habit, the proposal was made formally when he came to congratulate us. The practice became general; and though perhaps it marked a change less significant than that symbolised by the introduction of the Greek dual, it has had its effect. Henceforth between friends manners were to depend on feelings rather than conventions.

I have set down in some detail these salient memories because I was one of Lytton's early friends. Friends we remained—I might say cronies—friends close enough to quarrel and make it up, but the sayings and doings of later life, when Lytton had become a public character, are matter for a biographer rather than a memorialist. Nevertheless, having recorded these *juvenilia*, I should like to say a word, or rather my word, about the writer whom I admired, but also knew intimately, and of whose art and scope I am perhaps as good a judge as another. His attitude to life was informed by that genius for good sense which is apt to express itself in what sounds like paradox to the general; and Lytton's good sense came sometimes as a shock to the early twentieth century much as Wilde's came to the 'eighties' and early 'nineties'. I remember his petrifying a party of Highland sportsmen by replying to a *Punch* artist, who, after pompously deprecating the habit of lynching negroes, had added, 'but you know what it is they lynch them for'.—'Yes, but are you sure the white women mind as much as all that?' An apology for lynching made with an air of gentlemanlike prudery, was the sort of thing that made Lytton angry. For he could be angry though he rarely lost his temper. Against the popular conception of him as a sublimely detached person sitting stroking his beard, godlike and unmoved, contemplating the fussy activities of this disintegrating ant-hill which men call Earth, I have nothing to say except that it is not true. To me it is sympathetic: it is rational; it is pretty; but it is not true. They likened him to Gibbon and Voltaire, his style owes something to both—but only from the Frenchman was he directly descended. That famous irony and that devastating sarcasm were not the fruits of an immense indifference coupled with a mild Gibbonian surprise, but sprang, like Voltaire's, from indignation. It was not because he thought of them as insects that he made so many eminent Victorians look small; but because in his heart he could not help comparing them with full-sized human beings. Lytton Strachey was no more indifferent and passionless than Voltaire himself. He might have taken *Écrasez l'infâme* for his motto: I am not sure that he did not.

Like all moralists he had his standards, unlike most he kept his temper and was never self-righteous. His standards came of no wretched personal fads or conventional prejudices but were based on an acute

LYTTON STRACHEY AND THE AUTHOR
AT CHARLESTON

sense of the past. It is this sense which conditions his attitude to the Victorians: for to him the Oxford of Newman and the London of Mr. Gladstone were not more real than the Paris of the Encyclopædists nor as sympathetic as the Athens of Pericles. And if you believe in the continuous identity of the race, if you believe that the human heart and brain have not contracted nor the glands dried up, if you believe that the Athenians in their passionate search for truth and their endeavour to realise their ideal were using faculties similar to those bestowed on liberals and conservatives, and if you have admired the broad grin of fatuity conferred by the scientific century on itself, why then you will have a subject for high and bitter comedy, out of which, if you happen to be Lytton Strachey, you may create a work of manifest beauty and implicit admonition.

It is legitimate to regard this humorous and witty historian, who contrives to enlighten without for a moment boring, as the descendant of Voltaire, provided you do not forget that he is at nearest great-great-grandson. Between them lie those discoveries of psychology which made it impossible for Lytton Strachey to treat life with the intellectual confidence of his ancestor. Life, he knew, was something of which the dimmest comprehension—to say nothing of the least amelioration—is more difficult than to the mind of the eighteenth century appeared its complete explanation and perfection. Overlook the fact that he defended Rousseau on the ground that Rousseau was 'a modern man', and as such incomprehensible to his contemporaries, and you mistake inevitably his point of view. The idea that he was insensitive to that side of life for which Rousseau suffered seems fantastic to anyone who knew him well; and the notion that he misjudged the Victorian age, as the revenant he is sometimes supposed to have been must have misjudged it, is absurd. In his criticism of men, of their conduct and motives, there is no failure to appreciate or sympathise with their modernity; and the 'age of progress', with all its good and bad luck, is weighed fairly in the balance and found, by comparison with the greatest—silly.

So it is a mistake to call Lytton Strachey '*dix-huitième*'. He belongs to no particular school: all one can say is, he was of the great tradition, which does not mean that he was old-fashioned or reactionary. The tradition (as you may have heard) is a live thing, growing always, growing and spreading like a tree; and the ape who would creep back to the trunk is as surely lost as the fool who would detach himself from the twig. Lytton was not at odds with his age; if he could see that there was much to be said for the Whig oligarchy and the system it maintained, he could see that there was much to be said for Social-ism too. In art or life or politics always it is silly to be crying for last month's moon, and even sillier to cut loose from the tradition and play at being Adam and Eve. Lytton was a good deal less silly than most of us. His attitude to life, and therefore his art, was based on a critical appreciation of the past, an inter-est in the present, and a sense of human possibilities —the amalgam bound together and tempered by a fine pervasive scepticism. He judged men and their doings, as he judged books, out of knowledge, sym-pathy and doubt; and because he understood what human beings had achieved he was not indifferent to their fate.

Having said so much of Lytton's attitude to life, I should like to say a word about the manner in which he expressed it. Naturally not in the manner in which Voltaire did justice to *le grand siècle*, nor that in which Gibbon unrolled the doom of the Roman empire, did this modern tell his tale. His style, though like most good styles it acknowledges its ancestry, is as personal as that of any well educated author of his time. To hear some critics talk you might suppose it was precious; whereas, in fact, Lytton was rather careless about words. Yet minute attention to words is, I take it, the essence of preciosity. In the prose of an author whose acute sense of words induces a tendency to this defect or ornament —I know not which to call it—you will generally find a concatenation of half-buried metaphors which often escapes the notice of casual readers. You will find words conditioning words by recondite influences: the artist having been so intensely aware of their precise and original meanings that he has felt bound to relate each to some other which recognises the original meaning and honours the implicit association. Thus do the sentences of the more elaborate stylists tend to become a series of almost imperceptible cognate relations; and these relations, forced on the attention of the insensitive, tend to annoy. Let me give a glaring example: 'If anyone were so sanguine, a glance at the faces of our Conscript Fathers along the benches would soon bleed him'. Lytton Strachey would hardly have written that, though it is not to be supposed that he was less aware than Sir Max Beerbohm of the meaning of the word 'sanguine'. Similarly, anyone as sharply and incessantly conscious of the exact and original meaning of words as Sir Max would be unlikely to speak of 'this singular opinion' when he meant this unusual and slightly ludicrous one: but Lytton does, and so, for that matter, does Gibbon.

Writing in sentences rather than words, and in paragraphs rather than sentences, Lytton comes nearer to Macaulay than to Gibbon, and is, I should say, freer, though more elaborate, than Macaulay. The paragraph is his pattern, and he a mosaicist on the grand scale, willing, I mean, to compose out of the oddest bits. To the intrinsic quality of the cube he is indifferent almost, provided it does its work: ready-made phrases, exclamatory interjections, dramatic aposiopesis and frank journalese serve his turn: and so masterly is his art that he makes all tell, a lump of broken bottle here foiling there a die of purest *lapis*. He is a master but a dangerous one to learn of. No precious author and very few careful stylists would write: 'The light thrown by the Bible upon the whole matter seemed somewhat dubious' —'the influential circles of society'—'an excellent judge of horse-flesh'. In full dress Gibbon would never have written: 'Ward forced him forward step by step towards—no! he could not bear it;' nor I think would Macaulay. But Dr. Johnson himself might have observed with pleasure that, 'Dyspeptic by constitution, melancholic by temperament, he could yet be lively on occasions, and was known as a wit in Coburg'. For my part, I would change nothing in Lytton's style; the stock phrase and the costumier's adjective used for purposes of irony and sarcasm become delicate weapons in the hand of a master: only I would observe that they are much too treacherous to be played with by girls and boys.

I have tried to indicate in a few paragraphs—and the attempt was impertinent no doubt—what was Lytton's attitude to life and how he chose to express it. To describe the effect of this attitude on the age in which he flourished will be the task of some historian, and him I would gladly help out with a few anecdotes illustrating Lytton's reforms in the matter of free speech could I recall any that were at once significant and printable. The business ought not to be too risky seeing that what seemed downright smut to Edwardian gentility sounds conversational enough today. But either my memory or my courage fails me. Oblivion will not be cheated by my indiscreet revelations; and, anyhow, it was through his writings that Lytton's influence was spread widely, though perhaps a trifle thin. It was felt most deeply by his friends of course, and by them maybe was most effectively disseminated. With them he created a peculiar atmosphere—an atmosphere conditioned naturally by the person he happened to be with. He was extraordinarily sympathetic and provoked confidences. Gradually he must have come to know his friends' secret thoughts about most things, including themselves. Yet there was seldom anything tense in a conversation with Lytton; it drifted hither and thither in that pleasant atmosphere, gay, truthful (cynical if you will—the terms are interchangeable almost), amusingly and amusedly censorious. Lytton brought a literary and historical flavour into his talk so that, if the past were discussed sometimes as though it were the present, the perplexities and misfortunes of his contemporaries were treated often as though they came from the pages of Saint-Simon or Horace Walpole. But always there was that atmosphere, that sense of intelligent understanding mingled with affection, which induced his companion to give of his or her best in a particular way from a particular angle. I should despair of resurrecting the ghost of an idea of what I have in memory were it not that a lady, speaking of him soon after his death, let fall a melancholy but illuminating remark which seems to me to suggest the quality of his company, 'Don't you feel', said she, 'there are things one would like to say and never will say now?' And by this she did not mean affectionate things, flattering things, things that would have shown Lytton what one felt for him or thought of him, but mere comments on life or books or art or acquaintances or historical characters, little jokes and little ironies, paradoxes that were almost true and truisms masquerading as inventions, things to which the climate would have given a peculiar relish, things that now will never come to life.

Of this peculiar quality is any taste to be found and enjoyed in his writing? Yes, I think so. Sometimes when, with demurest deference, he exposes the outrageous follies of mankind as though he were recording the fruits of profound cogitation and ripe political wisdom—as indeed he often is—one catches an echo of his voice. And sometimes, when he indulges a turn for that subtle kind of fun which is the extension into the universal of a private joke, one fancies oneself back at Tidmarsh. The family joke, coterie humour, we know: in every school and college, in every clique and set, are sources of merriment which for the outside world do not exist. But there are writers—and in this English writers are perhaps especially happy—who can make a coterie of all the world. The esoteric joke depends, not only on common experience but on common assumptions; and there are writers—Sterne, Charles Lamb, Byron, Peacock—who persuade us, apparently without trying, to accept theirs and divine them even. Though we have been told very little about their favourite butts, we laugh at them mercilessly because we laugh with the marksman. And already are we so much in Lytton's humour that when, on the fourth page of his essay, he remarks of Dr. Arnold that 'his legs, perhaps, were shorter than they should have been', we know that it is all up with the headmaster of Rugby.

Unless he was feeling ill, as too often he was, Lytton with his intimate friends, or with people to whom he had taken a fancy, was delightful; but his company manners could be bad. I do not know whether it was vanity or some more recondite motive that made him unwilling to speak, or give any sign of taking an interest in the conversation, when he could not be sure of appearing as he wished to appear. Once or twice he has been with me in France, and once or twice in my flat in the company of French or French-speaking people and on such occasions he could be downright grumpy. Yet he spoke French no worse than many I have heard disporting themselves cheerfully in that language: possibly his skin was thinner than theirs. Be that as it may, in practical matters—and a party is a practical matter—Lytton was not helpful. He was something self-conscious and he was not generous. I do not mean that he was stingy, though, having been till near the end of his life rather hard up, he was always careful of his money; I mean that he was sparing of praise, a trifle envious maybe, and disinclined to put himself out for or make himself useful to others. Assuredly, he was not inconsiderate, but I suppose he was rather selfish and a thought arrogant. He took care of number one, as my old nurse used to say, and I do not blame him.

Lytton could love, and perhaps he could hate. To anyone who knew him well it is obvious that love and lust and that mysterious mixture of the two which is the heart's desire played in his life parts of which a biographer who fails to take account will make himself ridiculous. But I am not a biographer; nor can, nor should, a biography of Lytton Stachey be attempted for many years to come. It cannot be attempted till his letters have been published or at any rate made accessible, and his letters should not be published till those he cared for and those who thought he cared for them are dead. Most of his papers luckily are in safe and scholarly hands. The habit of cashing in on a man's reputation while it is still warm grows apace, and—but, to avail myself of Strachean aposiopoesis, it is time to make an end.

It was towards the end of November that I came back from Venice in 1931. A day or two after my return Lytton dined with me. He was feeling ill and went away early saying, 'let us meet again very soon when I am better'. So we dined together on the following Friday and enjoyed one of those evenings which Lytton contrived to turn into works of art. Next day I went into Wiltshire, and at Paddington discovered that Lytton, with his sister Philippa and some other relations I think, was travelling in the same coach. He came to see me in my compartment, where I was alone, and we had some talk, mostly I remember about my tussle with the Commissioners of Inland Revenue, who, as usual, were behaving disagreeably. At Reading he rejoined his party. At Hungerford I watched him walk along the platform on his way out. That was the last time I saw Lytton.

IV

MAYNARD KEYNES

IN a memoir called 'My Early Beliefs' Lord
Keynes, describing the company he kept at Cambridge, finds a word or phrase to fit each of his
friends: 'Moore himself was a puritan and a precis-
ian', he writes, 'Strachey (for that was his name at
that time) a Voltairean, Woolf a rabbi, myself a
nonconformist, Sheppard a conformist and (as it
now turns out) an ecclesiastic, Clive a gay and amiable dog, Sydney-Turner a quietist, Hawtrey a dog-
matist and so on'. Now Clive may have been gay and
amiable and a dog, but Maynard can have known
it only by hearsay; for, oddly enough, at Cambridge
we never met. Or did we meet for a moment, before
dinner, before a debate? I think not; though I distinctly remember Edwin Montagu telling me that
he had invited a brilliant freshman, just up from
Eton, who would be of great value—when we had
gone down—to the Liberal Party in the Union.[1]
That was in the late autumn of 1902, and that was
the first I heard of Maynard. That we did not know
each other may be accounted for perhaps by the fact
that I spent a good part of my last, my fourth, year
(October 1902–3) in London working at the Record
Office, and when I was in Cambridge lived mostly

[1]In my last year I seem to have grown out of my early contempt for politics.

42

with my old friends in Trinity, not accompanying Lytton Strachey on his excursions into King's. Be that as it may, certain I am that the first time I met Maynard to talk to was in the summer of 1906, when Lytton brought him to my chambers in the Temple. He was then, I surmise, sitting for the civil service examination, and wearing, I am sure, a light green Burberry and a bowler hat.[1]

Our acquaintance must have improved steadily. In February 1908 my elder son was born; and, as in those days it was customary for a young mother to remain in bed for perhaps a month after giving birth to a child, I took to inviting some agreeable friend who after dinner would entertain the convalescent with an hour's conversation. Maynard was one of the three or four who came. Nevertheless we cannot yet have been what I should call intimate since I remember feeling, not exactly shy, but conscious of the fact that this was the first time I had dined with him en tête-à-tête. He was still a clerk in the India Office, living in one of those dreary blocks of flats near St. James's Park Station; but a few months later he returned to Cambridge, and though during the next year or two I saw him much in company I

[1]May I, while correcting one mistake, irrelevantly call attention to another? On page 79 of 'Two Memoirs' Maynard writes—'Many years later he (D. H. Lawrence) recorded in a letter which is printed in his published correspondence, that I was the only member of Bloomsbury who had supported him by subscribing for Lady Chatterley.' This, if I am to be reckoned a member of Bloomsbury, is, like so many things that Lawrence said, untrue. My subscription copy, duly numbered 578 and signed, stands now in my book-case.

rarely saw him alone. He stayed with us in the country; he was with us at Guildford in July 1911 and he it was who, having as usual secured first look at *The Times*, told us that the Lords had passed the Parliament Act: when he took Asheham for the Easter holidays my wife and I stayed with him. Evidently in August 1913 we were on easy and amiable terms for we shared a tent on a camping-party, organised by the Olliviers of course—the Brandon Camp: I recall most vividly the discomfort. Maynard minded less, he was a better camper-out than I. On the other hand he was an even worse lawn-tennis player. We played occasionally on the hilly courts of Gordon Square—he and I, Gerald Shove, Phillip Morrell and sometimes Adrian Stephen. But Maynard was so feeble that though we always gave him for partner, Phillip, by far the best of the bunch, we could not make a game of it. Maynard was dropped.

This must have been just before the first war, in the summer of 1914, when Maynard was lodging in Brunswick Square. During the winter he had served on a Royal Commission on Indian currency and consequently had begun to make friends in high places. A new Maynard, who accompanied but never displaced the old, was emerging—a man of great affairs and a friend of the great. Also, I fancy, it was about this time or a little earlier that he took to speculating. According to an account he once gave me—in whimsical mood I must confess—Maynard, who at Cambridge and in early London days had barely glanced at 'Stock Exchange Dealings', grew so weary —this is what he told me—of reading the cricket-scores in *The Times* that, while drinking his morning tea, he took to studying prices instead. You may believe it or not as you choose: anyhow it was a digression from what I was saying, that already before the war Maynard had come into contact with a part of the political and high official world. Some of us shook our heads, not over the new interests but over the new friendships. Would they not encourage the growth of what we were pleased to consider false values? Would he not soon be attaching more importance to means (power, honours, conventions, money) than to ends—i.e. good states of mind (*vide Principia Ethica passim*)? Would he not lose his sense of proportion? But when Maynard, having invited to dinner two of his big-wigs (Austen Chamberlain and McKenna I seem to remember), discovered at the last moment that all his Champagne had been drunk by Duncan Grant and his boon companions— Duncan's mid-day Champagne-parties in Brunswick Square were a feature of that memorable summer— he took it well enough. His sense of values appeared to be intact. And I will not doubt he realised that a subsequent party to which he and Duncan Grant invited the St. John Hutchinsons—Mrs. Hutchinson was Duncan's cousin—Molly MacCarthy and myself was much greater fun.

In September 1914 Maynard was with us at Asheham; and it pleases me to remember that the great man—and he was a great man—who enjoyed for years an international reputation for cool and detached judgment, rebuked me sharply for refusing to believe in the Russian-troops-in-England fairy tale and for surmising that the war would not soon be over. The fact is, of course, that Maynard's judgment would have been as sound as his intellect was powerful had it really been detached; but Maynard was an incorrigible optimist. I am not likely to forget the infectious confidence with which he asserted in 1929 that the Liberals were bound to have more than a hundred seats in the new House of Commons and would probably have a hundred and fifty (in fact they had 59); for he backed his opinion by a gamble on the Stock Exchange in which he involved some of his impecunious friends—I was not one of them. With considerateness as characteristic as his confidence, when he realised the awkwardness of the scrape into which his optimism had led them, he shouldered their liabilities. In 1939, towards the middle of July, when he was about to leave for a cure at Royat, he asked me whether I thought war would break out that autumn or whether there would be 'another hullabaloo'. ('Hullabaloo' seems to me quite a good name for Munich). I said that, having committed ourselves, foolishly in my opinion, to defend Poland, and Hitler being obviously determined to invade Poland forthwith, I supposed war before winter was inevitable. This time Maynard did not exactly rebuke me, but he did call me a 'pessimist'.

During the 1914–18 war I saw a good deal of him, especially during the later part, when he and I, Sheppard and Norton, shared 46 Gordon Square. It seems not generally to be known—though Mr. Roy Harrod has not attempted to conceal the fact— that Lord Keynes was a conscientious objector. To be sure he was an objector of a peculiar and, as I think, most reasonable kind. He was not a pacificist; he did not object to fighting in any circumstances;

he objected to being made to fight. Good liberal that he was, he objected to conscription. He would not fight because Lloyd-George, Horatio Bottomley and Lord Northcliffe told him to. He held that it was for the individual to decide whether the question at issue was worth killing and dying for; and surely he was entitled to consider himself a better judge than the newspaper-men who at that time ruled the country. He was surprised and shocked when Mr. Asquith gave way to their clamour. His work at the Treasury, which by 1917 had become of vital importance, kept him in contact with the more important ministers, and he saw right through Lloyd-George. He detested his demagogy. I remember his cutting from a French paper—*Excelsior* presumably—a photograph of 'the goat' as he always called him, in full evening dress and smothered in ribbons, speaking at a banquet in Paris; and I remember his writing under it 'Lying in state'. He pinned it up in the dining-room at forty-six. Later, in the supposed interests of the Liberal Party, he collaborated with 'the goat' who had become for certain left-wing papers and politicians a sort of 'grand old man'. No good came of that. As for his conscientious objection, he was duly summoned to a tribunal and sent word that he was much too busy to attend.

There are those who maintain that Maynard's importance during the war and familiarity with the great bred that cocksureness which was his most irritating characteristic. I do not agree. The influence of the great on Maynard was slight compared with Maynard's influence on them. The cocksureness was always there; circumstances evoked and possibly stimulated it. Certainly the habit was provoking. It was also amusing. Late one night towards the end of the first war I remember his coming up to my room in Gordon Square where Norton and I were talking quietly about, as likely as not, the meaning of meaning. He was elated; he had been dining; what is more, he had been dining with cabinet ministers. The question had arisen—'Who finally defeated Hannibal?' No one knew except Maynard and he told them it was Fabius Maximus: 'unus homo nobis cunctando restituit rem' he declaimed, and I hope he translated it for the politicians though for us he was good enough to leave it in the original. Of course it was not the cunctator but Scipio Africanus who finally defeated Hannibal at the battle of Zama, as I obligingly pointed out. Maynard disregarded my correction in a way that did perhaps ever so slightly suggest that someone who had been dining with cabinet ministers knew better, and continued to expatiate on the pleasures of the evening, his little historical triumph, the excellent cooking and above all the wine.

Maynard laid down the law on all subjects. I dare say I minded too much: many of his friends took it as a joke. But I do think it was silly of him; for by dogmatising on subjects about which he knew nothing he sometimes made himself ridiculous to those who did not know him well and to those who did annoying. Cocksureness was his besetting sin, if sin it can be called. Gradually it became his habit to speak with authority: a bad habit which leads its addicts to assume that the rest of us are ready to assume that their knowledge must be greater than ours. Maynard knew a good deal about a great many things, and on several subjects spoke with warranted authority. Unfortunately he got into the habit of speaking with authority whether it was warranted or not. He acquired—I do not say he cultivated—a masterful manner; and when he spoke of matters about which he knew little or nothing with the confidence and disregard for other people's opinions which were perhaps excusable when he was talking about economics or probability of rare editions, instead of appearing masterly he appeared pretentious. That, too, was a pity, for he was not pretentious; he made no boast of his superior knowledge and expected no praise for it, he merely assumed it. For my part, I was exasperated most often by his laying down the law on painting and painters; but I will not draw an example of his misplaced self-confidence from his pronouncements on art, because, æsthetic judgments being always questionable, though I am sure that his were often wrong, I am far from sure that mine are always right. Instead, I will recall a conversation—or should I say an exposition?—which remains extremely clear in my memory, and provides an instance of misplaced self-confidence the misplacedness of which is not open to dispute.

He had been staying with one of his rich city-friends—for in those days (the early 'twenties') there were still rich men in England: he had been staying in Hampshire I think but I am not sure, certainly in the south, and he returned to Charleston, the house in Sussex which for a while he shared with my wife, myself and Duncan Grant, and told us all about it. It had been a shooting party; Maynard himself never handled a gun, but he told us all about it. He told us what is done and what is not done; he told us when you might shoot and when you might not shoot, he told us how to shoot and what to shoot. And as he was under the impression—all this happened long before he had a farm and a wood of his own—that his party had been shooting grouse in Hampshire or thereabouts with rifles, you can imagine the sort of nonsense he made of it. Now it so happens I was brought up in a sporting family: I have possessed a game-licence since I was sixteen and walked with the guns since I was a child; and I do believe I have killed every game-bird in the British Isles except a capercailzie and some of the rarer duck. But if you suppose that these facts would have daunted Lord Keynes, all I can say is—you have got the great economist wrong.

My insistence on Maynard's cocksureness may have given the impression that he was spoilt by success. If so, I have given a false impression. Maynard floated happily on a sea of power and glory and considerable wealth, but never went out with the tide. Two stout anchors held him fast to shore: his old friends and Cambridge. This Mr. Roy Harrod has made clear in his excellent biography. Cabinet Ministers and *The Times* might praise, but if he had an uneasy suspicion that Lytton Strachey, Duncan Grant, Virginia Woolf and Vanessa Bell did not share their enthusiasm, public flattery might appear something to be ashamed of. When he came to Charleston with Lady Keynes for the first time after his peerage had been announced he was downright sheepish. 'We have come to be laughed at' he said.

And what was Cambridge thinkng? Maynard cared passionately for his country, but I believe he was at greater pains to improve the finances of King's than to rescue those of the British Empire. If this be a slight exaggeration, that artistic temperament, from which I should like to be supposed to suffer, must bear the blame; but that stern, unbending economist, Mr. Roy Harrod, has made it clear to all who read that Keynes valued the good opinion of his old friends far above that of the majority or the great. Mr. Harrod, it seems to me, gives an excellent account of his subject—I had almost said his 'hero' —which should be read for its own sake and perhaps as a corrective to mine. Nevertheless I understand the feelings of those old and intimate friends who say —'Maynard was not really like that, he was not like that at all'. That is what old friends will always say of official biographies; and they will be right. Mrs. Thrale, who knew Johnson far longer and far more intimately than Boswell knew him, doubtless said as much. And of course Mrs. Thrale was right. Only she forgot that it was Boswell's business to write a biography, to depict a man in all his activities and in his relations to all sorts of people, while it was her privilege to record a personal impression.

I, too, am recording a personal impression. I am trying to remember little things that have escaped the notice of my betters. Such things are trivial by definition, and sometimes derogatory; but, though they may be beneath the dignity of history, they matter a good deal in daily life. My recollections, I foresee, run the risk of appearing spiteful. To counteract this appearance I could of course pile up well

merited compliments. But of what use would it be
for me to expatiate on the power of Maynard's intellect and his services to humanity when writers far
better qualified have done it already and done it
with authority? Nevertheless, to escape the charge
of malignity, let me say here and now what maybe
I shall have occasion to repeat. Maynard was the
cleverest man I ever met: also his cleverness was of
a kind, gay and whimsical and civilized, which made
his conversation a joy to every intelligent person who
knew him. In addition he had been blest with a
deeply affectionate nature. I once heard him say,
humorously but I believe truly, at dinner, before a
meeting of the memoir club, 'If everyone at this
table, except myself, were to die tonight, I do not
think I should care to go on living'. He loved and he
was beloved. He did not love, though he may have
rather liked, me; and I did not love him. That
should be borne in mind by anyone who does this
sketch the honour of a reading.

In great things he was magnificently generous;
generous to his country, generous to his college, generous to servants and dependents, particularly generous to his less fortunate friends (I know two charming young men who may or may not know that they
were educated—and highly educated—partly at his
expense). In small things, however, like many who
have enjoyed the advantages and disadvantages of a
serious, non-conformist upbringing, he was careful.
Also, financier that he was, he loved a bargain. One
summer's evening in 1919 he returned to Charleston
from a day in London bearing a heavy parcel which
contained innumerable minute tins of potted meat.

He had bought them at a sale of surplus army-stores and he had bought them at a penny a piece. The private soldiers had not liked the stuff, and therein had shown good taste. I teased Maynard by pretending that the meat had been condemned as unfit for human consumption: and indeed, the bargain-hunter himself could barely keep it down. But at a penny a tin. . . . Again, I remember being with him at Lewes races, and asking a farmer of my acquaintance for 'a good thing'. Maynard did not want 'a good thing'; what he wanted was the best bet. He wanted a bargain in odds. This rather complicated notion puzzled my friend, and we left him puzzling. For I did not attempt to explain that what Maynard had in mind was that there might be some horse in some race against which the odds were longer than need be, or rather, book-makers being what they are, less short than might have been expected. If there were a starter at a hundred to one which might just as well have been offered at sixty-six to one, that horse, though standing no apparent chance of winning, was the horse for Maynard's money. What he wanted was not a winner but a bargain.

Lytton Strachey used to say—'Pozzo has no æsthetic sense'.[1] That was an exaggeration perhaps.

[1] Mr. Roy Harrod writes in a note: 'For many years in Bloomsbury Keynes was familiarly known by the name of Pozzo, having been so christened by Strachey after the Corsican diplomat, Pozzo di Borgo—not a diplomat of evil motive or base conduct, but certainly a schemer and man of many facets'. But it was not only, nor chiefly, of the Corsican diplomat that Lytton and those who used the nickname were thinking. The Italian word 'pozzo' has more than one meaning, and to English ears carries various suggestions.

What may be said confidently is that he had no innate feeling for the visual arts. Had he never met Duncan Grant he would never have taken much interest in painting. He made a valuable collection because generally he bought on good advice; when he relied on his own judgment the result was sometimes lamentable. Lamentable it would have been had he relied on his own judgment to the end when he wrote that piece in *The New Statesman* about Low's drawings; for in the original version, not only had he compared Low with Daumier, he had likened him to Daumier, had almost equalled him with Daumier. What he insisted on retaining is sufficiently tell-tale.

'We all know that we have amongst us today a cartoonist in the grand tradition. But, as the recognition, which contributions to evening papers receive by word of mouth round the dinner-table, cannot reach the modest cartoonist, one welcomes a book like this as an opportunity to tell Low how much we think of him and how much we love him. He has the rare combination of gifts which is necessary for his craft—a shrewd and penetrating intelligence, wit, taste, unruffled urbanity, an indignant but open and understanding heart, a swift power of minute observation with an equally swift power of essential simplification, and, above all, a sense and talent for beauty, which extracts something delightful even out of ugliness. One may seem to be piling it on, but Low really has these things, and it is a great addition to our lives to meet the tongue and eye of a civilized man and true artist when we open the *Evening Standard*.

Last summer Low and Kingsley Martin made a trip to Bolshieland, and this agreeable book is the outcome. Low's pencil and charcoal sketches are reproduced by some process which, whatever it may be, looks like lithograph and thereby reinforces the comparison between Low and the lithographers of the old *Charivari* of Paris— Gavarni and Daumier and their colleagues. They are *illustrations* in the literal sense of the word—pictures of the inside and of the outside of things at the same time.' (Review of 'Low's Russian Sketchbook'—*New Statesman and Nation*, Dec. 10, 1932).[1]

What one tried to point out, and Maynard could not understand, was that no two artists—to be for a moment polite and dishonest—could be much more unalike than Daumier and Low. To begin with, Low is not an artist. He possesses a prodigious knack of inventing visual equivalents for political situations and ideas; and ekes out their meaning with tags which have often the neatness of epigrams. It is a remarkable gift. But those equivalents have no æsthetic value—no value in themselves. The line is as smart and insensitive as the prose of a penny-a-liner. Daumier, who was one of the great draughtsmen of the nineteenth century, lacked entirely that gift which in old days made us buy the *Evening Standard* to see what Low was up to. Having made a beautiful drawing, which might or might not suggest some crude bit of social or political criticism, Daumier as often as not, could think of no legend to put under it. The drawing, you see, was not an illustration of something else but a work of art complete in itself. So he left the business of putting in the patter to Philipon or some other clever fellow in the office.

[1]Gladly I take this opportunity of thanking Mr. Kingsley Martin, the editor of *The New Statesman*, who was kind enough to have this review hunted down and transcribed for my benefit.

This distinction to Maynard seemed fanciful, as it must seem to anyone who has no real feeling for visual art. Even in literature his untutored judgment was not to be trusted. During the last war he returned from America with a find—a great new novel. He had discovered a modern master, and he had brought the masterpiece home with him. It was Bemelmans' 'Now I lay me down to sleep', a piece of comicality that might, or might not, while away an hour in the train.

That Maynard Keynes has benefited all the arts by the creation of the Arts Council is a title to glory and a notorious fact which proves nothing contrary to what was said in the last paragraph. It would prove, if further proof were needed, that he was one of those uncommon human beings who have devoted great powers of organisation to good purposes. Maynard's gifts were always at the service of civilization, and by long and affectionate association with artists —do not forget that Lady Keynes was a brilliant ballerina and an interesting actress—he came to realise acutely that of civilization the arts are an essential ingredient. Also this achievement, the creation of the Arts Council in time of war, of a war in which he was playing an important and exhausting part, proves—but again what need of proof?—his boundless energy and versatility, as well as his capacity for making something solid and durable out of a hint. God forbid that anyone should imagine that I am suggesting that it was I who gave the hint. At that time anxious questionings as to the future of the arts in a more or less socialist state were to be heard on all sides. I drag myself into the picture only because I recall a conversation with Maynard which led to my writing, at his suggestion, an article in *The New Statesman* of which, at that time, he was part-proprietor and, unless I mistake, a director. My argument was that, much as I disliked the idea of a Ministry of Fine Arts, the creation of such a Ministry would be, when private patronage had been destroyed by economic egalitarianism, the only means of saving the arts from extinction. The argument was neither striking nor novel; what was remarkable was that Maynard, in the midst of his preoccupations, should not only have devised but realised an institution which might nourish the arts without handing them over to civil servants and politicians. So far his contrivance has worked and worked well. Whether it will continue to evade the embrace of death—of politicians I mean—remains to be seen.

Those who have said that Maynard Keynes had no æsthetic sense may seem to have forgotten his prose. He had a fine, lucid style in which he could state persuasively and wittily the interesting things he had in mind. When he attempted to express the more delicate shades of feeling or to make a picture out of observations rather than ideas, he was, in my opinion, less convincing. Those famous portraits of Clemenceau, Wilson and Lloyd-George have never seemed to me quite the masterpieces they have seemed to other, and perhaps better, judges. They are lively and telling but scarcely subtle I think. To my taste his best book is *Essays in Persuasion*, and the best portrait he ever drew that of Alfred Marshall. In that long biographical notice, reprinted in *Essays in*

Biography, his knowledge and his culture, which, though limited, had been garnered and sifted by an extraordinarily powerful understanding, are most skilfully employed to enlighten what in other hands might have appeared a dull subject. The result, if not precisely beautiful, is more than pleasing: in the exact sense of the word it is admirable.

I said that his culture was limited: such judgments are always relative, and perhaps I should try to be more explicit. As has been intimated, in the visual arts his taste was anything but sure and his knowledge amounted to nothing. Some believe he appreciated music, but I have never discovered the foundations of their belief. Literature is another matter. At Eton Maynard had been reared on the classics, and of the Greek and Latin authors remembered as much as clever people who have enjoyed what are called the advantages of a public school education can be expected to remember. I have heard that he was a fair German scholar, but of that I cannot speak. He had very little French and no Italian. Of English he had read much, both verse and prose. He liked poetry; but he enjoyed it as a well educated man of affairs rather than as an artist or an æsthete. One had only to hear him read aloud —and he was fond of reading poetry aloud—to feel that the content was what he really cared for. His commerce with the English historians would have been more profitable if his memory had been more retentive. He had a capacity for forgetting, and for muddling, dates and figures, that was astonishing and sometimes rather tiresome—tiresome because, with his invincible cocksureness, he could not dream of admitting that he mistook. To the end of his life he continued to study—or perhaps, towards the end, merely to take an interest in—mathematics and philosophy. Presumably he understood Wittgenstein as well as anyone understood him—except Professor Ayer. He never called himself a Logical Positivist. Of his economic theories and constructions, that is to say of the great work of his life, I am too ignorant to speak. I should be able to say more about his theory of Probability than that it served him ill at Monte Carlo, since in the years before the first war I often heard him talk about it. And after that war, when he took up the manuscript of his old disertation with a view to making a book, he would—I suppose because we were living in the same house— occasionally hand me a much corrected sheet saying —such was his lack of memory—'can you remember what I meant by that?' Alas, figures and symbols had crept into the argument and my miserable inaptitude for sums made me unhelpful. Anyhow I am not equipped to criticise so abstruse a theory, but I understand that Ramsay made a rent which caused all the stitches to run.

I dare say most readers will think I have said enough to disprove my statement that Maynard's culture was limited. Maybe I used the wrong word and should have said 'provincial'. To explain what I mean by that, perhaps I may be allowed to draw on my homely but vivid memories. At Charleston it was our habit to sit after dinner in an oblate semicircle before a curious fire-place, devised and constructed by Roger Fry to heat with logs a particularly chilly room: strange to say, it did. Each of us would be reading his or her book, and someone was sure to be reading French. Also it so happened that, just after the old war, stimulated I think by Aldous Huxley, I had become interested in the life and through the life the plays of Alfieri; wherefore, Alfieri leading on, I might be reading some early nineteenth century Italian. Thus, towards bed-time, could spring up talk about French or Italian ways of thinking, feeling and living. In such discussions one could not but be struck by Maynard's inability to see a foreign country from inside. France, Italy, America even, he saw them all from the white cliffs of Dover, or, to be more exact, from Whitehall or King's combination room. Compared with (say) Roger Fry, who was often of the company, he seemed ludicrously provincial. And that may be what I had in mind when I called his culture limited.

In spite of all the little annoying things that have stuck in my memory, my recollection of Maynard, vivid and persistent, is that of a delightful companion. I miss him; and I understand the feelings of those who more than miss, of those for whom the wound caused by his death never quite heals and may at any moment become painful. What I miss is his conversation. It was brilliant: that is an obvious thing to say but it is the right thing. In the highest degree he possessed that ingenuity which turns commonplaces into paradoxes and paradoxes into truisms, which discovers—or invents—similarities and differences, and associates disparate ideas—that gift of amusing and surprising with which very clever people, and only very clever, can by conversation give a peculiar relish to life. He had a witty intellect and a verbal knack. In argument he was bewilderingly quick, and unconventional. His comment on any subject under discussion, even on a subject about which he knew very little, was apt to be so lively and original that one hardly stopped to enquire whether it was just. But in graver mood, if asked to explain some technical business, which to the amateur seemed incomprehensible almost, he would with good-humoured ease make the matter appear so simple that one knew not whether to be more amazed at his intelligence or one's own stupidity. In moments such as these I felt sure that Maynard was the cleverest man I had ever met; also, at such moments, I sometimes felt, unreasonably no doubt, that he was an artist.

That Maynard Keynes was a great man is generally admitted; but in private life no one could have been less 'great-manish'. He was never pompous. His greatness no doubt revealed itself most impressively in economics—the work of his life—in organisation and negotiation; but of greatness in such matters I am not competent to speak. Nor yet, alas! am I entitled to speak of what to some was his most memorable quality: for me his cleverness was what counted most, but to a few privileged men and women who knew him through and through his supreme virtue was his deeply affectionate nature. He liked a great many people of all sorts and to them he gave pleasure, excitement and good counsel; but his dearest friends he loved passionately and faithfully and, odd as it may sound, with a touch of humility.

V

ROGER FRY

'YOU knew him well, why don't you give us your picture of him?' said an American friend with whom I was talking about Roger Fry. Because, said I, Virginia Woolf wrote a biography which, besides being as complete an account of Fry's life as for the present it would be seemly to publish, happens to be a masterpiece: I have no notion of entering into competition with one of the great writers of my age. Of course I knew well enough that what my friend had in mind was something utterly unlike Mrs. Woolf's biography; what he expected of me was an appetising lecture, fifty-five minutes of lively gossip, a chapter from my unpublished memoirs. But here again a lion was in the way: for though, as a matter of fact, I did jot down soon after Fry's death, for the amusement of my friends and his, a handful of anecdotes intended to illustrate just one facet of his nature—the lovably absurd, I felt that to enjoy these fantastic tales it was necessary to have known the hero and to have known him well. Now Virginia Woolf made us know him so well that she was able to avail herself of my collection—which was of course at her service—dropping delicately here an absurdity there an extravagance with telling effect: but I am not Virginia Woolf. I cannot bring the dead to life, and so I cannot effectively retell my own stories. All I can do is to give, or try to give, the impression made on me by the man, the critic and the painter, drawing more on my recollection of what he said and did than on what he published, which is after all accessible to all and I hope familiar to most. For his ideas I must go sometimes to his books; but of his character and gifts I will try to give an account based on what I remember of his sayings and doings.

'How did Roger Fry strike you?' That, I suppose, is the question. It is not easily answered. That fine, old sport of analysing characters and reducing them to their component qualities or humours is out of fashion, and was, I admit, as a method, unsubtle. Still, no one who knew Roger is likely to quarrel with me if I say that some of the things that come first to mind when one thinks of him are intelligence, sweetness, ardour and sensibility; nor I believe will it be denied that one of the first things to catch the attention of anyone who was coming acquainted with him was likely to be his prodigious and varied knowledge. To be sure, the very first thing that struck me was his appearance. He was tall—about six foot I dare say; but did not look his height. Maybe he stooped a little; he was well made, by no means lanky, anyhow he certainly did not give the impression of a very tall man. What one noticed were his eyes which were both round and penetrating—an uncommon combination—and were made to appear rounder by large circular goggles. One noticed his hair too—once black, I believe, but greyish when I met him—which, long, rebellious and silky, somehow accentuated his features which, in profile at all events, were very sharply defined. He was clean shaven. There was something the air of a judge about him, but still more the air of one who is perpetually surprised by life—as indeed he was. At moments he reminded me of a highly sagacious rocking-horse. He wore good clothes badly. Obviously they had been made by the right tailor, but there was always something wrong with them. It might be a too decorative tie fashioned out of some unlikely material, or a pair of yellow brown sandals worn when black shoes would have been appropriate. His hats were peculiar; broad-brimmed, round, Quakerish and becoming. Only in full evening dress—white tie, white waistcoat, boiled shirt and collar—did he appear smart. Then, with his silvery hair carefully brushed, he looked infinitely distinguished.

So much for the impression made at first meeting. Acquaintance ripening to friendship, you would probably note a restless activity of mind and body. Ardent he was, as I have said, intelligent, sensitive, sweet, cultivated and erudite: these qualities and attainments revealed themselves sooner or later, and soon rather than late, to everyone who came to know him, and of them I must speak first. But what charmed his intimate friends almost as much as his rare qualities was his boundless gullibility: of that I shall speak later.

I have said that his knowledge was what might well have struck you in the beginning. One was surprised by the amount he knew before one realised that it was a mere means to something far more precious—to culture in the best sense of the word. Roger Fry was what Bacon calls 'a full man'; but his various erudition was only a means to thought

GROUP

Frances Marshall, Quentin Bell, Julian Bell, Duncan Grant, Clive Bell,
Beatrice Mayor, Roger Fry and Raymond Mortimer

and feeling and the enrichment of life. Knowledge he knew added immensely to the fun of the fair, enabling one to make the most of any odd fact that comes one's way by seeing it in relation to other facts and to theories and so fitting it into the great jig-saw puzzle. But he never cared much to be given a result unless he could learn how that result had been obtained; and therein you will recognise one of the essential qualifications of a scholarly critic. At Cambridge his studies had been scientific: that is something to have in mind for it helps to an understanding of the man, his merits and some of his defects. He took a first in the Natural Science tripos. To do that, I am assured, requires more than smattering a little Botany and cutting up a few frogs: to have done it is, I suspect, to have given the mind a bent which the most varied and thrilling experiences of later life will hardly rectify.

I shall ask you to bear in mind, then, that Roger Fry was a man of science by training and to some extent by temper. I shall not ask you to bear in mind that he was intelligent and lovable, because intelligence and charm are the very oil and pigment in which the picture of his life is to be painted. These qualities, I hope, will make themselves felt without demonstration as my tale proceeds. His old friends will not be surprised if I do not insist on them; what may surprise some is that I did not put first among his qualities, Sensibility. That Fry had acquired exquisite sensibility was clear to all who knew him or read his writings or listened to his lectures, and clearer still to those who worked with him. To watch, or rather catch, him—for in such matters his meth-

ods were summary—disposing of a foolish attribu-
tion, was to realise just how convincing a decision
based on trained sensibility and knowledge can be.
I have seen a little dealer, with all due ceremony,
reverence and precaution, produce from a triply
locked safe what purported to be a Raphael Madon-
na; I have seen Fry give it one glance or two and
heard him say sweetly but firmly 'an eighteenth-
century copy and a bad one at that'; and I have
seen the dealer, himself for the moment convinced,
fling the picture back into the safe without so much
as bothering to lock the door. Such was the force of
Fry's sensibility—trained sensibility supported by
intelligence and knowledge. His possession of that
has never been called in question so far as I know.
What perhaps he did not possess, in such abundance
at all events, was that innate sensibility, that hank-
ering after beauty, that liking for art which resembles
a liking for alcohol, that 'gusto' as Hazlitt would
have called it, which is the best gift of many second-
and third-rate painters and of some critics even—
Théophile Gautier for instance. In a later chapter I
shall try to recall the joy of wandering about Paris,
a boy just down from Cambridge, with the Canadian,
J. W. Morrice—a typical good second-rate painter
(first-rate almost)—and of being made to feel beauty
in the strangest places; not in cafés and music-halls
only (in those days, about 1904, the classic haunts of
beauty), but on hoardings and in shop-windows, in
itinerant musicians singing sentimental romances, in
smart frocks and race-meetings and arias by Gounod,
in penny-steamers and sunsets and military uni-
forms, at the *Opéra comique* even, and even at the

Comédie française. With Roger Fry I have been privileged to travel in many parts of Europe, and from him I have learnt to discover uncharted subtleties and distinguish between fine shades of expression; but I do not think he could have found beauty where Morrice found it. Perhaps Roger possessed in the highest degree sensibility of a methodical kind, what I have called 'trained sensibility'; whereas Morrice had the sensibility of an artist—innate. I do not know.

His first approach to art was so hampered by family tradition, lofty and puritan, that it was I dare say inevitable that he should make some false starts and fall into some pits from which a normal, barbarous upbringing might have saved him. Also the climate of Cambridge in the ' 'eighties', and even later, was not altogether favourable to growth of the æsthetic sense. Also he was reading science. All this I take into account: and all this notwithstanding I do feel, re-reading the story of his early years, that his blunders of commission and omission, his baseless enthusiasms and blind spots, were not those of a very young artist but of an intellectual at any age. Assuredly the admirations and anathemas of the very young are never to be brought up against them; but in 1892 Fry was twenty-six and, what is more, had for some time been an art-student, which makes it hard to believe that, had sensibility been innate, he could have spent months in Paris—at Jullian's too—without feeling a thrill for the Impressionists and could have found in the Luxembourg nothing more exciting than Bastien Lepage.[1]

[1] It should be remembered, however, that the Caillebotte collection had not yet been installed.

I spoke of family tradition lofty and puritan: the puritan strain in Roger's character his friends might like but could not ignore. To his hours of abandon even it gave an air of revolt. His paganism was protestant—a protest against puritanism. Intellectually the freest of men, and almost indecently unprejudiced, he made one aware of a slight wrench, the ghost of a struggle, when he freed his mind to accept or condone what his forbears would have called 'vile pleasures'. It is on this streak of puritanism the devil's advocate will fasten when Roger comes up, as come up he will, for canonisation. He was open-minded, but he was not fair-minded. For though, as I have said, he was magnificently unprejudiced, he was not unprincipled; and he had a way of being sure that while all his own strong feelings were principles those of others, when they happened to cross his, were unworthy prejudices. Thanks to his puritanical upbringing he could sincerely regard his principles as in some sort the will of God. From which it followed that anyone who opposed them must have said, like Satan, 'Evil be thou my good'. People who happened not to agree with him found this annoying.

Few of us are all of a metal; most, as Dryden puts it, are 'dashed and brewed with lies'. The best founded even are flawed with some disharmony. The cup is just troubled with an 'aliquid amari', and the bitterness will now and then catch in the throat and spoil the flavour of life as it goes down. A tang of puritanism was in Roger's cup: it was barely appreciable, yet to it I believe can be traced most of his defects as man and critic. Not all: there are defects that can be traced to his scientific training and temper, but here there is gain to record as well as loss. The pure unscientific æsthete is a sensationalist. He feels first; only later, if he happens to be blest—or curst—with a restless intellect, will he condescend to reason about his feelings. It would be false and silly to suggest that Roger Fry's emotions were at the service of his theories; but he was too good a natural philosopher to enjoy seeing a theory pricked by a fact. Now the mere æsthete is for ever being bowled over by facts: the facts that upset him being as a rule works of art which according to current doctrine ought not to come off but which somehow or other do (e.g. the Houses of Parliament or the works of Kipling). The æsthete, sensationalist that he is, rather likes being knocked down by an outsider. He picks himself up and goes on his way rejoicing in an adventure. Roger Fry did not altogether like it. He entered a gallery with a gereralisation in his head— a generalisation which, up to that moment, was, or should be, a complete explanation of art. He was not the man to deny facts, and he was much too sensitive to overlook the sort I have in mind; but I do think he was inclined to give marks to pictures which, because they were right in intention, ought to have been right in achievement, and sometimes, I think, he was rather unwilling to recognise the patent but troublesome beauty of works that seemed to be sinning against the light. Nine times out of ten this tendency towards injustice was due to a puritanical aversion from charm, and to counter it the spirit of science had made him magnificently open-minded. He was the most open-minded man I ever met: the only one indeed who tried to practise that fundamental precept of science—that nothing should be assumed to be true or false until it has been put to the test. This made him willing to hear what anyone had to say even about questions on which he was a recognised authority, even though 'anyone' might be a schoolboy or a housemaid: this also made him a champion gull—but of that later. Had he fallen in with a schoolboy—a manifestly sincere and eager schoolboy—in the Arena Chapel at Padua, and had that boy confessed that he could see no merit in the frescos, Roger would have argued the question on the spot, panel by panel: and this he would have done in no spirit of amiable complacency. Always supposing the boy to be serious and ardent, the great critic would have been attentive to the arguments and objections of the small iconoclast: convinced, I suppose, he would have modified his judgment and, if necessary, recast his æsthetic.

About that æsthetic, which gave him so much trouble, I shall soon have a word to say. But first let me give an example of open-mindedness and integrity which will, I hope, make some amends for what I have said or shall say concerning his slightly biased approach to works of art. Always he had disliked Indian art: it offended his sense of reasonableness and his taste. Late in life, having enjoyed opportunities of studying more and better examples may be, or perhaps merely having studied more happily and freely examples that were always within his reach, he changed his mind. That done, the next thing to do was to 'own up'. And 'own up' he did in a discriminating lecture. When you remember that at the time of writing this palinode Roger Fry was getting on for seventy and was the foremost critic in Europe, I think you will agree that he gave proof of considerable open-mindedness and a lesson to us all. The scientific spirit is not without its uses in the appreciation of the fine arts: neither is character.

Indeed he was open-minded; which is not to say, as jealous fools were at one time fond of saying, that he was a weather-cock, slave to every gust of enthusiasm. It is a memorable fact, to which Sir Kenneth Clark sorrowfully calls attention in his preface to *Last Lectures*, that, try as he would, Fry could never bring himself greatly to admire Greek sculpture. He would have been glad to admire it: for Greek civilization, for the Greek view and way of life, for Greek prose and verse, philosophy and science, he felt what all intelligent and well educated people must feel. He realised that Athens was man's masterpiece. And so, towards the end of his life, he went with three friends —one an accomplished Hellenist and all highly intelligent—to see whether he could not prove himself wrong. The will to admire was there: but honesty, but fidelity to his personal reaction, proved the stronger. He found Greek sculpture, whether archaic or of what is called 'the great age', comparatively dull. And he said so.

Roger Fry was troubled by æsthetics; anyone who cares for art yet cannot keep his intellect quiet must be. Roger cared passionately, and positively enjoyed analysing his emotions: also he did it better, I think, than anyone had done it before. Having analysed he went on to account for his feelings, and got into that fix which everyone gets into who makes the attempt: *experto credite*. Art is almost as wide as life; and to invent a hypothesis which shall comprehend it may be as difficult, just as it may appear as simple, as to explain the universe. The place where Roger stuck is where we all stick. There is a constant in art just as, once upon a time, there was supposed to be a constant in life. I have a notion they called it 'C': anyhow that was a long time ago. But I feel pretty sure that in those far off days the difference between Organic and Inorganic was determined by the presence or absence of a definable somewhat; and still it is permissible to say that a work of art cannot exist unless there be present what I used to call 'significant form', and you may call by any name you please— provided that what you mean by your name is a combination of lines and colours, or of notes, or of words, in itself moving, i.e. moving without reference to the outside world. Only, to say that, is no more to answer the question 'What is art?' than to chatter about 'C' is, or ever was, to answer the question 'What is life?' Renoir, painting pictures of girls and fruit, concentrated his attention exclusively on their forms and colours. But implicit in those forms and colours, for Renoir inseparable from them, was appetisingness—the feeling that girls are good to kiss and peaches to eat. Easy enough to see that when a painter sets out to make you feel that his girls would be nice to kiss he ceases to be an artist and becomes a pornographer or a sentimentalist. Renoir never dreams of trying to make you feel anything of that sort; he is concerned only with saying what he feels about forms and colours. Nevertheless, he does feel, consciously or subconsciously, embedded in those forms and colours, deliciousness. All that he feels he expresses. Now all that an artist expresses is part of his work of art. The problem is turning nasty, you perceive; complicate it, multiply instances and diversify them, and you will be near where Roger stuck. He never quite swallowed my impetuous doctrine—Significant Form first and last, alone and all the time; he knew too much, and such raw morsels stuck in his scientific throat. He came near swallowing it once; but always he was trying to extend his theory to cover new difficulties—difficulties presented, not only by an acute and restless intellect, but by highly trained sensibility playing on vast experience. Need I say that his difficulties were always ahead of his explanations? In wrestling with them he raised a number of interesting questions; better still—far better—he threw a flood of brilliant light on art in general and on particular works. Read again that masterly chapter in *Transformations* called 'Some Questions in Æsthetics', a matter of fifty pages, in which he goes deeper into the subject than anyone had gone before or has gone since—I am not forgetting Max Eastman whom I greatly admire. You will find the destructive criticism entirely satisfying; you will be enlightened by the analysis of æsthetic experience; you will enjoy seeing the finest mince-meat made of Mr. Richards's simple-minded psychological explanations, which boil down to the absurd conclusion that our responses to works of art are the same as our responses to life; and when it comes to justification let Fry speak for himself:

'As to the value of the æsthetic emotion—it is clearly infinitely removed from those ethical values to which Tolstoy would have confined it. It seems to be as remote from actual life and its practical utilities as the most useless mathematical theorem. One can say only that those who experience it feel it to have a peculiar quality of "reality" which makes it a matter of infinite importance in their lives. Any attempt I might make to explain this would probably land me in the depths of mysticism. On the edge of that gulf I stop.' (*Vision and Design*, p. 199).

Certainly his wrestlings helped to give muscle to the body of Fry's criticism; but to the building of that body went many rare aliments—trained sensibility, intellect, peculiar knowledge, wide general culture, the scientific spirit and honour. Virginia Woolf speaks of 'his power of making pictures real and art important'. Words could not give better a sense of just what it was Roger Fry did for my generation and the next. Having learnt to feel intensely the beauty and glory and wonder of a work of visual art he could, so to speak, unhook his emotion and hold it under, I will not say a microscope, but an uncommonly powerful pair of spectacles. That done, he could find, and sometimes invent, words to convey feelings and analyses of feelings into the apprehension of the reader—or listener: it was even better to be a listener than a reader. I am not thinking of those unforgettable conversations and discussions before particular works of art in churches and galleries, but of his lectures. Roger Fry's lectures were his best critical performances: he was the perfect lecturer almost. And the lecture with slides is the perfect medium for pictorial exegesis, permitting, as it does, the lecturer to bring before the eyes of his audience images of the objects about which he is speaking, thinking and feeling. To hear a lecture by Roger Fry was the next best thing to sight-seeing in his company. He stuck but loosely to his text, allowing himself to be inspired by whatever was on the screen. It was from a sensation to a word. Almost one could watch him thinking and feeling.

To say the excruciatingly difficult things Fry set himself to say he was obliged to work language pretty hard. In my opinion he worked it well. His prose was lucid and lively, and on occasions he could be delightfully witty and verbally felicitous. His biographer glances, critically but affectionately, at his habit of repeating favourite phrases. The fault is unavoidable in the prose of an art-critic since there is no vocabulary of art-criticism. If such terms as 'plastic sequence', 'plastic unity', 'inner life', 'structural planes' keep cropping up, that is because they are the only symbols available for subtle and complex things which themselves keep cropping up. It is essential to understanding that readers or listeners should know precisely what the critic is referring to; and only by repeatedly describing in the same terms the same concepts can he hope to give these terms anything like generally accepted significance. To some extent the art-critic must create his own vocabulary.

Writing, as a fine art, was Roger's foible. Of prose and verse rhythms he was indistinctly aware; but he liked spinning theories about them. Of his translations of Mallarmé the less said the better: the one significant thing about them is that he believed them to be adequate. They have made me think of Bentley editing Milton; for, after all, Bentley was a great, a very great critic, and in some ways understood Greek poetry as it never had been understood by a modern. Having named Milton I find myself thinking of some gibberish Roger once wrote—for the benefit of intimate friends only—gibberish which did possess recognisable similarity of sound with the *Ode on the Nativity* but did not possess what he firmly believed it to possess, i.e. all, or almost all, the merits of the original. The gibberish was, of course, deliberate gibberish—a collection of sounds so far as possible without meaning. It was highly ingenious, and I am bound to reckon the theory behind it pretty, seeing that it was much the same as one I had myself propounded years earlier as an explanation of visual art. Only, at the time Roger's experiment was made we were deep in the 'twenties' and the fine frenzy of Post-Impressionism was a thing of the past. There was now no controversial axe to grind. Simply, Roger liked the theory because he felt it was one in the eye for 'magic'. It came from the heart rather than the head and he wanted to believe it. Now it was this gibberish, and his opinion of it, and the passion with which he defended his opinion, that finally opened my eyes to a truth which had, I suppose, always been plain to those who did not love him: Roger's feeling for poetry was puritanical. The charm, the romance, the imagery, the glamour, the magic offended the quaker that was in him; wherefore he was very willing to believe that all that signified could be reduced to clean, dry bones.

Having said so much about writing and lecturing, I must say something, I suppose, about painting. It is an unenviable task; for, preposterous as it must

seem to those who know him only by his achievement, Roger Fry took his painting more seriously
than he took his criticism. It was the most important
thing in his life, or at any rate he thought it was. He
said so and his friends were bound to believe him;
yet some of them wondered: surely he knew that he
was the best critic alive, and, at the bottom of his
heart, can he have believed that he was a very good
painter? He knew that those whose opinion he
valued did not think so. To me it seems that his early
work, especially his water-colours and paintings on
silk, are his happiest productions. They are frankly
eclectic; the influence of some master, of some English water-colourist as a rule, being acknowledged at
every turn. But in most of these works—things done
before 1910 shall we say?—there are pleasing qualities which later I seek in vain. Unashamed, in those
unregenerate days, he could utilise his knowledge,
and exploit his taste, the delicacy of his perceptions,
his sleight of hand. All these assets contributed to a
tentative style which did in some sort express a part of
his nature. The Post-Impressionist revolution which
set free so many of his latent capacities overwhelmed
these modest virtues. It set free his capacity for living
and enjoying, but it did no good to his painting. On
the contrary, that movement which was to liberate the
creative powers of all those young and youngish artists who possessed any powers worth liberating, that
movement of which in this country he was the animator, did Fry's painting harm, driving it into un-
congenial ways. He tried to paint in a manner which
he understood admirably and explained brilliantly
but could not make his own. No longer decked in the

77

rather antiquated finery which had fitted his temper on one side at any rate, his painting gift appeared naked, and we perceived to our dismay that it amounted to next to nothing. His very energy and quickness, qualities elsewhere profitable, here served him ill. He worked too fast. Neither had he that ruminating enjoyment which lingers over a subject till the last oozings of significance have been tasted, nor yet the patience which will elaborate a design to its last possibilities. I have seen him, out of sheer conscientiousness, or in some desperate hope of a miraculous revelation, work on at a picture to which he knew he could add nothing, for all the world like an examination-candidate who has written all he knows and vainly strives to improve the appearance of his paper by writing it all over again. Roger knew that he had added nothing. Maybe he knew too much.

Roger Fry was a good, though impatient, craftsman, proper of his hands and quick to learn a trade. His best productions in this sort are the white pots and plates he made for the Omega; and it is to be hoped that a few will be preserved in some public collection, for they grow rare. But no sooner did he think it necessary to embellish a chair or a table or a chest of drawers, to beautify a curtain, a lampshade or a frock, than something went wrong. There must have been a devil, I have sometimes fancied, a demon born of puritanism and pampered in young 'artistic' days, which lurked in his sub-consciousness and on favourable occasions poked up its nose. At any rate, in all that he did for the Omega, with the exception of those plain white pots and plates, I taste an unpleasant flavour—a flavour redolent of 'artistry'. That was the devil's revenge; and perhaps it was this same evil spirit that forbade Fry the paradise of creation. From that delectable country he was excluded; he could not reach the frontiers because where art begins some perverse sub-consciousness or self-consciousness arrested him. What was it precisely? I hardly know. Could he have believed—no, he could not have believed nor thought either—but could he have hoped, in some dark corner of his being inaccessible to reason, that style could be imposed? A horrid fancy: that way lie art guilds and gowns, sandals, homespun and welfare-work, and at the end yawns an old English tea-room. If Roger had finished a picture before he had begun a work of art, that may have been because he could not practise what he preached so well—that in creating all the horses must be driven abreast, that you cannot hitch on style or beauty as an ostler used to hitch on a tracer. And if I am asked why Roger Fry's painting seems dead, all I can say is what Renoir said when asked whether art comes from the head or the heart: '*des couilles*' he replied.

But if Roger Fry was not an artist, he was one of the most remarkable men of his age, besides being one of the most lovable. This his biographer has established; his other friends can but bring a few flowers to the monument and cherish the inscription. I first met him appropriately enough in the morning train from Cambridge to King's Cross. It was early in 1910, a moment at which Fry was in a sense beginning a new life. The tragedy in which the old had ended, the courage and devotion with which that tragedy had been fought and for a while warded off,

Mrs. Woolf has most movingly recounted. In 1910 Roger Fry was in his forty-fifth year: one life was ending and a new, and perhaps more exciting, about to begin. Indeed, it was a moment at which everyone felt excitement in the air: had not I—even I—just sat down to describe the general state of affairs in an *opus* to bear the pregnant title *The New Renaissance*, an *opus* of which the bit I did publish three years later, a book called *Art*, would have formed a mere chapter. Certainly there was stir: in Paris and London at all events there was a sense of things coming right, though whether what we thought was coming could properly be described as a 'renaissance' now seems to me doubtful. The question is academic: as usual the statesmen came to the rescue, and Mr. Asquith, Sir Edward Grey and M. Viviani declared war on Germany. But in 1910 only statesmen dreamed of war, and quite a number of wide-awake people imagined the good times were just round the corner. Miracles seemed likely enough to happen; but when Roger Fry told me that morning in the train that he proposed to show the British public the work of the newest French painters, I told him that I would be proud to help in any way I could but that his scheme was fantastic. Not that there was any question of my being of serious use—Roger never needed an *État-Major*; but as I had written in praise of Cézanne and Gauguin and other 'revolutionaries' he thought I might as well give a hand. Anyhow, I was put on a committee which did nothing, and late that summer I joined Roger and Desmond MacCarthy in Paris: in the autumn opened the first Post-Impressionist exhibition.

Of this exhibition and the next Fry was, as everyone knows, the original and moving spirit: 'as everyone knew' perhaps I should have said. For lately a story has been put about that it was not Roger Fry who introduced the Post-Impressionist masters to the British public and stimulated that enthusiasm for their work which persists. Even it has been suggested that the credit should go to Mr. Samuel Courtauld, which is of course sheer nonsense. Far from being a pioneer, Sam Courtauld—I speak with some authority as a fairly close friend—was a little behind the times. It was in 1922 that he began to collect Post-Impressionist paintings; before that date he had been buying work of quite another kind—pictures by D. Y. Cameron for instance. In 1911 I do not think Roger Fry knew him; but before 1920 at latest he (Courtauld) had been strongly urged by Roger Fry, or at Fry's instigation, to buy pictures by Cézanne, Van Gogh and Gauguin, which already were beyond the reach of the small collectors who coveted them.

Mr. Douglas Cooper in a valuable introduction to his catalogue of the Courtauld Collection—a masterpiece of exact and brilliant scholarship—has inexplicably misjudged the public reaction to the Post-Impressionist exhibitions of 1910–11–12 and consequently has misunderstood the sentiment of the succeeding decade. Of the first exhibition he writes: 'But today one cannot help feeling that it was an unfortunate exhibition, for it presented a distorted view of Post-Impressionist developments and, by virtue of its own inconsistencies, had the effect of frightening the English public away from rather than of encouraging it to take an active interest in modern French art.'

This is not true. Rich collectors, directors and their trustees may well have been frightened—Mr. Courtauld himself was frightened I dare say—but the younger members of the art-loving public were for the most part wildly enthusiastic. And the enthusiasm endured. During the next ten years, war notwithstanding, the interest in modern French art never flagged; also throughout those years Roger Fry was the animator. When, immediately after the war Sir Osbert Sitwell brought over from Paris a scratch lot of pictures collected by Zborowski, the supply hardly met the demand. For that matter, already at the first and second Post-Impressionist exhibitions almost all the cheaper pictures found buyers. And here, maybe, we touch on one of the causes of Mr. Cooper's misconception. He was writing of the Courtauld collection and consequently thinking of big prices. True it is that rich collectors and trustees of public galleries held aloof till prices had become not big but preposterous; and that, though he did not begin till 1922, Mr. Courtauld was the second, or perhaps the third, in this country to buy expensive Post-Impressionist pictures. Roger Fry was not to blame for that. The art-loving public is not composed exclusively of rich men; chiefly it is composed of men and women of moderate means, and already in 1910 the works of Cézanne, Gauguin and Van Gogh were beyond those means, as, in 1912, were the more important works of Matisse and Picasso. Nevertheless, though not impressive purchasers, the admirers of the Post-Impressionists and of contemporary French painting were enthusiastic and numerous.

Mr. Cooper complains that the first Post-Impressionist exhibition came to the public as a shock. It should have been led up to gradually. Here speaks the historian rather than the art-lover; for though Mr. Cooper loves art he adores chronology, and chronology he feels was slighted. Probably it was. There are scholars who think that exhibitions should be organised for historians rather than amateurs. Roger Fry was not one of them. He was content to show a number of fine pictures and encourage people to enjoy them. They did enjoy them.[1]

One result of the first Post-Impressionist exhibition was that Roger Fry became the animator and advocate of the younger British painters; but not the master. Few young painters mistook him for a master, though to him they looked for advice and encouragement and sometimes for material support. With his fine intellect, culture and persuasive ways he became spokesman for modern art—our representative in the councils of the great; for he could place his word where he would. *The Times* felt bound to print letters from him in large type on the leader page. Even fine ladies, even the Prime Ministress, had to pretend to listen. And, under the wand of the enchanter, with his looks, his voice, his infinite variety and palpable good faith, those who began to listen found themselves becoming converts. It was now, in these last years of peace, that France became

[1]In writing these paragraphs I have made free with a longish review I contributed to *The Times Literary Supplement* (March 26, 1954).

for him what for the rest of his life she remained—
his second country; and there he made friends, deep,
affectionate and charming, who later were to do
much to lighten the gloom of declining years. At
home, too, between 1910 and '14 he was making
friends, some of whom were to grow into close companions and collaborators; and of these most, it is to
be noted, were of a generation younger than his own.
They were, I think, gayer, more ribald, more unshockable, more pleasure-loving and less easily impressed by grave airs and fine sentiments than the
friends—whom, by the way, he never lost nor ceased
to love—with whom he had grown to middle age.
It was from these younger people that he learnt to
enjoy shamelessly almost—yes, almost. Their blissful
adiabolism helped him to ignore the nudgings of the
old puritan Nick. And this I like to count some small
return for all they learnt from him. He taught them
much: amongst other things, by combining with an
utterly disinterested and unaffected passion for art a
passion for justice and hatred of cruelty, he made
them aware of the beauty of goodness. That virtue
could be agreeable came as a surprise to some of us.
Like all satisfactory human relationships, these new
friendships were matters of give and take; and I
know who gave most. Nevertheless, between the first
Post-Impressionist exhibition and the first war I have
a notion that Roger Fry changed more than he had
changed in all the years between Cambridge and
that exhibition.

I have suggested that one reason why Roger was
unable to elaborate a work of art and knocked off
too many works of craft was that his boundless en-

ergy induced impatience. This energy, allied with prodigious strength of will, was terrifying; and it is not surprising that his enemies, and his friends too when they chanced to be his victims, called him ruthless and obstinate; for it is provoking to be driven straight into a field of standing corn because your driver cannot admit that his map may be out of date or that he may have misread it. Of this energy and wilfulness an extract from my unpublished notes may perhaps give some idea. So, 'I recall a cold and drizzling Sunday in August: I cannot be sure of the year. Roger is staying with us at Charleston, convalescent; for, like many exceptionally robust and energetic men, Roger was a valetudinarian. I remember hearing my wife say, probably at breakfast, that she suspected him of intending to be motored some time in the afternoon to Seaford, eight or nine miles away, where dwelt his curious old friend, Hindley Smith; but that she, the weather being vile, the road slippery, the car open and ill-humoured, had no intention of obliging him. Just before lunch Frances Marshall (Mrs. Ralph Partridge) who also was staying with us, and possessed, like my wife, what most would deem a will of iron, told me she had a headache and meant, the moment lunch was over, to slip off to bed, if that could be done without causing commotion. In any case she was not going to play chess with Roger. For my part I never cared about playing chess with Roger; if, by any chance, one succeeded in some little plot for surprising his queen or rook—and setting traps is what amuses all thoroughly bad players such as I—he would dismiss the strategem as 'uninteresting', retract a series of moves—generally to his own advantage—and so continue till on scientific and avowable principles he had beaten one to his satisfaction. Anyhow, on this dark and dismal Sunday, lunch finished, Roger sprang to his feet—all invalid that he was he could spring when the occasion seemed to demand action —exclaiming: "Now Frances for a game." And, as soon as Frances had been allowed to lose in a way of which he could approve, again he sprang: "Now, Vanessa, we've just time to go and see Hindley Smith." Vanessa went like a lamb.'

I have spoken of Roger's open-mindedness, of his readiness to listen to anyone he thought sincere: that was fine. His aptitude for discovering sincerity in unlikely places was fine, too, I suppose; but sometimes it landed him in difficulties. Not to mince words, he was a champion gull: gullibility was the laughable and lovable defect of a quality. Stories illustrating this weakness abound; one or two, which, I am proud to say, are drawn from my notes, appear in Virginia Woolf's biography. If I venture to impose yet another on your patience, the excuse must be that it illustrates, or at least adumbrates, more than one characteristic.

The scene is laid in a studio in the south of France. It is a cold spring day and we are sitting round a stove drinking tea. Roger has recieved a letter; to be sure he received it several days ago and it has been kept ostentatiously secret ever since. It is from an American book and picture dealer in a small, private way of business. It is highly important and extremely confidential, but Roger must speak or burst. Well, of course the writer wanted money—a good deal of money. Why he wanted so much will appear. In Vienna, in what was rather vaguely termed 'the archives', someone had discovered certain papers. These turned out to be no less than the secret papers of Roger Bacon—and in fact some writings of his, not in the least secret, had been unearthed several months earlier—but these *secret* papers proved beyond doubt that the admirable friar had foreseen everything—flying-machines,motor-cars,telephones, wireless, high explosives, poison gas—all the modern conveniences in short. Now for some reason not very clearly defined these documents were extremely damaging to the Papacy: also the Pope had forbidden their publication. They could be published only in the United States, and there only if some millionaire could be induced to buy them and print at his own expense. Surely Mr. Roger Fry, former adviser to the Metropolitan Museum and to Mr. Pierpont Morgan, would know of a likely purchaser. For until they were purchased these world-shaking documents could not be made public. That was clear; and even when they had been purchased they must be smuggled into America. Such is the influence of the Church.

You might have thought there were other possibilities. At that time Austria herself was a republic under social-democratic government, as was Germany. Russia was just over the way, and there seemed no reason to suppose that something damaging to the Vatican would necessarily be banned in Moscow. Also, there was France, a land of tempered liberty, to say nothing of England. So you might have thought: you would have thought wrong. None of these countries would do: to America the precious papers must be conveyed, though at frightful personal risk and incalculable expense. There indeed they could be printed, but only if rich collectors were sufficiently public-spirited to buy them, *en bloc* or severally; for only when they had been bought and paid for, in dollars, could the picture-dealing bookseller undertake the perilous, but for the future happiness of mankind essential, task of making their contents generally known.

Having told this long story with a long face Roger concluded that something must be done. Vainly was it suggested to him that if safety from the Inquisition were all that was needed there could be no call to go so far afield as Fifth Avenue or Wall Street: besides, was it likely the Pope would consider anything written in the thirteenth century fatal to his prestige in the twentieth? Roger was not to be shaken. He had swallowed the tale, hook, line and sinker. The Jew was an honest Jew, manifestly the victim of priestly intrigue and powerful obscurantism. So to no purpose did I doubt whether anything Roger Bacon might be found to have said was likely to prove more difficult to get round than what had already been published by Bayle or Hume or Voltaire, or, for that matter, Darwin: in vain did I wonder why these manuscripts could not be printed till they had been sold. Roger was not impressed. Only he felt, as one could see, that we were all surprisingly unfair. Indeed he was shocked, as he admitted in a letter, that anyone as intelligent as my son, Julian, should have supported me in my notorious and stupid scepticism.

Inevitably one so gullible and so often gulled grew suspicious—not of the crooks, but of old friends and well meaning acquaintances. To make matters worse, Roger had no turn for practical psychology. A poorer judge of men I have seldom met, and it goes without saying he piqued himself on penetration. He was as ready as Rousseau to believe in *conspirations holbachiques*, and was given to explaining plots which he supposed to have been woven against him, and had in truth been woven in his own imagination, by facts and motives which his friends knew to be non-existent. Does this sound sinister? It was not; for his attention could be diverted with the greatest ease from private grievances to general ideas or, better still, to particular events—in plain words to gossip. In both he delighted; also his mind was far too nimble, his capacity for enjoyment too keen, his taste too pure, his sense of fun too lively, for him to dwell long on petty troubles. He was not much like Rousseau after all. But suspicious he was, and in his fits of suspicion unjust. He could be as censorius as an ill-conditioned judge: possibly the trait was hereditary. Then it was that the puritan came out from hiding undisguised and made him believe that those who differed from him must be actuated by the foulest motives. In such moods it was that he suspected those who opposed him of having said, like Satan, 'evil be thou my good'; also, it seems to me, these moods grew more frequent with the years, bringing with them a perceptible loss of magnanimity. So it seems to me. Or was it that some of his old friends were growing touchy? That explanation is admissible too.

OLD FRIENDS

In this discursive chapter I hope to have given some idea of the qualities that made Roger Fry one of the most remarkable men of his age. A combination of intellect and sensibility, extensive culture not in the arts only but in history and science as well, dexterous manipulation of a fine instrument, and an unrivalled power of getting close in words to thoughts and feelings, made him indisputably our first critic. In fact he was more than the first critic of the age; so far as I can judge from my readings in three languages he was one of the best writers on visual art that ever lived. There may be Russians or Germans who have responded more delicately and analysed their responses more acutely, who have contrived to come nearer the heart of the matter; if so, I shall be glad to study their works as soon as they have been translated. Add to these gifts, which were as one may say open to the public, those with which in private he charmed his friends, a playful intellect for instance, free fancy and a sense of fun, along with taste in food and wine, and you have beside a great critic a rare companion. Men I have known who possessed tempers to me more congenial, but none better equipped to please generally. His was, on the whole, a happy disposition, and a cause of happiness in others. One permanent anxiety beset him: it was the child of his virtues. He dreaded, especially during the last years of his life, the collapse of civilization. For civilization he cared nobly; and the prevalence of its mortal enemies—fanaticism, superstition, dogmatism, unreasonableness, the cult of violence and stupidity, contempt of truth and the ways of truth—dismayed him. In naming these vices I have indicated his virtues, which were their contraries. He was a man of many virtues; what is more, in practice he contrived to make them amiable.

VI

VIRGINIA WOOLF

THAT I should have been amongst the first, perhaps the very first, to write a full dress article on Virginia Woolf is neither surprising nor important. I believe it was published in America, possibly in *Vanity Fair* under Frank Crowninshield's rule; but I am not sure. Because I should like to be sure, I mention the matter at the very beginning of this chapter. I should like to know to whom I ought to apologise for making free with his or her property. I have lost track of the thing; and all I can discover is a dirty manuscript written presumably in 1922 or 23 since it ends with an elaborate criticism of *Jacob's Room*, described as 'Mrs. Woolf's latest novel'. For the rest, it is a longish piece of five thousand words or so, but was I dare say cut down for publication. I should be amused to see how it looks in print, though I cannot say that in manuscript it reads particularly well: maybe at the time it seemed interesting because so little was known of the subject. Be that as it may, I shall not hesitate to make use of this manuscript if any bit seems worth salving; and perhaps the criticism is not worthless after all, for I do remember that when, some years later, a French writer produced an appreciation, his victim was amiable enough to tell me that it was a poor thing of which the best part was a paraphrase of what I had already published. Naturally I remember the compliment, but now, looking at it suspiciously, I cannot quite decide from which hand it comes.

As I was saying, that I should have been one of the first to sing the praises of Virginia Woolf is not surprising. I had known her since she was a girl of twenty, and in the years between my marriage to her sister in 1907 and her marriage to Leonard Woolf in 1912 I was to some extent her literary confidant. From earliest days I admired her reviews in *The Times Literary Supplement, The Cornhill* and *The Guardian*, and perhaps that was why she took me into her confidence and showed me short imaginative pieces few, if any, of which have been printed. Why should they have been? To me they were thrilling because they revealed—so I thought and thought rightly— in a person I cared for, genius; but to a coldly critical eye perhaps they would have seemed no more than a gifted girl practising. During these years we met regularly, once a week I dare say, to talk about writing generally and her writing in particular; with pleasure I remember that already I possessed sufficient sense of proportion to say nothing about mine. And yet we contrived to quarrel occasionally: we were both young. I call to mind some famous rows: and I have by me a picture post-card from Siena, written many years later, with an inky cross against a spot on the fortezza and beneath this legend— 'Here Clive quarrelled with his sister-in-law'.

However, it is neither about our bookish talks nor yet about her books that I want to say my word, though doubtless I shall have said something about the latter before I have done. What I want to do is something much more difficult. I want to give an idea, an adumbration, of the most remarkable person I have known intimately. I cannot hope perfectly to succeed; the task is beyond my powers, and would, I fancy, be beyond the powers of any writer unless he were an artist possessing gifts comparable with those of his subject. Yet for a professional critic who has known and known well a genius—a genius who worked magic not only in art but in life; for such a critic, so fortunately placed, to despair of giving any account of the impression made on him, would be in my opinion poor-spirited. I will do my best. Two people I have known from whom emanated simply and unmistakably a sense of genius: the other is Picasso. With Picasso I have been acquainted for fifty years almost, and at one time I saw a good deal of him; but I do not pretend to have known him well. Picasso I would not attempt to describe, though later I may have some tales to tell about him. Nevertheless, had I never seen a picture by Picasso I should have been aware of his genius: I knew him well enough for that. Similarly, had I never read a book by Virginia I should have been aware of hers. It has been my fortune to be friends with a number of very clever people: Maynard Keynes, the cleverest man I ever met, Roger Fry, Lytton Strachey, Raymond Mortimer, Jean Cocteau. None of them cast the peculiar spell I am trying to characterise. The difference between these very clever people and the less clever, between Roger Fry and me for instance, was it seemed one of degree rather than kind. There was no reason in nature why I should not have been as bright as Roger, only I happened not to be. I can imagine myself as bright as Roger; I cannot imagine myself in the least like Virginia or Picasso. With Roger's understanding and mental processes mine were of a kind: I thought and reasoned and invented and arrived at conclusions as he did, only I thought and reasoned and invented less well. But Virginia and Picasso belonged to another order of beings; they were of a species distinct from the common; their mental processes were different from ours; they arrived at conclusions by ways to us unknown. Also those conclusions or comments or judgments or flights of fancy or witticisms, or little jokes even, were true or convincing or effective or delightful for reasons that are not the reasons of logic nor yet of our well tried common-sense. Their standards, too, were of their own creation: yet spontaneously we appraised by those standards, which for the moment we not only accepted but appropriated, whatever they chose to offer. Their conclusions were as satisfying as the conclusions of mathematics though reached by quite other roads; for though they might seem to have postulated that two and two made five their answers always came out right. All this is clumsy and perhaps beside the point. The point is that half an hour's conversation with Virginia sufficed to make one realise that she had genius.

I want in this attempt to describe Virginia to dispel certain false notions. One result of the publication of extracts from her diary (*A Writer's Diary*, Hogarth Press) has been to confirm an opinion already current, the opinion that Virginia's nature was harsh and unhappy. Nothing could be further from the truth. Yet, though the inference drawn from the

published diaries is false it would be excusable had
not the editor, Mr. Leonard Woolf, been at pains
to put readers on their guard. On the very first page
of his preface he writes: 'At the best and even un-
expurgated, diaries give a distorted or one-sided portrait of the writer, because, as Virginia Woolf herself remarks somewhere in these diaries, one gets into
the habit of recording one particular kind of mood
—irritation or misery say—and of not writing one's
diary when one is feeling the opposite. The portrait
is therefore from the start unbalanced, and, if someone then deliberately removes another characteristic, it may well become a mere caricature.'

Someone did remove another characteristic. The
editor, himself, very properly cut out a number of
passages which were much too personal, not to say
libellous, to be published while the victims were
alive.

Despite this warning, there are those who find
confirmation in these diaries of what they wish to
believe and retell the old tale—Virginia Woolf was
gloomy and querulous; so I will add a few sentences
to what her husband has said clearly enough. More
often than not the diary was written in moments of
agitation, depression or nervous irritation; also the
published extracts are concerned almost entirely
with her work, a subject about which she never felt
calmly. Indeed, creating a work of art, as the diary
shows, was for Virginia a cause, not only of moral
but of physical exasperation—exasperation so intense
that often it made per positively ill. I should not be
surprised if some lively journalist had dubbed the
book 'Screams from the torture-chamber', for truly

VIRGINIA WOOLF AT TWENTY

much of it must have been written when the author felt much as one feels at the worst moments of toothache. Even so, were the unpublished part (the published is not a twentieth of the whole) before the reader, it is certain that his idea of the writer would change completely. Of this unpublished part I know only scraps; and even these will not be printed for some years I surmise. Nor can I choose but rejoice; for amongst pages of gay and brilliant description will be found many disobliging comments on the sayings and doings and characters of her friends—of whom I was one. Wherefore here and now I should like to interpose a caution. Those comments and descriptions, those that I have read or heard read, though always lively and amusing are not always true.

Sooner or later Virginia's diaries and letters will be printed. They will make a number of fascinating volumes: books, like Byron's letters, to be read and re-read for sheer delight. In the midst of his delight let the reader remember, especially the reader who itches to compose histories and biographies, that the author's accounts of people and of their sayings and doings may be flights of her airy imagination. Well do I remember an evening when Leonard Woolf, reading aloud to a few old friends extracts from these diaries, stopped suddenly. 'I suspect', said I, 'you've come on a passage where she makes a bit too free with the frailties and absurdities of someone here present'. 'Yes', said he, 'but that's not why I broke off. I shall skip the next few pages because there's not a word of truth in them'.

That Virginia possessed the poet's, and dreamer's,

faculty of 'making Cables of Cobwebbes and Wild-
ernesses of handsome Groves' will surprise no one
who has read her books; what may surprise is that
she should have employed this faculty not only in
art but in life. I have gone so far as to conjecture—
and it was going rather far I admit—that at times
she saw life and to some extent experienced it as a
novel or rather as a series of novels, in which anyone
of her friends might find him or herself cast, all unawares, for a part. Yours might be a sympathetic rôle,
and in that case all you said and did would be seen
through roseate lenses, your banal comments would
be transmuted to words of wisdom or subtle intuition, your ungainly gestures would acquire an air of
dignity and significance. Sometimes, however—in
my case generally—it was quite the other way. But
for better or for worse one's character, conduct and
conversation had to fit in to a picture which existed
in the artist's imagination. To one's surprise, often
to one's dismay, one found oneself the embodiment
of a preconceived idea.

I felt so sure that there was something in my
theory that I propounded it to one of Virginia's
friends, from whom I heard a story to confirm my
suspicions. This friend happened to be a lady, elegant and aristocratic to be sure, but unconventional
to the verge of eccentricity. Her manners certainly
were all that manners should be; but she was a rebel
at heart, and her conversation and way of life would
have shocked her mother profoundly and did shock
her more sedate relations. No one could have been
less like a leader of Victorian society. Nevertheless,
in one of those marvellous romances which were a

part of Virginia's everyday existence, that is what this wayward individual—Lady X shall we call her? —had to be: the typical leader of rather old-fashioned 'Society', exquisite and soignée (as she was) but also classically correct, smooth and sure of herself, running true to form in a world of dukes, ambassadors and orchids. To give a sharper point to this imaginary relationship—the friendship of a *grande dame* and a novelist—Virginia, who besides being one of the most beautiful was one of the best bred women of her age, cast herself in the rôle of a tough, uncouth, out-at-elbows Bohemian—of genius. And such was the spell she threw, such the cogency of her imagination, that many a time poor Lady X found herself, not only playing up to the rôle assigned to her, but positively accepting Virginia in the rôle she had allotted to herself. Am I not justified, then, in beseeching a vast posterity of enchanted readers to be on their guard?

To return for a moment to that silly caricature— Virginia the gloomy malcontent—let me say once and for all that she was about the gayest human being I have known and one of the most lovable. I was going to add 'besides being a genius'; but indeed these qualities were elements of her genius: in that sense she was all of a piece. I am not suggesting that she was faultless, or that those who have suspected her of being a little jealous on occasions or unwilling to 'brook a rival near the throne' were merely malevolent gossips. Only her jealousies and lapses of sympathy were of such a peculiar kind that it is difficult to understand them and easy to exaggerate. I do not pretend to understand them entirely, and so will give an example or two, leaving the reader to provide his own explanation. Someone said in her presence that it must be very tiring for her sister, a painter, to stand long hours at the easel. Virginia, outraged, I suppose, by the insinuation that her sister's occupation was in any way more exacting than her own, went out at once and bought a tall desk at which she insisted on standing to write. But this was when she was very young, and the very young are apt to be touchy. Surely she was guilty of excessive touchiness when she complained—a friend having told her I had said in a letter that she was looking well (she had been ill)—that 'Clive thinks I have become red and coarse'. It was a sort of jealousy, no doubt, that made her deprecate her friends pursuing the arts or professions which seemed in some way to put them in competition with herself. From time to time she would regret that Duncan Grant had not accepted a commission in the Black Watch—'I feel sure he would have been a remarkable soldier' (so do I). I believe she herself felt that she had gone a little far when she told me that Lytton Strachey should have been an Indian civil servant; but perhaps she was right when she persuaded Molly MacCarthy to write me a letter (to which I replied beginning 'Dearest Virginia') pointing out that critics were mere parasites on art and that my abilities (such as they were) would be much better employed at the bar. I think there was a sort of jealousy in all this, but I also think there was a sort, a very odd sort, of Victorianism. Sometimes it seemed to me that Virginia had inherited from her immediate ancestors more than their beauty and intelligence. Every good Victorian knew that a young man should have a sensible profession, something solid and secure, which would lead naturally to a comfortable old age and a fair provision for the children. In her head Virginia knew perfectly well that to give such advice to Lytton or Duncan was absurd; but Virginia, like the merest man, was not always guided by reason.

I said 'the merest man' because Virginia was, in her peculiar way, an ardent feminist. What is more, some of her injustices and wanton denigrations can be traced, I think, to female indignation. In political feminism—the Suffrage Movement—she was not much interested, though I do remember that once or twice she and I went to some obscure office where we licked up envelopes for the Adult Suffrage League. But, as you will have guessed, it was not in political action that her feminism expressed itself: indeed she made merciless fun of the flag-wagging fanaticism of her old friend Ethel Smythe. What she minded most, perhaps, was what she considered male advantages, and especially advantages in education. Readers of *A Room of One's Own* will remember an amusing, but none the less bitter, comparison of lunch in King's with dinner at Girton; and intelligent readers will have felt that the comparison is to be carried a great deal further. Also she resented the way in which men, as she thought, patronised women, especially women who were attempting to create works of art or succeed in what were once considered manly professions. Assuredly Virginia did not wish to be a man, or to be treated as a man: she wished to be treated as an equal—just possibly as a superior. Anyhow the least suspicion of condescension irritated her intensely and understandably. She grew angry and lashed out; and her blows fell, as often as not, on innocent noses. She could be monstrously, but delightfully, unfair; and witty blows below the belt sometimes leave nasty bruises. Neither male nor female can be wholly objective about *Three Guineas*; but for my part I feel sure it is her least admirable production.

Virginia's feminism was genuine and ardent, yet I do not think it played a great part in her life. Certainly the tantrums to which it gave rise were rare and transitory; and I will make bold, and bold it is, to say that hers was a happy nature. I know all about those fits of black despair; she had something to be desperate about, seeing that always hung over her the threat of collapse if she indulged too freely her ruling passion—the passion to create. Writing was her passion and her joy and her poison. Yet, I repeat, hers was a happy nature and she was happy. As for her gaiety—does this seem significant? My children, from the time they were old enough to enjoy anything beyond their animal satisfactions, enjoyed beyond anything a visit from Virginia. They looked forward to it as the greatest treat imaginable: 'Virginia's coming, what fun we shall have'. That is what they said and felt when they were children and went on saying and feeling to the end. And so said all of us. So said everyone who knew her. 'What fun we shall have' and what fun we did have. She might be divinely witty or outrageously fanciful; she might retail village gossip or tell stories of her London friends; always she was indescribably entertaining; always she enjoyed herself and we enjoyed her. 'Virginia's coming to tea': we knew it would be exciting, we knew that we were going to laugh and be surprised and made to feel that the temperature of life was several degrees higher than we had supposed.

I have not yet said what I want to say, I have not succeeded in giving an idea of Virginia's high spirits and lovable nature, so let me try another method. Barbara Bagenal was a girl of whom Virginia was fond; but Barbara Bagenal would be the last to claim that she was one of Virginia's closest friends. However, Barbara was down on her luck: she had been looking forward to a grand holiday, six weeks in Spain, and a day or two before she was to start she had been struck down by scarlet fever. That was a disaster with the misery of which Virginia could sympathise, and she showed her sympathy to some purpose. To her unhappy friend in hospital she wrote, and wrote precisely the sort of letters anyone in hospital would like to receive. The nurses insisted on burning most of them, but here is one that escaped.

Hogarth House. 24th June 1923

My dear Barbara,

'I should have written to you before, but I have had so many disasters lately from writing letters that nothing short of death or bankruptcy will in future draw one from me. I hope scarlet fever isn't about as bad as going bankrupt. I have often thought of you in your hospital,

as I take my way about the streets in comparative freedom. Yet I would have changed places with you last
Sunday fortnight, when Ottoline completely drew the
veils of illusion from me, and left me on Monday morning to face a world from which all heart, charity, kind-
ness and worth had vanished. How she does this, in 10
minutes, between 12 and 1, in the best spare bedroom,
with the scent of dried rose leaves about, and a little
powder falling on the floor, Heaven knows. Perhaps after
37 under-graduates, mostly the sons of Marquises, one's
physical life is reduced, and one receives impressions
merely from her drawl and crawl and smell which might
be harmless in the stir of normal sunlight. Only is the
sunlight ever normal at Garsington? No, I think even
the sky is done up in pale yellow silk, and certainly the
cabbages are scented. But this is all great rubbish. We've
had a desperate afternoon printing, and I'm more in
need of the love of my friends than you are. All the 14 pt.
quads have been dissed into the 12 pt. boxes! Proof taking has been made impossible; and Eliot's poem delayed
a whole week. I'm sure you'll see that this is much more
worth crying over than the pox and the fever and the
measles all in one.[1] Do you have horrid old gamps who
come and cheer you up? By which I mean tell you stories
about their past grandeur, and how they have come
down in the world, or they wouldn't be nursing the likes
of you—by which they mean that you haven't got silk
chemises. I could write you a whole page about their
talk, but refrain. Here is a quotation from a letter I've
just had from Roger[2], in Salamanca. "I was really rather
surprised to see Saxon Turner approach the table at
Segovia where I was seated with one Trend, a Cambridge musician; he approached the table in perfect
style with just a little guttural noise, a sort of burble,

[1]Mrs. Bagenal was suffering from scarlet-fever only.
[2]Roger Fry.

which expressed everything that the moment demanded, and sat down, and we went about very happily for some days. He became quite talkative. And really what a nice creature he is.'' So our poor old Saxon is moving among the living. He disappeared in such gloom, owing to your loss, that I've since thought of him as a kind of seagull wailing forlornly round the coast on windy nights. You won't be lacking in letters from him. And they will tell you every detail. London is spasmodically gay, that is to say I dine out in humble places and went to the opera one night, and one night to the Italian puppets, and one night to see Nessa,[1] and another to dine with Maynard.[2] Leonard is frightfully busy. We meet on the stairs oftener than anywhere, and I'm not sure that the glories of the *Nation*[3] are quite worth so much energy. Mrs. Joad is doing very well—much better to be honest than dear old Ralph, but then she is a daily worker, enthusiastic sanguine, and much impressed by small mercies.[4] If only she didn't scent herself, rather cheaply, I should have nothing to say against her. She is a character so entirely unlike my own that I can't help gaping in astonishment as we sit at lunch. Fancy playing tennis in Battersea Park! Fancy having a mother who lives at Harpenden! Fancy eating up all the fat, because it's good manners! Carrington insisted on meeting her. I don't think they received good impressions of each other.'

(I must omit a passage which contains scurrilous, and probably untrue, reflections on a person now alive).

[1]Vanessa Bell.
[2]Maynard Keynes.
[3]Leonard Woolf was at that time literary editor of *The Nation*.
[4]Mrs. Joad was working for the Hogarth Press, where she succeeded Ralph Partridge and Barbara Bagenal herself.

'Duncan was very severely treated by Simon Bussy in the *Nation*. Nevertheless he has sold almost every picture, I hear; and they say this will revive poor Roger's miseries about his own failure; but Roger, of course, is far the nicest human being of any of us, and will as usual be incomparably more generous than one could suspect Christ to be, should Christ return, and take to painting in the style of Cézanne at the age of 56. Clive, who has nothing Christlike about him, has had to give up eating tea, because, when Lady Lewis gave a party the other night and Rosenthal played Chopin, a waistcoat button burst and flew across the room with such impetuosity that the slow movement was entirely spoilt.[1] The humiliation, which would have killed you or me—the room was crowded with the élite of London—only brushed him slightly—he won't eat bread and butter any more; but his spirits are superb, and he says that life grows steadily more and more enchanting, the fatter one gets. Mr. Bernard Shaw almost agreed to review his book for the *Nation*;[2] and said so on a post card, but Clive is very touchy about post cards from Bernard Shaw and has never forgiven Carrington, nor ever will.'[3]

(With deep regret I omit a particularly entertain-

[1] I don't think it happened quite like that. For Rosenthal read Rubinstein, probably.

[2] Strange, if true; the only thing I published about that time was a little essay *On British Freedom*, it seems unlikely that Bernard Shaw would have heard of it.

[3] Carrington had sent me a card, purporting to come from Bernard Shaw and complaining of something I had said about him in print. I was taken in. Carrington and Logan Pearsall Smith were the hoaxers in chief of the age. Personally, I never cared for practical jokes and hoaxes; but when I described them as 'fools' wit' Pearsall Smith took it in bad part. May I add that Carrington and I remained fast friends to the day of her death?

ing paragraph which contains statements that may well be true but are certainly libellous).

'I hope you realise that though I am chattering like a pink and yellow cockatoo (do you remember Mrs. Brereton's poem, Pink and yellow, pink and yellow?) I'm a chastened raven underneath: I mean I am very much concerned at your miseries, which besides being in themselves odious, show a mean malignity on the part of Providence which makes me, for once, a Christian and a believer. If there was not a God, of course you would have gone to Spain with Saxon: as it is, there you are in bed at Maidstone. Our only alleviation of HIS afflictions is to send you our latest, *Talks with Tolstoi*—a very amusing book, even when it has passed through the furnace, which I suppose it must do, before reaching you.[1]

'Leonard is still trying to take proofs in the basement. I have cheered myself up by writing to you, so please don't say that I've plunged you into despair, as another invalid did the other day, when I cheered myself up by writing to her.

'Please get well, and come and see me. Barbara Chickybidiensis is one of those singular blooms which one never sees elsewhere, a rare and remarkable specimen.[2] I wish I could write an article for Outdoor Life about you, and get £50. £25 should then be yours. Love to Nick. Let me know how you are.

Yr. V.W.'

[1] No: it would have to pass through the furnace—if it passed through the furnace at all—after and not before reaching the invalid.

[2] Walking in the garden at Rodmell, Virginia had noticed a flower which struck her as not quite a common nasturtium. She enquired the name. Out came Barbara with 'Tropaeolum Canariensis'. So grand a name, delivered with such authority, by so small a creature, took Virginia's fancy, and she christened her flower-like little friend 'Barbara Chickybidiensis'.

That Virginia should have written such a letter to one who, as I have said, would not claim to have been of her nearest and dearest, will give some idea of her thoughtful and affectionate nature: the letter itself gives a taste of her gaiety, spirits and power of invention.

But of course it was in conversation that her gaiety poured out most abundantly. Her talk, as my friend Raymond Mortimer would say, was 'dazzling'. It was unlike any other I have heard, though at moments that of Jean Cocteau, at his best, has reminded me of it. To describe conversation is notoriously impossible, and to report it verbatim is not easy. I know it is supposed to be the secret of Boswell's success, but I have sometimes wondered whether Johnson did say exactly what Boswell makes him say. I, at any rate, cannot report conversations word for word: and when I have told the reader that the quality of Virginia's came in part from the apparent whimsicality and from the unexpectedness of her notions and comments, partly from a happy choice of words and constructions, hardly at all from the manner of delivery, but chiefly from sheer magic, I believe I shall not have brought him much nearer the heart of the mystery. The melancholy fact is that till her familiar correspondence has been published, even a vague idea of the fun and spirit of Virginia's talk can hardly be gained by those who did not know her. As the correspondence—or the best part of it—cannot yet be published, admirers must try to catch a taste of the delicious treat that was her company from passages such as this: '. . . To show how very little control of our possessions we have—

what an accidental affair this living is after all our civilization—let me just count over a few of the things lost in one lifetime, beginning, for that seems always the most mysterious of all losses—what cat would gnaw, what rat would nibble—three pale blue canisters of book-binding tools? Then there were the bird cages, the iron hoops, the steel skates, the Queen Anne coal-scuttle, the bagatelle board, the hand organ—all gone, and jewels too. Opals and emeralds, they lie about the roots of turnips. What a scraping paring affair it is to be sure! The wonder is that I've any clothes on my back, that I sit surrounded by solid furniture at this moment. Why, if one wants to compare life to anything, one must liken it to being blown through the Tube at fifty miles an hour—landing at the other end without a single hair pin in one's hair! Shot out at the feet of God entirely naked! Tumbling head over heels in the asphodel meadows like brown paper parcels pitched down a shoot in the post office! . . .'

This fragment from that enchanting soliloquy, *The Mark on the Wall*, may perhaps give a hint of what it was like when Virginia indulged in a flight of fancy, as she often did. Of her full length books I think *Orlando* gives the best idea of her with her elbows on the tea-table letting herself go. I am not sure that it is not my favourite of all her works, though of course I do not consider it the best. That, no doubt, is *The Waves*. Indeed, if I were writing as a critic, instead of what they call a 'fan', I should be inclined to say that *The Waves* and perhaps *To The Lighthouse* were the only perfect masterpieces she ever produced. To me *The Waves* seems perfect;

whereas I perceive that a stern critic could pick a hole or two in most of the others, and more than two in *Orlando*. Only, if he find fault with *Orlando*, he must find fault with *Tristram Shandy* too; and it seems a pity, should one have the luck to possess a sense of beauty and a sense of humour, to accept grudgingly either of these exquisite satisfactions.

Just now I pictured Virginia with her arms on the tea-table. The image came to mind naturally enough. Often I think of her in the dark dining-room at Rodmell or at the round painted table of Charleston, childishly revelling in cakes and honey, enjoying them as she enjoyed the accompanying gossip and nonsense, herself the life and inspiration of the party. The 'tea-table' I said, and so saying unintentionally gave myself an opportunity of putting a stop to one of the most preposterous lies that ever came into circulation. A year or so before the war I found myself in Paris sitting at dinner next an attractive young French woman who turned out to be a passionate admirer of the novels of my sister-in-law. Naturally she questioned me, and naturally I supplied information of the banal kind one does supply on such occasions. Amongst other things I told her that the artist was handicapped by the constant menace of a nervous disorder which, when it attacked her, made any sort of intellectual effort impossible and reduced her to a state of agitated misery. 'Ah yes', said my pretty neighbour, 'Ah yes', and said it with a sorrowful, meaning look which was not meant to escape me. Quite at a loss, I exclaimed,

'What on earth are you driving at?' 'Well', she said, 'Well, everybody knows—whisky'.[1]

As my old nurse would have said, you could have knocked me down with a feather. As soon as I had recovered my balance I explained that normally Virginia never touched alcohol of any sort, for she did not much like it. Indeed it was a standing joke —every set of intimate friends has its standing jokes —that 'Clive always makes me drunk', by which she meant that when she dined with me I would, if I could, cajole her into drinking a glass of wine or half a glass at any rate. The fact that this grotesque fabrication appears to have been accepted as true by people who certainly wished Virginia no ill, should be, I suppose, a warning to biographers. I have a fondness for gossip and am perhaps too willing to give mongers the benefit of a doubt. But this bit positively shocks me, not because I object to people getting drunk, but because the notion of Virginia as a dipsomaniac is absurd beyond the limits of absurdity. So I trust that anyone who does me the honour of reading this paragraph, and happens to hear the lie repeated, will do truth the honour of contradicting it flatly.

In my attempts to sketch the characters of other old friends I have adopted the classic method of recalling particular sayings and doings which seemed

---

[1]As I have admitted that I cannot report a conversation verbatim, let me further admit that the only words faithfully reproduced here are 'Ah' and 'Whisky': we were talking French.

notably characteristic and pinning them down; but with Virginia that method will not do. Everything she said or did, the way she propounded a theory or uttered an exclamation, the way she walked or dressed or did her hair (not very securely), the way she cut a cake (not very neatly), or laughed or sneezed, was peculiar and characteristic. Admirers in search of a memorable image will find my account inadequate, and admirers will be right. As I have sadly admitted more than once, until all the letters and diaries have been published they cannot hope to possess anything like a portrait of the artist: all they can do is to seek her in her books, and these, though of course expressive, do not reveal the whole nor perhaps the most fascinating part. Still, when they have enjoyed her art for its own sake, some are sure to begin wondering just how much of the artist it really does reveal. I will help them in their quest if I can. And now it seems to me possible that by extracting certain passages from that essay—written with Virginia just round the corner and in the knowledge that it would be read and criticised by her—by extracting passages, or elaborating them, I may put the curious on a profitable track.

I then said that what made Virginia Woolf's books read queerly was that they had at once the air of high fantasticality and blazing realism. This, I think, is true, and the explanation may be that, though she is externalising a vision and not making a map of life, the vision is anything but visionary in the vulgar sense of the word. Her world is not a dream world; she sees, and sees acutely, what the reviewer in a hurry calls 'the real world'—the world of Miss Austen and George Eliot, of *Madame Bovary* and *War and Peace*. It is a perfectly comprehensible world in which no one has the least difficulty in believing: only she sees it in her own way. She sees life more purely than most of us see it; and that may mean that sometimes she sees it less passionately. Sometimes she seems to be watching through a cool sheet of glass two lovers (say) on a bench in the park: she will know well enough what they are saying and know (not feel) what they are feeling; she will miss not one subtle, betraying gesture; she will be aware of the romance, but she will not share the romantic emotions. In the strictest sense of the word she is a seer. More often than not her creative impulses spring from her sense of a scene. And this pure, this almost painterlike, vision sets her far apart from the common or garden realists, her contemporaries.

Of course literary art cannot be much like painting; for it is out of words that writers must create the forms that are to clothe their visions, and words carry a significance altogether different from the significance of lines and colours. Virginia, as a matter of fact, had a genuine and highly personal liking for pictures.[1] But her sense of visual values revealed itself most clearly, and characteristically, in a feeling for textures and the relations of textures. She would pick up a feather in the fields and set it in an appropriate wine-glass against a piece of stuff carelessly pinned to the wall, with the taste and 'rightness' of a Klee, if not a Picasso. But that, though I

[1]Herself, she occasionally made drawings, which are said to show considerable talent. They accompanied letters which I have not seen.

hope it may be of interest to some of her admirers, is beside my immediate point. What I am trying to say is that her vision, and superficially her style, may remind anyone, as it reminded the French critic, M. Abel Chevalley, of the French Impressionists. Her vision may remind us of their passion for the beauty of life, loved for its own sake, of their abhorence of sentimentality, and of their reputed inhumanity; while technically her style may remind incorrigible seekers after analogy of little touches and divisions of tone. We are familiar with the way in which Renoir and Monet proclaim their sense of a garden blazing in the sun. It is something that comes to them in colours and shapes, and in shapes and colours must be rendered. Now see how an artist in words deals with a like experience.

'. . . How hot it was! So hot that even the thrush chose to hop, like a mechanical bird, in the shadow of the flowers, with long pauses between one movement and the next; instead of rambling vaguely the white butterflies danced one above another, making with their white shifting flakes the outline of a shattered marble column above the tallest flowers; the glass roofs of the palm house shone as if a whole market full of shiny green umbrellas had opened in the sun; and in the drone of the aeroplane the voice of the summer sky murmured its fierce soul. Yellow and black, pink and snow white, shapes of all these colours, men, women, and children were spotted for a second upon the horizon, and then, seeing the breadth of yellow that lay upon the grass, they wavered and sought shade beneath the trees, dissolving like drops of water in the yellow and green atmosphere, staining it faintly with red and blue. It seemed as if all gross and heavy bodies had sunk down in the heat motionless and lay huddled upon the ground, but their voices went wavering from them as if they were flames lolling from the thick waxen bodies of candles. Voices. Yes, voices. Wordless voices, breaking the silence suddenly with such depth of contentment, such passion of desire, or, in the voices of children, such freshness of surprise; breaking the silence? But there was no silence; all the time the motor omnibuses were turning their wheels and changing their gear; like a vast nest of Chinese boxes, all of wrought steel turning ceaselessly one within another, the city murmured; on the top of which the voices cried aloud and the petals of myriads of flowers flashed their colours into the air.'

No one, I suppose, will deny the beauty of that. No one ever has denied that Virginia Woolf chooses and uses words beautifully. But her style is sometimes accused, injuriously, of being 'cultivated' and 'intellectual'—obviously such criticism would be inapplicable here—especially by people who themselves are not particularly well off for either culture or intellect. Cultivated it is, in the sense that it reveals a finely educated mind on terms of easy acquaintance with the finest minds of other ages; and perhaps it is cultivated also in the sense that to enjoy it a reader must himself be pretty well educated. No doubt it makes unobtrusive reference to and recalls associations with things of which the unlettered dream not. Intellectual? Yes, it is intellectual in that it makes demands on the reader's understanding. However, it is not difficult in the way that the style of philosophers and philosophic writers must be difficult, since it is for visions and states of mind and not for logical processes and abstract reasoning that this author finds verbal equivalents. She has no call to chop logic so her prose can be musical and coloured; also as she has no taste for violence it can be cool. Though colder far, the lyrical passages in her novels are nearer to the last act of Figaro, to that music which gives an etherial sense of a summer night's romance, than to the second act of Tristan which gives . . . Well, the over-sexed will appreciate the art of Virginia Woolf hardly; the fundamentally stupid never.

Yet it cannot be denied that reasonable people have complained—'Virginia Woolf's novels make stiff reading'. Generally, I think, any trouble they may have in following the movements of her mind is caused not by eccentricity of expression but by the complexity of what is being expressed. For just as there are subtleties of thought which a philosopher cannot, with the best will in the world, make as plain as a police-court statement, so there are subtleties of feeling which an artist cannot express as simply as Tennyson defined his attitude to Lady Clara Vere de Vere. Those who in moments of vexation call her writing unintelligible are, I suspect, unless merely thick-witted, making the mistake that was made by the more enlightened opponents of Impressionism. They are seeking noon at twilight. They are puzzled by a technique which juxtaposes active tones, and omits transitions which have no other function than to provide what modern painters and Virginia Woolf and perhaps the majority of serious contemporary writers hold to be unnecessary bridges. For my part, I shall not deny that I am a little old for jumping, or that in literature I love a bridge, be it merely a plank. My infirmities, however, are unimportant. The important thing is that Virginia Woolf's words and phrases are chosen deliberately, with exquisite and absolute precision, to match her meaning, and that they form a whole which perfectly envelops her vision.

I have tried, by recalling memories and touching on her art, to give what I confessed at the outset would be no more than an adumbration of Virginia Woolf. It now seems to me, re-reading what I have written, that I have failed—and this is perhaps my worst omission—to convey a sense of her magic— for Virginia was a magician in life as well as in art. Can I mend matters, I wonder, by calling to mind at this eleventh hour something that happened many years ago when, after one of her recurrent collapses, she was sent by her doctor to a convalescent home kept by an amiable and commonplace woman called, shall we say, Miss Smith? Although Virginia was ill and intellectually and emotionally below normal her magic within a day or two had done its work; Miss Smith was transformed. Nothing like this had happened to her before; suddenly life, which she had found drab and dreary, had become thrilling and precious. Every moment counted; for everything seemed exciting or amusing. Positively the poor woman started, on the sly, to struggle with the poets; but soon discovered that she had no need for books, her own life, coloured by the presence and idle talk of her patient, having grown poetical. For the first, and I dare say last, time she was living intensely. As she tried to explain to me one after- noon when Virginia, whom I was visiting, was taking a rest, for the first time in her life she felt of consequence to herself; she was aware of her own existence, she said, and all the trivial things that made up that existence had significance too. The magician had cast her spell, and Miss Smith, like any poet, was seeing the world in a grain of sand. Whether the spell endured after the magician had departed I do not know; I should think it unlikely. But during a month or six weeks 'the world' for Miss Smith was 'so full of a number of things' that she, the matron of a nursing home, 'was as happy as' a queen: and I dare say a good deal happier.

This transformation seemed miraculous because the transformed was what is called 'a very ordinary woman'. But the effect of Virginia on her closest friends was not different in kind. I remember spending some dark, uneasy, winter days during the first war in the depth of the country with Lytton Strachey. After lunch, as we watched the rain pour down and premature darkness roll up, he said, in his searching, personal way, 'Loves apart, whom would you most like to see coming up the drive?' I hesitated a moment, and he supplied the answer: 'Virginia of course'. Be sure her magic would have worked on him as it had worked on Miss Smith.

VII

ENCOUNTERS WITH T. S. ELIOT

IT would be better, of course, if he were to record his encounters with me, for in that way students, besides enjoying a bit of prose by our best living poet, might learn the exact truth: the author of *Mr. Apollinax* is surely one to remember dates and details. So far as I can remember, it was in the summer of 1916 that first we met. Bertrand Russell asked me to look out for a man called 'Eliot' who had just come, or was just coming, to England, and had been his best pupil at Harvard: he may have said 'My only good pupil', but if so, doubtless he exaggerated as philosophers will. Eliot came to dinner at 46 Gordon Square, where I was living with Maynard Keynes; however, I was alone that night, and so after dinner the poet and I sat in my room at the top of the house and talked about books. I was not sure that he altogether liked my enthusiasm for Mérimée's stories and Horace Walpole's letters; but for my part I liked him so much that I determined, there and then, to make him acquainted with some of my friends. Soon afterwards I introduced him to Roger Fry and Virginia Woolf, both of whom were to play parts in later encounters.

Virginia liked Tom from the first and appreciated his poetry: also she teased him. Roger was excited and enthusiastic, and, as usual when excited, constructive. He it was who urged Eliot to elucidate the text of *The Waste Land* with explanatory notes. Eliot met him half-way: he supplied notes, but whether they are explanatory is for others to decide. Between Virginia and myself somehow the poet became a sort of 'family joke': it is not easy to say why. To some people the combination of human frailties with supernatural powers will always appear preposterous, which is, I suppose, a roundabout way of saying that a poet is an oddity. To us at any rate this mixture, talent, in its rarest form, combined with studied primness of manner and speech, seemed deliciously comic. Besides, Virginia was a born and infectious mocker. I would receive a post-card, for in those happy days (the early 'twenties' maybe) there was no telephone at Charleston, my summer refuge: 'Come to lunch on Sunday. Tom is coming, and, what is more, is coming with a four-piece suit'. This came from Rodmell, five or six miles away, where Leonard Woolf still lives, where Eliot was a frequent visitor, and whence frequently he was brought to Charleston for a meal. One of these meals, a dinner-party, he will hardly have forgotten.

He will remember it not so much for what was said as for what was done. We had been sent a brace of grouse. My wife, who takes my opinion on sporting matters and on no others, enquired whether this would be enough for a party of eight. I said it would not, and that a bird between two was a fair allowance. She thinks she may have confused this estimate with something I had once said about snipe—two a mouth. Anyhow more grouse were ordered, and, when the soup-plates had been cleared away, entered three platters supporting sixteen birds—ten on table and six on the sideboard. Even the inventor of Sweeney appeared to think this unusual. The evening was not to end, however, without its contribution to scholarship; for somebody wondered whether anything was known of Mrs. Porter and her daughter beyond the fact that they wash their feet in soda water. 'These characters are known', said the master, 'only from an Ayrian camp-fire song of which one other line has been preserved:

And so they oughter.

Of such pieces, epic or didatic', he continued, 'most have been lost, wholly or in part, in the mists of antiquity; but I recall one that is generally admitted to be complete:

Some say the Dutch ain't no style, ain't no style,
But they have all the while, all the while.'

And this reminds me of a poem I once wrote, on T. S. Eliot, in French, and sent to Virginia on the back of a post-card. It is unlikely to have been saved: it was called *Sur le tombeau de Tom.*

I am getting a little out of date. If I met Eliot in 1916, it must have been in '17 that I went to Garsington for an Easter party taking with me some ten or dozen copies of the last, and perhaps the first, publication of the Egoist Press, 'The Love Song of J. Alfred Prufrock'. Anyone with a taste for research can fix the date, for the book, or brochure rather, had just appeared and I distributed my copies hot from the press like so many Good Friday buns. Who were the recipients? Our host and hostess, Philip and Lady Ottoline Morell, of course. Mrs. St. John Hutchinson, Katherine Mansfield, Aldous Huxley, Middleton Murry, Lytton Strachey perhaps, and, I think, Gertler. Were there others? Maria Balthus for instance (later Mrs. Aldous Huxley). I cannot tell: but of this I am sure, it was Katherine Mansfield who read the poem aloud. As you may suppose, it caused a stir, much discussion, some perplexity. I wonder how many of us have kept our copies. Mine I have stowed in some secret place where I cannot now lay hands on it. Already it must be worth a deal of money; for, not only is it the first edition of a fine poem by a fine poet, of one of his earliest works too, but, unless I mistake, the brochure itself is bound in a trashy yellow jacket and is badly printed on bad paper. Misprints, if I remember right, and letters turned upside-down are discoverable. In a word, it is the sort of thing for which bibliophiles give hundreds. But though it must be amongst my most valuable mislaid possessions, I esteem it less than certain envelopes addressed, after the manner of Mallarmé, in verse, and addressed to me. Of these I own several, which, by taking pains, I could bring to light; but happily I may spare myself a dusty search since only the other morning arrived what will serve to give a taste of my correspondent's mettle.

> *O stalwart SUSSEX postman, who is*
> *Delivering the post from LEWES,*
> *Cycle apace to CHARLESTON, FIRLE,*
> *While knitting at your plain and purl,*

ENCOUNTERS WITH T. S. ELIOT

Deliver there to good CLIVE BELL,
(You know the man, you know him well,
He plays the virginals and spinet),
This note—there's almost nothing in it.

For the benefit of the author I may say that this
pleasantry gave satisfaction to the postman invoked.
He considered it 'clever'. He was not quite sure
about the 'spinet', but knew that I was fond of a bit
of shooting: it was not true about the 'virginals' he
hoped.

At Sunday evening performances, especially those
given by the Phœnix Society, I used to admire Mr.
Eliot's faultless dress, white waistcoat and all:
whether at an evening party, or in the country (you
will remember the 'four piece suit') or in the city,
always the poet made himself inconspicuous by the
appropriateness of his costume.

Flowed up the hill and down King William Street
To where Saint Mary Woolnoth kept the hours
With a dead sound on the final stroke of nine.
There I saw one I knew, and stopped him, crying: 'Stetson!'

I might have cried 'Tom: cry you mercy, I took you
for a banker'. And a banker he was in these early
days; at least he worked in a bank. How characteristic! And how wise! Instead of doing as most young
poets of promise do, eking out a living with journalism, which slacks the sacred strings, thus too often
belying the promise, Eliot stuck to his desk—in King
William Street or thereabouts, and found time of an
evening to say all that he deemed worth saying. I

doubt whether in his poems—his plays are another thing—he has written a slovenly or an otiose line. He has kept his honour as bright as La Bruyère kept his.

If T. S. Eliot were not a famous poet, he would be known as a remarkably clever man. This cleverness comes out delightfully in conversation, and it came out rather unexpectedly one night at a birthday party given in her riverside house by Mrs. St. John Hutchinson. She had invited, so she said, the ten cleverest men in London to meet the ten most beautiful women: those who were not invited are not obliged to consider her judgment infallible. After supper we pulled crackers; and Lady Diana Cooper, having surreptitiously collected the riddles in which, along with caps and whistles, crackers used to abound, mounted a chair and announced that she would now put our wits to the test. She read the riddles aloud, and almost before the question was propounded pat came the answer from two of the guests: Maynard Keynes and T. S. Eliot. You might have supposed that a certain sedate primness of speech, inherited maybe from a line of New England ancestors, would have put Eliot at a disadvantage. It did. Luckily, Maynard Keynes, when excited, sometimes developed a slight stutter. He stuttered ever so little on this occasion but he stuttered sufficiently; the handicaps were equal, and the two cleverest of the clever ran neck and neck all the way. It is only fair to add that Aldous Huxley might have come in a better third had not righteous indignation provoked by the imbecility of the conundrums, in some measure balked the stride of his lofty intellect.

ENCOUNTERS WITH T. S. ELIOT

If in this little chapter—a mere hand wave and
doffing of the hat to an old and illustrious friend—
I have done nothing to explain the nature of his gift,
I shall not apologize. Anyone who cares enough
about poetry to read tittle-tattle about a poet needs
no help from a tattler.

VIII

BLOOMSBURY

THERE is mystery in the word, and money too perhaps. Or is it merely for fun that grave historians and pompous leader-writers no less than the riff-raff of Fleet Street and Portland Place chatter about the thing? 'The thing', I say, because that is the least committal substantive I can think of, and it is not always clear whether what the chatterers are chattering about is a point of view, a period, a gang of conspirators or an infectious disease. Beyond meaning something nasty, what do they mean by 'Bloomsbury'? Assuming, as seems reasonable, that they all have in mind, amongst other things, a gang or group or clique (for without human beings you cannot well have a point of view or a doctrine, and even an epidemic needs 'carriers'), I invite them to name the men and women of whom this gang or group or clique was composed. Who were the members of Bloomsbury? Let them give the names: then they may be able to tell us what were the tastes and opinions held in common by and peculiar to the people to whom these names belong, what, in fact, is or was the 'Bloomsbury doctrine'.[1]

---

[1] *The Times Literary Supplement* (20 August 1954) published a long review of a book the name of which escapes me. This review, or essay rather, was entitled 'The air of Bloomsbury'; and is by far the most intelligent and penetrating piece that has been written on the subject. There were errors of fact to be

BLOOMSBURY

But we must not ask too much—and it is much to think clearly and state one's thoughts perspicuously —of columnists and broadcasters, so to *The Times Literary Supplement* and a Fellow of All Souls I turn. The *Supplement* has before now castigated Bloomsbury in reviews and even in a leading article; while only the other day I caught one of the most prominent fellows of the glorious foundation writing in *The Times* of 'Bloomsbury historians'. From such high courts we may expect clear judgments. I implore the *Supplement*, I implore Mr. Rowse, to give categorical answers to a couple of straight questions: (*a*) Who are or were the members of Bloomsbury? (*b*) For what do they, or did they, stand?

I have been stigmatized as 'Bloomsbury' myself, and the epithet has been applied freely to most of those who are, or were—for many are dead—my intimate friends, so, if it be true that something that can fairly be called 'the Bloomsbury group' did exist, presumably I am entitled to an opinion as to who were the members and what were their thoughts and feelings. Of course I am aware that people born in recent years and distant lands hold opinions clean contrary to mine. By all means let them enjoy a Bloomsbury of their own invention; only, should

sure, errors there must be in an appreciation by someone who is not himself a part of the society described, by someone who was neither an eye nor an ear witness. But the essay, admirably written, reveals a remarkable power of understanding complex characters and peculiar points of view. It has value much beyond that of most ephemeral, or rather hebdomadal, criticism. And it is to be hoped that it will soon be published in easily accessible and durable form.

they chance to write on the subject, let them state clearly whom and what they are writing about. Otherwise historians unborn will flounder in a sea of doubt. Knowing that 'Bloomsbury' was the curse of a decade or two in the twentieth century, but unable to infer from a mass of woolly evidence who precisely were the malefactors and what precisely was the thing, some will be sure that it was a religious heresy, a political deviation or a conspiracy, while others, less confident, may suspect it was no more than a peculiar vice.

So, having appealed to the highest authorities for simple answers to simple questions, I now repeat my request to the smaller fry. Let everyone have his or her notion of 'Bloomsbury'; but let everyone who uses the name in public speech or writing do his or her best to say exactly what he or she intends by it. Thus, even should it turn out that in fact there never was such a thing, the word might come to have significance independent of the facts and acquire value as a label. I dare say Plato would have been at a loss to discover the connection between his philosophy and the epithet 'platonic' as used by lady-novelists and reviewers in the nineteenth and twentieth centuries; nevertheless in refined conversation the word now has a recognised meaning. 'Bloomsbury' may yet come to signify something definite, though as yet few people, so far as I can make out, understand by it anything more precise than 'the sort of thing we all dislike'. Wherefore I repeat, let publicists and broadcasters be explicit. That is my modest request: which made, I will give what help I can by telling all I know.

IN THE GARDEN AT CHARLESTON
Duncan Grant, Morgan Forster, Clive Bell,
Mrs. St. John Hutchinson

BLOOMSBURY

The name was first applied to a set of friends by Lady MacCarthy—Mrs. Desmond MacCarthy as she then was—in a letter: she calls them 'the Bloomsberries'. The term, as she used it, had a purely topographical import; and the letter, which doubtless could be found at the bottom of one of five or six tin boxes, must have been written in 1910 or 1911. But the story begins earlier. It begins, as I have recorded in an earlier chapter, in October 1899 when five freshmen went up to Trinity—Cambridge, of course—and suddenly becoming intimate, as freshmen will, founded a society as freshmen almost invariably do. It was a 'reading society' which met in my rooms in the New Court on Saturdays at midnight, and here are the names of the five original members: Lytton Strachey, Sydney-Turner, Leonard Woolf, Thoby Stephen, Clive Bell.[1] After he had gone down, and after the death of his father, Thoby Stephen lived at 46 Gordon Square, Bloomsbury, with his brother Adrian and his two sisters Vanessa (later Vanessa Bell) and Virginia (later Virginia Woolf). These two beautiful, gifted and completely independent young women, with a house of their own, became the centre of a circle of which Thoby's Cambridge friends were what perhaps I may call the spokes. And when, in 1907, the elder married, the circle was not broken but enlarged; for Virginia, with her surviving brother Adrian, took a house in nearby Fitzroy Square: thus, instead of one *salon*— if that be the word—there were two *salons*. If ever

---

[1] I maintain that A. J. Robertson was also an original member, but he disclaims the honour—or dishonour.

such an entity as 'Bloomsbury' existed, these sisters, with their houses in Gordon and Fitzroy Squares, were at the heart of it. But did such an entity exist?

All one can say truthfully is this. A dozen friends —I will try to name them presently—between 1904 and 1914 saw a great deal of each other. They differed widely, as I shall tell, in opinions, tastes and preoccupations. But they liked, though they sharply criticised, each other, and they liked being together. I suppose one might say they were 'in sympathy'. Can a dozen individuals so loosely connected be called a group? It is not for me to decide. Anyhow the first World War disintegrated this group, if group it were, and when the friends came together again inevitably things had changed. Old friends brought with them new and younger acquaintances. Differences of opinion and taste, always wide, became wider. Close relationships with people quite outside the old circle sprang up. Sympathy remained. But whatever cohesion there may have been among those who saw so much of each other in Gordon Square and Fitzroy Square, among Lady Mac-Carthy's 'Bloomsberries' that is, by 1918 had been lost. That was the end of 'old Bloomsbury'.

Now I will try to name these friends. There were the surviving members of the Midnight Society. Thoby Stephen had died in the late autumn of 1906: Leonard Woolf was in Ceylon between 1904 and 1911: remained in Bloomsbury Lytton Strachey (who, in fact, lived in Hampstead), Saxon Sydney-Turner, Clive Bell. There were the two ladies. Add to these Duncan Grant, Roger Fry, Maynard Keynes, H. T. J. Norton and perhaps Gerald Shove, and I believe you will have completed the list of those of the elder generation who have been called 'Bloomsbury'. Certainly Desmond and Molly Mac-Carthy and Morgan Forster were close and affectionate friends, but I doubt whether any one of them has yet been branded with the fatal name. So much for the old gang.

As I have said, after the war a few men of a younger generation became intimate with most of us. I will do my best to name these, too; but as the new association was even looser than the old, the classification will be even less precise. First and foremost come David Garnett and Francis Birrell, both of whom we—by 'we' I mean the old Bloomsberries —had known and liked before 1914. Immediately after the war, by a stroke of good luck, I made the acquaintance of Raymond Mortimer;[1] and about the same time Lytton Strachey, lecturing at Oxford, met Ralph Partridge. I do not know who discovered Stephen Tomlin: but I remember well how Keynes brought Sebastian Sprott and F. L. Lucas from Cambridge to stay at a house in Sussex shared by him with my wife, myself and Duncan Grant. I think it may have been through Francis Birrell that we came to know a brilliant girl from Newnham, Frances Marshall (later Mrs. Ralph Partridge).

Now whether all or most of the people I have named are the people publicists have in mind when they speak of 'Bloomsbury' is not clear. In fact that

[1]Raymond Mortimer reminds me that, after the first war, he was brought to 46 Gordon Square by Aldous Huxley. That was our first meeting.

is one of the questions I am asking. But from words let fall in broadcasts and articles I infer a tendency to lump together the two generations and call the lump 'Bloomsbury'. We can be sure of nothing till the journalists and broadcasters and the high authorities too have favoured us with their lists. I have given mine; and so doing have given what help I can and set a good example. I have named the friends who were intimate before 1914 and have added the names of those, or at any rate most of those, who became friends of *all* these friends later. Naturally, with time and space at their familiar task, the bonds of sympathy loosened—though I think they seldom snapped—and so the friends of 'the twenties' were even less like a group than the friends of the pre-war period. That, as I have said, has not prevented some critics lumping them all together, and calling the combination or compound, which it seems exhaled a mephitic influence over the twenties, 'Bloomsbury'. It is impossible, I repeat, to know whom, precisely, they have in mind; but, assuming their list to be something like mine, again I put the question: What had these friends in common that was peculiar to these friends?

Not much, I believe you will agree, if you will be so kind as to read my chapter to the end. For beyond mutual liking they had precious little in common, and in mutual liking there is nothing peculiar. Yes, they did like each other; also they shared a taste for discussion in pursuit of truth and a contempt for conventional ways of thinking and feeling—contempt for conventional morals if you will. Does it not strike you that as much could be said of many

BLOOMSBURY

collections of young or youngish people in many
ages and many lands? For my part, I find nothing
distinctive here. Ah, say the pundits, but there was
G. E. Moore the Cambridge philosopher; Moore
was the all-pervading, the binding influence; 'Moor-
ism' is the peculiarity the Bloomsberries have in
common. I should think there was G. E. Moore;
also the influence of his *Principia Ethica* on some of
us was immense—on some but not on all, nor perhaps on most. Four of us certainly were freed by
Moore from the spell of an ugly doctrine in which
we had been reared: he delivered us from Utilitarianism. What is more, you can discover easily
enough traces of Moorist ethics in the writings of
Strachey and Keynes and, I suppose, in mine. But
not all these friends were Moorists. Roger Fry, for
instance, whose authority was quite as great as that
of Lytton Strachey was definitely anti-Moorist. So,
in a later generation, was Frances Marshall who,
beside being a beauty and an accomplished ball-
room dancer, was a philosopher. Assuredly Raymond Mortimer, Ralph Partridge and Stephen
Tomlin—all three Oxford men—were not devout
believers in *Principia Ethica*; while F. L. Lucas, who
in those 'twenties' may well have heard himself
called 'Bloomsbury', at that time called himself a
Hedonist. I doubt whether either of the Miss
Stephens gave much thought to the all important
distinction between 'Good on the whole' and 'Good
as a whole'. Also it must be remembered that Bertrand Russell, though no one has ever called him
'Bloomsbury', appeared to be a friend and was certainly an influence.

133

Lytton Strachey, I have agreed, was a Moorist. Of him I have written at some length elsewhere and have said that, being a great character, amongst very young men he was inevitably a power. But at Cambridge, and later among his cronies in London, his influence was literary for the most part. He inclined our undergraduate taste away from contemporary realism towards the Elizabethans and the eighteenth century. But when, about 1910, Roger Fry and I became fascinated by what was being written in France he did not share our enthusiasm. Quite the contrary: and as for contemporary painting, Lytton, who had a liking, a literary liking, for the visual arts, thought that we were downright silly about Matisse and Picasso, and on occasions said so.[1] It begins to look—does it not?—as though this thing called 'Bloomsbury' was not precisely homogeneous. Maynard Keynes, whose effect on economic theory was, I understand, immense, bore no sway whatever amongst his friends in the West Central district. They liked him for his cleverness, his wit, the extraordinary ingenuity with which he defended what they often considered absurd opinions, and his affectionate nature. They disliked other things. He had very little natural feeling for the arts; though he learnt to write admirably lucid prose, and, under the spell of Duncan Grant, cultivated a taste for pictures and made an interesting collection. Said Lytton

[1]Well do I remember Lytton drawing me aside and saying: 'Cannot you or Vanessa persuade Duncan to make beautiful pictures instead of these coagulations of distressing oddments?' Duncan Grant at that time was much under the influence of the Post-Impressionists and had been touched by Cubism even.

once: 'What's wrong with Pozzo'—a pet name for Maynard which Maynard particularly disliked—'is that he has no æsthetic sense'. Perhaps Lytton was unjust; but with perfect justice he might have said the same of Norton. On the other hand, Pozzo and Norton might have said of some of their dearest friends that what was wrong with them was that they were incapable of wrestling with abstractions. You see we were not so much alike after all.

I have done my best to name those people who certainly were friends and of whom some at any rate have often been called 'Bloomsbury'. I have suggested that the people in my list held few, if any, opinions and preferences in common which were not held by hundreds of their intelligent contemporaries: I emphasise the words 'in common'. Wherefore, if my list be correct, it would seem to follow that there can be no such thing as 'the Bloomsbury doctrine' or 'the Bloomsbury point of view'. But is my list correct? It should be. And yet I cannot help wondering sometimes whether the journalists and broadcasters who write and talk about Bloomsbury have not in mind some totally different set of people. There are critics and expositors, for instance that leader-writer in *The Times Literary Supplement*, who describe Bloomsbury as a little gang or clique which despises all that is old and venerable and extols to the skies, without discrimination, the latest thing whatever that thing may be—the latest in art or letters or politics or morals. Also, according to this school of critics, the writers of Bloomsbury delight in a private and cryptic language, unintelligible to the common reader, while mocking at whatever is clear and comprehensible. Now who are these crabbed and wilfully obscure writers who despise all that is old? Surely not those reputed pillars of Bloomsbury, Lytton Strachey, Roger Fry, Maynard Keynes, David Garnett? I beseech the *Supplement* to give us the names.[1]

There are other critics, of whom I know as little as they appear to know of the reputed pillars of Bloomsbury, who hold a clean contrary opinion. I write from hearsay; but I am told there are brisk young fellows, authorities on the 'twenties', whose distressing accents are sometimes heard on the wireless by those who can stand that sort of thing, who explain that in 'the twenties' there still existed in England a gang or group which for years had devoted itself to stifling, or trying to stifle, at birth every vital movement that came to life. Oddly enough this gang, too, goes by the name of Bloomsbury. Now who can these baby-killers have been? Obviously not Roger Fry who introduced the modern movement in French painting to the British public, nor Maynard Keynes, who, I understand, revolutionised economics. Nor does it seem likely that the critics are thinking of Lytton Strachey who, far from being reactionary, went out of his way to help the cause of Women's Suffrage when that cause was reckoned a dangerous fad, or of Leonard Woolf who was a Fabian long before British socialism had become what the Americans call a racket. Whom can these castigators of 'Bloomsbury' have in mind?

[1] A week or so after this leading article appeared Mr. Oliver Strachey made the same request, and received from the *Supplement* (31st July 1948) what I can only consider a disingenuous reply.

BLOOMSBURY

Clearly not Virginia Woolf who invented what amounts almost to a new prose form; nor, I hope, certain critics who, long before 1920, had appreciated and defended the then disconcerting works of Picasso and T. S. Eliot.

Once more I cry aloud: Who were the members of Bloomsbury? For what did they stand? In the interests of history, if common decency means nothing to them, I beseech the Bloomsbury-baiters to answer my questions; for unless they speak out and speak quickly social historians will have to make what they can of wildly conflicting fancies and statements which contradict known facts. Thus, disheartened by the impossibility of discovering opinions and tastes common and peculiar to those people who by one authority or another have been described as 'Bloomsbury', the more acute may well be led to surmise that Bloomsbury was neither a chapel nor a clique but merely a collection of individuals each with his or her own views and likings. When to this perplexity is added the discovery that no two witnesses agree on a definition of the 'Bloomsbury doctrine', historians are bound to wonder whether there ever was such a thing. At last they may come to doubt whether 'Bloomsbury' ever existed. And did it?

IX

PARIS 1904

EVERY biographer knows that the undergraduate years are, or were, the most important, the most 'formative' to use an up-to-date expression, in a man's life—that is of a man who enjoyed the fortune of having been educated at Oxford or Cambridge. To me came the luck of a second formative period, the luck of a year in Paris when I was between twenty-two and twenty-three. In this chapter I shall try to recall my first acquaintance with Paris, commemorating in the attempt two friends, Morrice and O'Conor.[1] Of French friends I shall say little or nothing, for at that time I had none—no real friends, I mean. In another place I will speak of Copeau and Vildrac, Derain and Segonzac, Cocteau, Georges Duthuit, Matisse and Picasso, whom I came to know later and may, I hope, call 'old friends' though I may not call them intimate. But with Morrice and O'Conor for a time I was intimate; and as at that time I was young they left deep impressions on my tender mind. Of those later friends, French friends it would be silly and impudent to attempt an appreciation such as I have attempted in the case of Lytton Strachey, Roger Fry or Virginia Woolf, and when you come to read what I have to say about

---

[1] Unlike those who have written about him O'Conor spelt his name with one 'n'. I have letters to prove it.

138

them—if, indeed you read so far—you will find I have nothing better to offer than a handful of anecdotes and memories. But of Morrice and O'Conor, though I was in daily company with them for a little while only, I can write more knowingly. They played as influential a part in my life as any of my Cambridge contemporaries; inevitably, seeing that they and Gerald Kelly were the first painters I knew really well. For, at the time I was meeting these three men every day almost I had seen but little of that admirable paintress who was to become my wife, and could profit little by occasional encounters with second-rate French artists for the very good reason that I understood their language imperfectly and spoke it abominably. Wherefore to these three English-speaking painters I owe a vast debt of gratitude. Unluckily for me some four months after I first met him Gerald Kelly disappeared from our quarter and hid himself in the wilds of Montmartre. It was left to Morrice and O'Conor to continue my education.

I took my Bachelor's degree in June 1902, and though, to my tutor's annoyance and George Trevelyan's amusement, I obtained only a second, my college—Trinity—thought proper to offer me the Earl of Derby studentship. Accordingly I set myself to collect material for a dissertation on British policy at the Congress of Verona, and divided the academic year—October 1902 to August 1903—between Cambridge and the Record Office. In the late summer of that year I went most unwillingly with my father to shoot at animals in British Columbia. When I returned to England in November I realised that if ever I was to make anything of my dissertation I must continue my studies, not in the Record Office, but in the *Archives*. So to Paris I went in January 1904; and having been honoured by the personal inspection and presumably the approval of one of M. Delcassé's underlings I was permitted to begin my researches. They did not go far: I visited the *archives* thrice I believe. Nevertheless, the year 1904 was one of the most profitable of my life. Instead of going to the *archives* I went daily to the Louvre.

Like any other well meaning English boy I took lodgings in a *Pension* with a view to acquiring a better knowledge of French than my expensive education had provided. The Pension was kept by one Madame B——, a youngish widow, tolerably handsome and as hard as nails. We got on together well enough. Her house stood in a street which I can no longer find, though it is said to exist, la rue Bouquet-de-Longchamps, just behind the Trocadéro. There I began to stammer and half understand French, thanks partly to Madame and partly to a captain of the Colonial army, home from Indo-China, on long leave I suppose: I forget his name. Luckily he was one of those people who delight in giving information. Madame had designs on him I fancied. He may have been her lover, but I doubt it. He ate but did not sleep in her house. Anyhow, during the weeks I spent under Madame B——'s roof—weeks in which as I have said I acquired a smattering of French, as well as some knowledge of the paintings in the Louvre and of the streets on the north bank of the Seine—all I knew of Parisian 'night-life' came from occasional outings with this captain. I remember going with him, over-dressed in our swallow-tails and white ties, to see Sarah Bernhardt in *La Sorcière*—a shocking bad play I feel sure; and I remember how disappointing I found as much of it as I could understand. The captain was even more disappointed because he was on the look out for '*les jolies femmes et les belles toilettes*', and he saw little of either amongst the dumpy, *endimanchées* bourgeoises who were swallowing tepid white coffee and sandwiches in the foyer. The captain was a dull companion and the Pension a dull place—good for acquiring the rudiments of French though—and the Trocadéro quarter was not my quarter at all; nevertheless there I might have stayed for the rest of the year had I not come to Paris with a letter from E. S. P. Haynes to a young painter called Kelly. Probably it was not till the end of February or early March, not till I was beginning to feel at home in Paris, that I ventured to forward this letter, but a few days later I was knocking at a studio door in the rue Campagne-Première, a *cul de sac*, a warren of studios, just off the Boulevard Montparnasse.

Kelly, who had come to Paris in 1901, was a few years my senior; but, having spent three at Cambridge (Trinity Hall) he was a very young painter still. Also he was a painter of promise; and it is my belief that had he known how 'to feed on the advancing hour', had he about this time or a little later flung himself neck and crop into the contemporary movement, he might have found that nourishment for his talent which Spain and Java—so it seems to me—just failed to provide. In my opinion he has not fulfilled his promise: in my opinion, I say, because I do not suppose for a moment that Sir Gerald Kelly, P.P.R.A., considers himself a failure. Nor perhaps is he; for my part, I believe he is at the moment under-rated. I have seen good things by him in odd places—a surgeon's consulting room for instance—and I believe I could make a selection from his work which would surprise those critics who treat him as a nonentity. One thing is certain, he is about the best president the Royal Academy has given itself since Sir Joshua Reynolds. He has raised that foundation from the depths of public contempt to respectability if not honour. Anyhow in 1904 Kelly was an artist of promise: he was also a man of wit, culture and ideas, far better educated and more alert than the majority of his companions in the quarter, and I think it was partly because he enjoyed meeting someone with whom he could talk books and a little—a very little—philosophy that he took a fancy to me. You may wonder why he did not prefer to talk about these things with the French. I wonder too. As for me, during these first months in Montparnasse I was not sure enough of my hold on the subtleties of the language to butt into cultivated conversations—flirting with models and shop-girls was about as far as I dared go; but Kelly, like most of those who dined at the *Chat Blanc*, spoke French—or so it seemed to me at the time—fluently and correctly. When I consider how seldom during my solitary sojourns in Paris—and such sojourns have been frequent during a period of fifty years—how seldom I find myself speaking English, I am puzzled by the persistence with which these fluently

French-speaking English and American artists of the quarter for the most part kept themselves to themselves. Of course when the company was international they did speak French and spoke it easily; but then the conversation was apt to be trivial. Seemingly they reserved their graver and subtler thoughts for expression in their native tongue. Some of them had French mistresses—kept mistresses; but very few had French friends. They did not take part in the intellectual life of Paris. There must be some explanation. Maybe I shall hit on it presently. Meanwhile I take note that not long ago, in June 1947 to be exact, I observed that my friend Matthew Smith, who, since he has spent years in France doubtless speaks French easily, seemed to be seeking out English-speaking companions. This suggests that the tradition persists but does nothing to explain it.

Kelly, I say, took kindly to me because he needed a companion a little younger than himself with whom he could discuss matters, other than painting, in which he took an interest. But I do not suppose that the friendship would have ripened as it did —too quickly perhaps—had he not discovered to his surprise that this Earl of Derby student, this mugger up of dates and writer of dissertations, cared passionately for pictures, especially for those of the Impressionists, and appeared to know something about them. Had he not acquired, before coming to Paris, lithographs by Lautrec, and since his arrival had he not bought—for five francs—an etching by Renoir? That, I surmise, was what rendered me worthy of being taken to dine at the *Chat Blanc*, and afterwards to drink at the *Café de Versailles*. The first evening

turned my head. When, after two more such evenings, Kelly suggested that I should leave my respectable *Pension* and take a room in the quarter I hardly
knew whether I was standing on my heels or on that
head. I trumped up an excuse for leaving the useful
Madame B—— and her genteel neighbourhood, and
some time in April found myself installed in the
Hôtel de la Haute Loire, an *hôtel meublé*, at the angle
of the boulevard Montparnasse and the boulevard
Raspail. (The ground floor subsequently became
Batty. What is it now? I don't know). In those days
the boulevard Raspail ended in the boulevard Montparnasse: not until some years later was it driven
down to the long unlovely rue de Rennes. Also in
those days Montparnasse was not the centre of night-
life it became later. There was no *Rotonde*, no *Select*,
no *Bal nègre*, no *Boule blanche*, though the scrubby
little café on which I looked from my bedroom window was called *Le Dôme*. Montmartre was still the
artists' quarter: Montparnasse was a dingy suburb
enlivened by English and American painters. To
give you an idea of its isolation I may say that a
visit to Montmartre—a visit some of us made from
time to time—was matter for planning. One would
walk across the Luxembourg gardens and lunch
perhaps in a delightful little café—*Le Café Fleurus*—
on the corner of the eponymous street, behind a
flowery grill, looking on to the gardens. That was
the first step: it brought one close to the Odéon,
whence started every half hour a famous omnibus
drawn by three greys abreast—Odéon–Clichy. And
so, seated on the Impérial, one crossed Paris in an
hour or less and finally climbed on foot to the Place

du Tertre to have a drink before knocking at the door of some friendly studio. Having gone so far one stayed to dine; and every now and then O'Conor, Morrice and I would meet by appointment in Arnold Bennett's flat and take him to a *triperie*.

That was a great treat for Arnold Bennett, so we thought at the *Chat Blanc*. (What the *Chat Blanc* was I hope to explain in time). We were giving Bennett a taste of real Parisien life; so we thought, and upon my word I believe he thought so too. For Arnold Bennett, about 1904, was an insignificant little man and ridiculous to boot. Unless I mistake he was writing the 'Savoir Vivre Papers' for 'T.P.'s Weekly', and had written one or two trifling and ninetyish novels: above all he was learning French and he took longer about it than anyone has ever taken before or since. There we found him sitting in his little gimcrack apartment—I forget in which street, possibly la rue Fontaine—amidst his Empire upholstery from Waring and Gillow, with a concise French dictionary on the table, Familiar Quotations, *Whitaker's Almanack* and Morley's monographs on Voltaire and the Encyclopædists—these he admired hugely. He was the boy from Staffordshire who was making good, and in his bowler hat and reach-me-downs he looked the part. He was at once pleased with himself and ashamed:

> 'One of the low on whom assurance sits
> Like a silk-hat on a Bradford millionaire.'

We rather liked him, but we thought nothing of his writing. I do not think much of it now.

OLD FRIENDS

The Hôtel de la Haute Loire, in which I had a
comparatively spacious bedroom and a minute *cabinet de travail*, lay midway between the two centres
of Parnassian life—the *Café de Versailles* and the *Closerie des Lilas*. At the west end of what I may call our
high street—the boulevard—stood the restaurant
Lavenue—and what to us was more important its
adjunct, Le Petit Lavenue; there, at the west end,
stood also the Café de Versailles facing the Montparnasse railway-station oddly perched on what
looked like a band-stand. Between the station and
Lavenue there was just room for the entrance to the
rue d'Odessa; and in the rue d'Odessa flourished
the all-important *Chat Blanc*. A quarter of a mile or
so away at the east end of the boulevard were the
Bal Bullier and that most delightful of cafés (now
smartened and ruined) La closerie des Lilas. This,
as everyone knows, was a house of fame and literary
repair; where Paul Fort and his colleagues of *Vers
et Prose* held session; where later I was to hear
Moréas declaim his 'Stances'; where was pointed
out to me André Gide.

It was fifteen or sixteen years later that I came
to know Gide: Copeau brought us together. But may
I, taking advantage of the licence traditionally
granted to rambling old memoir-writers, may I re-
count here and now the rather surprising episode
which was my acquaintance with him. I feel pretty
sure it was in the late autumn of 1919 that Copeau
made us acquainted; and the acquaintance, as you
will see, must have come to its unfortunate end before I abandoned the beautiful Hôtel Voltaire on
the *quai* for the gloomy but highly convenient and

less noisy recesses of the Hôtel de Londres. That more or less fixes the date for start and finish—the end of '19 to the summer of '22 or thereabouts. To show you how amiable Gide made himself I need give one instance only. I had invited him to meet an English lady at lunch chez Foyot—I remember being slightly pained when he watered the particularly good Burgundy I had ordered in his honour—and at coffee time he said he would like to commemorate the occasion by giving this charming lady an unpublished poem by Valéry which he thought would please her. It was a pretty, gallant little thing which, Gide supposed, would never be published. I am not sure he did not write it on a paper fan: the summer was hot, and in those days restaurants were apt to provide fans in hot weather. Anyhow, he wrote it out in his exquisite hand: I wonder whether the honoured recipient has it still. Some time later he and I lunched together at the Voltaire in the Place de l'Odéon, and Gide brought with him an extremely handsome and intelligent youth—let us call him 'Henri'. This youth had been reading a book of mine, with the greatest interest he said, and had noted points he would like to discuss. Of course I was flattered. 'Come to lunch with me one day next week', I said, 'and we will have it out'. 'It must be a Thursday or a Sunday', said 'Henri'—*jours de sortie*—which proves that he was still a student. 'Next Thursday', said I.

Next Thursday morning I was sitting in my untidy bedroom writing an article for *The New Republic* when who should be announced but 'Monsieur Gide'. We sat and talked a while, and then I said—

'I must wash and dress now for at one I am lunching, as you may remember, with "Henri".' 'En effet, en effet', said Gide, 'nous pourrions déjeuner ensemble—tous les trois'. We did, and needless to say there was no æsthetic discussion between 'Henri' and myself. But from that day Gide refused to speak to me. What is more, it took my friends in Paris some seven or eight years to persuade him that, given my abnormal normality, the intentions he attributed to me were out of the question. He was convinced at last, so my friends told me; but only once after that unlucky day did I hold converse with the master. I was dining alone, and probably reading *Le Temps*, in my habitual restaurant *Lafond* at the corner of la rue des Saints Pères: in came Gide with a party—mostly women and children it seemed to me: I believe they were going to the circus. He crossed to my table and said—I should like to have a word with you before we leave; shall I join you presently for a cup of coffee? Gide had something definite to say, he had a question to ask. 'Why does Aldous Huxley refer to me as a "faux grand écrivain"? he demanded; adding traditionally 'I have never done him any harm'. I could not say; but we passed the five minutes he had to spare well enough, speaking ill of Aldous presumably. Later I asked Aldous whether he had said anything of the sort. Yes, he had—some twenty years earlier in a magazine, possibly an undergraduate magazine. But Gide had the eyes of a lynx and the memory of an elephant.

Let me return to the Boulevard Montparnasse. Next door, or almost, to Les Lilas was an *Etablissement de Bains*, standing in a small garden, which, to me, was a place of some importance, seeing that in my hotel was neither bath-room nor hip-bath even. That was normal in 1904. A year and a half later, when I was living in St. Symphorien, a hamlet just across the river from Tours, the only way of coming at a bath was either to walk into the town or have a bath sent out to the hamlet.[1] As a rule I walked: but once, having fallen sick and been brought to convalescence by le docteur Pigeon—the youngest doctor in France according to himself—aided by a groaning table of drugs, I sent for a bath. Out came the water in a cylindrical boiler, with a smoking brazier hanging under it, drawn by a horse and accompanied by two stout *hommes d'équipe*. A long deep trough was borne into my room and the steaming water in cans; when I had returned to bed the water was withdrawn through the window by means of a pipe and the trough was carried coffinwise downstairs. Years later I recounted this surprising experience, as it seemed to me, to Othon Friescz, who assured me that it was not surprising at all. Indeed, he remembered that when he was a student, about the turn of the century, and inhabited the attic of a house—in Paris mark you!—wherein dwelt a lovely and promising young actress—he remembered, said he, that the young beauty had a bath sent in twice a week, and that when she was clean the spacious and scented tub was removed to the landing. Here, said he, as often as not it remained a while till the *hommes d'équipe* returned from lunch;

[1] It is now a large and flourishing suburb with an excellent restaurant.

and occasionally the under-washed and perhaps slightly amorous *rapin* would seize this opporunity and take a quick plunge. That at all events is what Friescz told me; but in story-telling, as in lapidary inscription, 'a man is not on oath'.

I was speaking—rather a long time ago I fear—of the *Chat Blanc* in the rue d'Odessa. There an upstairs room was reserved for an undefined group of artists, their friends, models and mistresses. Anyone might bring a friend whom he judged would be generally acceptable; and these friends became members, so to speak of the club. Mistakes were made sometimes. The only big-wig who came—and he came very rarely and to lunch only—was Rodin. I got into a scrape with him later for touching the drapery on a lay-figure in his studio. He paid me out too; for when I went with Thoby Stephen and O'Conor to offer incense one snowy *jour de l'an* he sent word that he was at home only to his 'amis les plus intimes'. I don't blame him. On the two or three occasions that I saw the great man at the *Chat Blanc* he was gracious enough. We all admired and fled him; for in conversation with us, his inferiors, he was tedious and unexpectedly pompous. Also he stank. His famous model Thérèse, to the splendour of whose forms the Hôtel Biron bears abundant witness, was a more regular and welcome attendant. So was Bonnat, not precisely a big-wig but an old painter whose connoisseurship we all respected: the collection he bequeathed to Bayonne proves how right we were. Two French artists pretty often to be found at dinner-time in our upper room were Ulmann,[1] a timid Whistlerian whose mistress had been a governess in Poland and never let one forget it, and Scott of *Illustration*. And then there was Madame Irma. So long as the Luxembourg gallery remained open, though stript of the Impressionists it was one of the most depressing spots in Europe, I entered from time to time to glance at a painting by Dugardier; for there, walking on the sands in a boater was his enchanting model, Irma. I wonder what has become of that picture. Probably it is in the depths of the *dépôt national*. Besides being a beauty, Irma was a wit, and a *très brave fille* to boot. A passionate cyclist, she was the first woman wearing bloomers with whom I ever sat down to dine; also she was the first I ever saw pick up her plate and lick it clean. I learnt much from Irma.

Three decorated Americans frequented the *Chat Blanc*: the painter, Alexander Harrison, who flaunted the rosette of glory, the sculptors Brooks and Bartlet, merely beribboned. We saw and heard a good deal of Stanlaus, a young and successful American illustrator; also of the Englishmen, Howard, Kite and Thompson. Thompson, whose paintings I never saw, was also a good pianist and a lady-killer; Howard (called Pompey) was mixed up somehow with the legation at the Hague; Kite—a follower of Lavery—was a joke, and Irma called him 'Joseph'.

I set down these recollections of the *Chat Blanc* some years ago, and have since read a delightful essay by Somerset Maugham in which he gives his

[1]So his name is written by Mr. Donald Buchanan in his biography of J. W. Morrice. I had imagined it was Huilman.

account of the goings on in that upper room. He frequented it, he says, in 1904; but I cannot help thinking it must have been earlier, unless it were in the first three months of 1904 only. From April to Christmas of that year I dined there about five nights a week, except during the holiday months of August and September, and I never met Maugham though often I heard him spoken of. It is impossible that I should have forgotten it had I met him: Somerset Maugham is not a man to be forgotten or overlooked. Besides, I remember distinctly the excitement of coming to know him some years later in London. He says that Anrold Bennett dined in the restaurant once a week. In my day he never came there, though, as I have said, Morrice, O'Conor and I occasionally called for him in his flat. (Let me, by the way, seize this opportunity of recommending to anyone who has not read it Maugham's description of that flat, which he thinks may have been in the rue de Calais). But what convinces me that he is describing a *Chat Blanc* of an epoch earlier than mine is his account of the intellectual atmosphere that prevailed there. 'We discussed', he says, 'every subject under the sun, generally with heat', and recalls a discussion of Heredia's poetry into which were dragged the names of Degas, Mallarmé and Charles-Louis Philippe. In my day the intellectual atmosphere had deteriorated sadly, partly perhaps owing to the disappearance of Maugham. Heated discussions on literary subjects were seldom if ever heard. Only a smutty story or a denigration of Whistler by O'Conor was likely to raise the temperature a little above normal. The name of Hérédia might have been pronounced;

Degas was mentioned from time to time no doubt
—but not nearly so often as Whistler, Conder or
Puvis de Chavannes. No one, I think, but O'Conor
would have read Mallarmé. Both he and I might
have read *Marie Donadieu*, but we should have
known better than to speak of so recondite a work
to Stanlaus or Root.[1]

The 'regulars' of whom I saw most were Kelly,

[1]I have called attention elsewhere to a trivial mistake made
by Mr. Buchanan, and I may add that Somerset Maugham
also spells O'Conor with two 'n's. But to tell the truth I here
mention Mr. Buchanan's slip only to give myself an excuse for
again mentioning his book and calling attention to an admirable account of Arnold Bennett at the *Chat Blanc* contributed
to that book by Sir Gerald Kelly:

'I used to dine once a fortnight', says Sir Gerald, 'or once
a week with Bennett, alternately in Montmartre where he
lived, or in Montparnasse, where I lived. We were both
poor and, of course, each paid on the principle of a Dutch
treat.

Thus I had introduced Bennett to the *Chat Blanc*. He liked
Morrice very much. I believe I am right in remembering that
Morrice didn't very much care for him. At that time Bennett
was rather a figure of fun. His teeth stuck out through his upper
lip. He talked through his nose, and with the most appalling
accent. He had, through nervousness or from vanity, the most
overbearing, showy manner, and mentally and physically his
favourite attitude was with his thumbs in the armholes of his
waistcoat. Everything comic amused Morrice and he could
find comedy when a great many people could not, but after a
little while (if I remember aright) he found Bennett a little
overwhelming. I think all my acquaintances at the *Chat Blanc*
found Bennett rather overwhelming, though he only came once
a fortnight or once a month. I have a kind of recollection that
I was criticised for having brought him.' (*James Wilson Morrice—A Biography*, by Donald W. Buchanan. The Ryerson
Press, Toronto).

O'Conor and Morrice. During the summer months of 1904 Kelly was, I suppose, my closest friend. As for his influence, I may say that, in imitation of one of his sartorial flights of fancy, I sported on occasions a Lavallière. Yes, I have been seen by people now alive wearing a Lavallière bow at the *Café de Régence*. Kelly worked hard during the day, and I do not think we ever went picture-gazing together. But we talked pictures, and from him I learnt something about the technique of oil-painting and lithography. Mostly, however, our conversation was bookish; and I have surmised that it was because Kelly found in me someone with whom he could gossip endlessly about English literature that he saw much of me. He read aloud admirably—he had won the Winchester Reading Prize at Cambridge—and sitting in his studio looking out on that long, romantic stable-yard—for that is what the rue Campagne-Première is—sometimes before dinner, more often late at night by the light of a *lampe à pétrole*, he would neatly articulate a poem by Browning or a chapter of Meredith—two of his favourites—part of an Elizabethan play, a bit of Milton or Keats, or an essay by Oscar Wilde—another favourite. It was sitting here in the late dusk of a long June evening that we came in for a little comedy that entertained us considerably and sticks in my memory. Opposite Kelly's studio lodged in a small apartment a young paintress whose name I must not reveal—let us call her Helen Vavasour—of no great talent but endowed with appreciable beauty and a turn for high-falutin that fairly took one's breath away. Well, on this calm evening, appeared beneath her window a young

American painter, an occasional diner at the *Chat Blanc*, who perhaps had been absent for a day or two since he carried a Gladstone bag. There, in the gloaming, he stood beneath her window and called discreetly, 'Helen', 'Helen'. Beautiful, tall and tragic Miss Vavasour came to the window, and this is what she said: 'I have eliminated the material'. Someone had been putting ideas into the girl's head, we surmised. Could it have been Kelly's brother-in-law Alaister Crowley? It doesn't sound like him. But one never knows: besides, Miss Vavasour may have got it wrong. Anyhow, there in the dusk stood the young American: I can see him now in his white flannel trousers—yes, white flannel trousers—his bag dropped beside him, bewildered, staring. And this, picking up his bag, is what he said: 'I suppose that means I can't sleep here tonight'. Off he marched.

I knew Crowley: he came sometimes to the *Chat Blanc*, and sometimes took his *apéritif* at the *Versailles*. Sitting there one evening and turning to me, he exclaimed suddenly: 'I will take you to dine at Paillard's'—Paillard was at that time one of the most fashionable and expensive restaurants in Paris. I was by no means dressed for the occasion, and this I pointed out. In fact I was extremely shabby, not to say grubby; so, as you may suppose, I took my seat at the table, to which we were shown by an elegant waiter, in a state of some uneasiness. Crowley disappeared for a moment and returned observing—'It will be all right, I have told the *maître d'hôtel* that you are a Russian prince'. When we left there was a dispute about the bill. After dinner Crowley offered to take me 'where he would not take everyone'.

In fact we went to the *Caveau des Innocents* and *L'Ange Gabriel* in *Les Halles*, two underground eating-houses which remained open all night for the porters and market-gardeners. I forget into which of the two we ventured first: whichever it may have been, as it was about ten o'clock, of course it was empty. To be exact, there were a couple of soldiers playing dominoes in a corner. 'They always keep soldiers on duty here', whispered Crowley, 'they dare not do less'. As I had drunk brandy enough already, and as it was obviously my turn to play host, I called for a bottle of white wine. 'Ah, you shouldn't have done that', said Crowley, 'they will see that we have money'. After living dangerously in one establishment for about twenty minutes, we moved to the other. Here a young gentleman did approach our table and asked permission to take our portraits. He made two heavy pencil drawings which we took away with us, and gave him in return two francs and a glass of wine. After that, we felt that honour was satisfied and thankfully returned to the *Versailles* for a glass of beer. Crowley seemed to feel that we had looked pretty steadily into the jaws of death. I could not share his emotions, but of course he may have been right.

The Canadian, J. W. Morrice, an excellent painter whose work, though fairly well known, is in my opinion still insufficiently admired, would be described, I suppose, as an Impressionist of the second generation. As a youth he had studied in a Canadian university and even taken a degree—at least I think he had: also he retained a taste for, and a taste in, the 'humanities' as he liked to call them. It goes

without saying that his father wished him to enter
the family business, which I have heard was highly
profitable, or to become a lawyer. Instead he crossed
to England, half hoping he once told me—but he
was drunk at the time—to become a professional
musician. He was an accomplished flautist, when he
could keep his breath, and a passionate lover of
music: I believe he told me that he had played in
the Hallé orchestra, but I do not think that can have
been true. How he came to France and under whom
he studied I do not know. He had been a friend of
Conder and an acquaintance of Lautrec; the influence of Harpignies, Manet, Monet and Whistler is
discoverable in his early and middle periods. He
must have known Bonnard and Vuillard, though he
never spoke of them to me; and I dare say he and
O'Conor were the only *habitués* of the *Chat Blanc* who
in 1904 had even heard of either of them, which
gives you the measure of our provincialism. Morrice
would have been about forty when I met him, and
all through his life his art continued to develop. As
early as 1911 or '12 he fell in with Matisse at Tan-
giers; and during the 1914–18 war saw much of
him. The art of Matisse had considerable influence
on that of Morrice. This is much to the credit of the
latter; for he was already a mature and fairly successful painter in another style. He preserved an
open mind and sensibility, and was capable of profiting by new methods and a younger man's vision.
But essentially he was a solitary artist. He had a
great deal of character, which is by no means the
same thing as having a strong character: he *was* a
character. Had he been more often sober, probably

he would have painted more and larger pictures, but I doubt whether he would have painted better. Many of his things are sketchy, I admit; but all are charming and personal.

Morrice was of the *Chat Blanc–Versailles* connection, but its cosy parochialism did not satisfy him. He liked knocking about Paris and sometimes he took me with him. From Morrice I learnt to enjoy Paris: to be sure I was a willing pupil. Also from Morrice I learnt more about pictures; and it was he who later advised me to look at Matisse. Here I cannot be sure of dates; but certainly it was before I had the surprise of being shown, in Florence, and at Mr. Berenson's table of all places, photographs of some drawing by that master. I think I was in Florence in the spring of 1908; I know that I had the honour of lunching with Berenson, and I remember that we did not lunch at *I Tatti*. Now I know why: *I Tatti* was undergoing alterations. Well do I remember admiring those photographs and maybe expressing my admiration tactlessly; for what I did not know at that time was that with the great critic the subject of Matisse was one to be handled gingerly. Some months earlier he had decided that a room at *I Tatti* should be decorated by a modern artist: he would give the *fauves* a chance of showing whether there was anything in them. This bold resolution boiled down to a choice between Matisse and Piot. The great man plumped for Piot; and at the moment I was going into indiscreet raptures over Matisse the Piot decorations were being concealed. After they had been executed and paid for, Mr.

Berenson discovered that he did not like them. *I Tatti* was uninhabitable.[1]

The Paris to which Morrice introduced me, the Paris of 1904, was still the Paris of the Impressionists. It was a city of horse-omnibuses and yellow *fiacres* and drivers with shiny white 'toppers'; of craftsmen working, with a 'hand' or two in their own shops; of good living and low prices. It was a Paris without a 'metro'; but those yellow fiacres would take you almost anywhere it seemed for a franc and a half: indeed, late at night, even though you were as far afield as Montmartre, you had only to spot a cab with a green light—which meant that the horse's stable was in Montparnasse—and the driver could generally be argued into taking you home for a franc, plus of course the standard tip of five sous. The *Café de la Paix* and the restaurant behind it were still the favourite cosmopolitan haunts. Morrice would say—'Let us go and drink a Pernod at the *Café de la Paix* and look at the *rastas* as O'Conor calls them'. In 1904 the echoes of the Dreyfus case were still audible; the Congregations were being

[1]The story goes—I do not vouch for it—that Berenson, having commissioned Piot to decorate his library (I think) went abroad. On his return, seeing what had been done, he gave orders that it should be obliterated. He had forgotten that the Italian government, with his approval—sanction should I say? —had made a law that no wall-paintings in Italy were to be destroyed. But Piot had not forgotten. Accordingly, Piot's decorations could not be destroyed but had to be concealed beneath boards and canvas at considerable expense. If the story be true, they must still be on the walls or ceiling at *I Tatti*, unseen but intact.

harried, or thought they were; I dare say Emile Combes was *président du conseil*.

This Paris was still full of little music-halls and *cafés chantants*; Morrice delighted in such places— places where waiters circulated taking orders for drinks during the performance, places where one kept one's drink in front of one on a ledge provided for the purpose. Even at the *Concert Rouge*, where a capable quartet played exclusively classical music, this pleasing habit obtained: *cerises au cognac* was the thing to order there. The *Concert Rouge* was a favourite with Morrice; it stood opposite Foyot and so was on his way from the *quais* to the *Versailles*. But he liked almost as well, though in a different way perhaps, *La Cigale*, a little Montmartrois music-hall decorated by Willette: it was there I feel almost sure I first heard Jeanne Granier. Morrice was one of those fortunate people who enjoy beauty as they enjoy wine; both were for him necessities and he was not too difficult about the vintage. Beauty he found everywhere; in streets and cafés and *zincs* (the word 'bar' was still a stranger in the French language) in shop-windows and railway-stations, in the circus and on penny-steamers. There is nothing surprising about that; all these were recognised beauty-spots in Impressionist days. But Morrice could take pleasure in an evening at the Opéra or the Opéra-Comique, and that was quite irregular. True to his generation he had a taste for Pernod, and was exceptional only in his taste for several in succession; but he would not drink them anywhere. He had the knack of discovering sympathetic *endroits*: sometimes it would be a large and superficially garish café, sometimes a discreet retreat. He might give you rendezvous for six o'clock at what then seemed a vast new *brasserie* on a populous *place* or in an almost undiscoverable Louis-Philippe box in a bye-street. Always the place had character; and always Morrice enjoyed it for what it was worth and made his companion enjoy it too. One of his favourite words was 'gusto', used, as he would observe with gusto, in the sense in which Hazlitt used it. He read little, but he enjoyed what he read. He read newspapers and he read poetry; and he enjoyed both. He enjoyed his round, merry mistress, Léa, but he kept her in her place, that is, on the fringe of his life. He enjoyed her meridional accent, and especially her impulsive habit of using the meridional expletive, *'Pardi'*.

As I have said, Morrice moved about Paris more than did most of the frequenters of the *Chat Blanc*. Topographically he was not of the quarter but of the centre rather, inhabiting the quai des Grands Augustins—number 35 if I remember right. Certainly his studio—a not very big room over-looking the river—must have been close to *La Pérouse*, for on the rare occasions when he settled down to work in the morning he would have the *plat du jour* and a bottle of wine sent up from the restaurant. The normal Parnassien—the hideous word Montparnois had not yet been coined—was unbelievably regional in those days. Only serious business or planned and premeditated pleasure took him far out of a territory bounded by the boulevard St. Michel, the rue Denfert-Rochereau, the cemetery, the Avenue du Maine, the rue de Sèvres and the boulevard St. Germain. The Gaîté Montparnasse and the Bobino were

his theatres; and when he had money to burn he
would take a girl to dine at the Taverne du Panthéon—dinner at the Panthéon (without wine)
might cost as much as five or six francs a head. An
excited party might press on to Bullier, a hundred
yards or so up the boulevard, but would hardly have
pushed down across the bridges. Morrice, however,
would go anywhere that was not too smart. It was
he who took me to the tart-parade at Olympia and
to dine at the Horse Shoe, an English House near
the Gare du Nord, familiar to students of Huysmans. Morrice had an 'emphatic gusto', to borrow
one of his favourite expressions, for a vaguely Dick-
ensian England and Scotch Whisky—especially if
they could be had in Paris. But he always maintained that the first Pernod of the evening tasted
better on the boulevards than anywhere else. I never
saw Morrice in evening clothes, and I doubt whether,
though well enough off, he possessed a tail-coat or
a dinner-jacket even. I suppose he would have been
called a Bohemian. He did not look like one, he
dressed *en bourgeois*: no Lavallière and wide-awake
for him, but a stiff white collar of the up and down
variety and a neat speckled tie. Only his head betrayed the artist, a pear-shaped, bald head with a
pointed beard and slightly mad eyes. I remember
saying timidly to O'Conor—timidly, for you must
remember that I had only just come to Paris from
Cambridge and that O'Conor was the most formidable figure in the quarter—I remember saying that
I thought Morrice the most remarkable of our companions at the *Chat Blanc*. 'He's the only one who
has character, if that's what you mean', growled

O'Conor. Kelly tells a story which may be true and is certainly illuminating. Early one summer morning a party was returning from a carouse when Morrice somehow or other fell into the gutter. There was nothing extraordinary in that: from time to time Morrice was knocked over by a horse and never seemed much the worse for it. But on this June morning it so happened that the gutter was a rippling stream; for they were washing the streets. There lay Morrice on his back gazing up out of the cold water into the dawn-lit sky and murmuring, with unmistakable gusto, 'pearly', 'pearly'.

O'Conor—Roderick O'Conor—was of course an Irishman. He came of a land-owning family which by his own account had done well enough out of the Land Purchase Act.[1] He was a swarthy man, with a black moustache, greying when I met him, tallish and sturdy. He carried a stick, and there was nothing Bohemian about his appearance. In 1904 he was over forty I suppose, and had not been in the British Isles for twenty years or more, so he told me. He told me too that somewhere in London he had a top-hat. He was highly intelligent and well educated, had read widely in French and English and was conversant with the Latin masters. At one time he seems to have known, if only a little, most of the more interesting French painters of his generation—the Nabi for instance: but the acquaintance had been allowed to drop. Why? I haven't a

[1]Mr. Buchanan says that O'Conor 'suffered from poverty'. This, I think, is an exaggeration. So far as I can remember O'Conor was sometimes hard up, but never poor.

notion. Sheer laziness perhaps. Misanthropic he certainly was; and I should say he was a solitary by temperament had he not taken undisguised pleasure in lunching almost daily in that autumn of 1904 with a callow youth from Cambridge, well educated to be sure and let us hope fairly intelligent. Yes, we lunched almost daily at *Le Petit Lavenne*; and, as Kelly had disappeared into Montmartre, O'Conor became my most intimate friend. He exhibited at the *Salon d'automne* and *Les Indépendants*, through which societies he must have preserved relations of some sort with the French artists. Indeed later, much later, when I was making friends with the painters of his generation and the next, I was surprised to find how often, when I pronounced his name, one of them would exclaim—'Le père O'Conor: tiens, qu'est-ce qu'il fait à présent?' What was he doing? I hardly knew how to reply, though we continued for twenty years and more to meet occasionally by appointment and dine at the *Alençon* (always in the quarter you perceive). I have suggested that he was solitary by choice; yet I remember once when I met him he said he had just returned from Italy, and added that he had stayed there picture-gazing until he began to feel lonely: evidently there was a degree of solitude which he could not stand. I suspect he was a tragic figure though he kept his tragedy to himself. Conscious of gifts—perhaps great gifts—he was conscious too that he lacked power of expression. His pictures—there is one in the room next to the study in which I am writing—were full of austere intention unrealised; incidentally, they were influenced by Cézanne at a time when the influence

of Cézanne was not widespread, when, in my part of
Montparnasse, his name was unknown. These pictures painted at the beginning of the century are
sometimes oddly like what daring young men were
to paint ten years later. His taste and judgment were
remarkable: already in 1904 he had noticed most of
those talents, plastic and literary, which in 1914 it
was still considered 'advanced' to recognise. From
time to time he would give me a book, and the authors he chose in 1904 or '5 were, if I remember
right, Claudel, Laforgue, Remy de Gourmont, Jules
Rennard and—unless I am confusing dates—Charles-
Louis Philippe. He certainly gave me, then or a little
later, the autobiography of Madame Sacher Masoch.
He was an accomplished book-hunter, and found
for me on the *quais* the 1882 large-paper edition of
Flaubert and a first edition of Mérimée's *Lettres à
une Inconnue*. His taste in pictures, if not precisely
catholic, was not as narrow as that of most painters.
He admired both Ingres and Delacroix, and must
have been one of the first to see something in the
douanier Rousseau. He spotted the *Chasse au tigre*
when it was shown at Les Indépendants and advised
me to buy it for a hundred francs. I was tempted,
but the picture seemed rather large to bring home
in a portmanteau. That he did not buy it himself
was possibly because he was hard up, probably because he had no place for it: already he possessed
paintings by Gauguin, Bonnard, Rouault and
Laprade amongst others. Of course there were
plenty of people in Paris in 1904 who knew all about
these painters and writers; but at the *Chat Blanc* I
do not think I ever heard the name of Cézanne or

Gauguin or Van Gogh pronounced. For O'Conor, when he dined there, never talked 'art', unless to deflate some overblown reputation—e.g. that of Whistler, Sargent, Conder Carrière or Cottet, all of whom passed for masters in the Anglo-American quarter. Generally he confined himself to comments on people and things, gruff and disobliging as a rule, and to grim jokes. It was only at our tête-à-tête *déjeuners*, sometimes followed by a round of the galleries, that he permitted himself a little enthusiasm about pictures and books.

The great event in O'Conor's life had been, I surmise, his friendship—a close friendship so far as I could make out—with Gauguin. They met at Pont Aven, during Gauguin's last sojourn in Brittany perhaps, or perhaps earlier; O'Conor dealt little in dates and let fall his recollections in stray sentences amidst conversations on alien topics. But I assume the friendship was pretty close because O'Conor possessed drawings by the master bearing affectionate and humorous inscriptions: also, at some time or other he lent Gauguin his studio in the rue Cherchemidi. What to me seems clear is that Gauguin's strength of character and convincing style of talk made a deep impression on the young, or youngish, Irishman, and I dare say it was the only deep impression he ever received from a fellow creature. That Gauguin had a way of talking and moving and looking which caught his imagination I feel sure: years later, in 1919 or 1920, when I invited him to meet Derain, O'Conor told me, solemnly almost, that he had never met anyone whose manner reminded him so much of Gauguin's. Now O'Conor did not much admire Derain's painting; he would have been at no pains to pay him a compliment, and assuredly he considered this judgment of his complimentary in the highest degree. So, if in his judgment Derain and Gauguin were in some subtle but significant way alike, I am inclined to believe that they were.

Pictures, books, music, drawings, photographs (mostly so far as I remember of works by Greco and Cézanne) filled O'Conor's life and his spacious but gloomy studio. He never put pen to paper if he could help it, and when obliged to do so wrote in a childish, irregular hand, rather surprising in a man of his culture and force.[1] An *amie* he had, kept severely in the background: I never saw her. The charming and gifted lady, whom I knew too little, and who mitigated the painful loneliness of his old age, can at this time have been no more than a child. He played the violin—to himself. Rarely did he make the immense effort of going to a concert, though he loved music.[2] You must remember there was no wireless in those days, and I doubt whether much classical music had been recorded for the gramophone. So he played to himself, badly. He might have bought a pianola: he did not, nor could he have dreamed of such a thing. In music his taste was austere, and he would snarl at Morrice for his 'romanticism' and 'laxity'. After a scolding from O'Conor, Morrice would say to me 'let us go tomorrow and hear some

[1]However I have ten or a dozen letters from him, some of them long and mostly about painting.

[2]Occasionally he passed an evening with Thompson listening to the piano.

lenient music', and off he would take me to hear *Traviata* at the Opéra Comique. But O'Conor remained in his quarter grim and uncompromising. Once only did I see him impressed by a human being, and that was by Virginia Woolf—Virginia Stephen to be exact. In 1904 she was very young and quite unknown, having published nothing: but O'Conor confessed after their first and, I think, only meeting—'she put the fear of God into me'.

As I came to know more people in Paris inevitably I saw less of Morrice and O'Conor, nevertheless I kept well up with them till 1914. Morrice I saw for the last time in the late autumn of that year. He had come to London, perhaps a little panic-stricken, but he did not stay long; for he found, so he told me, that the only thing to be done in an English winter was to sit indoors drinking whisky: 'it was always like that' he added. So he returned to France and improved his acquaintance with Matisse. Again they were together in North Africa. Matisse appreciated Morrice's painting and felt his charm, but I think he may have been disconcerted by his habits. He did not like it, I gather, when the Arab urchins took to following Morrice in the street shouting 'Whisky, Whisky'. When I returned to Paris in 1919 I tried to find Morrice. No one seemed to know where he was; only it was thought that he was rarely in town. Occasionally I heard tell of him from O'Conor; stories were repeated by Matisse or by Georges Duthuit; but it was not until I read Mr. Buchanan's book that I knew that he had died in Tunis in January 1924.

One day, in the late 'twenties' I suppose, I was

to lunch with Segonzac who was serving on the hanging committee of the *salon d'automne*. I chanced to fall in with O'Conor who had sent pictures to the exhibition and suggested that he should join the party. Segonzac said it would be delightful to see 'le père O'Conor' again, and as usual the qualification surprised me: I never thought of O'Conor in that way. Segonzac insisted on lunching *chez* 'Footit', an English bar kept by an ex-clown, or rather by an ex-clown's wife, which suited the taste of the French in a certain mood. It was *bien anglais*—it was indeed: a tough, over-cooked chop, watery potatoes and a bottle of tepid beer, to be consumed at a high counter instead of a table: *bien anglais*. O'Conor and Segonzac went back to the *Petit Palais*, and I stayed in the hope of getting into conversation with two pretty English girls who were manifestly out of their depth. Was that the last time I saw O'Conor? No, now I come to think of it, I saw him some years later, one Sunday afternoon when I was drinking a solitary *café crême* at *les deux Magots*: O'Conor and his amie passed by and stopped to have a word with me. That was the last. He went to live in the midi, married his mistress, and—so Matthew Smith tells me—died a good while ago.

X

PARIS IN 'THE TWENTIES'

STRANGE as it seems today, and will seem to future generations, in 1919 there were intelligent men and women who believed that an age of peace and prosperity lay before mankind. I hasten to say that I was not one of them. Like most people, however, I was happy, and there was much to be happy about. The war was over, that was the great thing. The slaughter, the hardship, the dictatorship of the press—for that is what government amounted to in the last years—the reign of terror and stupidity was over—for the time being. Once again civilized people in England would be allowed to lead civilized lives; and obviously one of the things they would wish to regain would be contact with civilized people in other countries. They would want to travel. As it happened, continental civilization came to us before we had a chance of going to it; for early in the summer of 1919 Diaghileff's troupe arrived in London, with *La Boutique fantasque* and *Le Tricorne*, with Picasso, Derain, Stravinsky and Ansermet, imparting, as the Russian ballet always did, its own culture and collecting its own public, both of which were international. Suddenly the arts became the preoccupation of Society (with the capital S) which twelve months earlier had been preoccupied with military and political intrigues. French became the language of the Savoy where Diaghileff, Massine,

Stravinsky, Picasso and Picasso's very beautiful and rather aristocratic wife were staying for the season. Abruptly and unexpectedly the wheels of civilization began to turn.

Picasso dwelt in the Savoy: for Derain we found a modest lodging in Regent's Square; and their ways of life in London were as distinct as their addresses. Madame Picasso had no notion of joining in the rough and tumble of even upper Bohemia. She and her husband lived in their fashionable hotel and went to fashionable parties, at which, if they happened to be evening parties, the latter appeared 'en smoking'. Derain never went beyond a blue serge suit. Even on the first night of *La Boutique*—and never before or since have I beheld such a scene of white-tied, tail-coated enthusiasm—when at last Diaghileff and Massine forced him in front of the curtain Derain was still wearing that suit; so inevitably he was wearing it at the extremely smart supper-party given afterwards in his honour. I remember coming home from that party, Derain, Ansermet and I in a 'taxi', all the better for the evening may be, and driving round and round Gordon Square pursuing some momentous argument about I know not what. Ansermet, I should explain, who had come to conduct the orchestra, played a leading part in the adventures and festivities of that memorable summer.

The Picassos, I have said, went mostly to fashionable parties; however they went to one that was pretty shabby. I shared a house then—number 46 Gordon Square—with Maynard Keynes, who early in the year had gone to Paris for the peace-confer-ence, out of which he had walked in a state of well justified indignation. He and I decided that for once Picasso should meet a few of the unfashionable. We, in our turn, would give a supper-party. From the ballet we invited the Picassos, Derain, Lopokova and Ansermet. We did not invite Diaghileff; but we did invite some forty young or youngish painters, writers and students—male and female. Maynard, Duncan Grant, our two maids and I waited on them. Picasso did not dress. We rigged up a couple of long tables: at the end of one we put Ansermet, at the end of the other Lytton Strachey, so that their beards might wag in unison. I remember that Aldous Huxley brought with him a youth called Drieu La Rochelle—that ill-starred and gifted writer, whose memory it seems is still under a cloud, but whom I, for my part, shall never cease to regret.

This London prelude to Paris in 'the twenties' was necessary because, when I went to Paris for a couple of months or more in the autumn of 1919, intending to see pictures and old friends, I made a host of new ones; and with most of these new friends—my friends of 'the twenties'—I became acquainted through Derain whom I met for the first time that summer in London. With Picasso my acquaintance was older, though it was never so intimate. I had known him since 1911 or thereabouts. I believe it was Gertrude Stein who took me to his studio overlooking the *cimetière Montparnasse*: I remember Picasso said he liked the view. (This, by the way, should help to fix a date—I never knew Picasso in Montmartre). Gertrude Stein and her brother Leo were then living together in the rue Fleurus and collecting

pictures by Matisse and Picasso. It was mere chance
—so at least it has always seemed to me—that they
were not collecting works by Monsieur Untel and his
gifted sister: for neither, so far as I could make out,
had a genuine feeling for visual art. Miss Stein, as
everyone knows, became a famous patron—a valuable patron at a critical moment she certainly was
—and a famous propounder of riddles. Leo took to
psycho-analysis and Futurism and had his day of
notoriety. The truth seems to be that they were a
pair of theorists—Leo possessing the better brain and
Gertrude the stronger character, and that for them
pictures were pegs on which to hang hypotheses.
They took up Matisse and Picasso; but, as I have
dared to suggest, they might just as well have taken
up something quite different, something that provided an even better peg. And, in fact, Leo did take
up the Italian Futurists, while Gertrude took up Sir
Francis Rose. It was their brother, or cousin perhaps,
Michael who loved painting; and it was in his house,
in the rue Madame, before the first war, that I saw
a superb collection of early Matisse—up to 1912 say
—which enabled me to follow and appreciate the
development of that master's art.

Having mentioned Matisse, may I elongate a digression which is perhaps pardonable in a chapter
even more discursive than those which have gone
before, and speak of our first meeting and tell a tale.
For Matisse, too, I met before the 1914–18 war;
whereas in 'the twenties' I saw very little of him.
I was taken to his studio at Clamart by Bréal and
Simon Bussy: Roger Fry was of the party. I remember the pictures, and I remember a small conserva-

tory full of exquisite flowers which often provided 'motifs' for those pictures; but of the artist himself, as he appeared at that first meeting, I remember very little. Much later I came to know him fairly well, and I shall try to give some account of him in the course of this memoir. But already, at the time of which for the moment I am writing (about 1912 or '13) he must have been famous and prosperous too, for he had taken to riding in the Bois —in brown top-boots. And thereby hangs the tale. It is one that Matisse used himself to tell, so there can be no harm in repeating it. Those who have seen him will realise that Matisse had not the figure for equitation; and one day what you would have expected to happen did happen: he fell off. He was a little—a very little—hurt; he took a cab and drove straight to the family doctor; then he drove home. Meanwhile the doctor had telephoned to Madame Matisse—but this of course Matisse did not know—to say that the injury amounted to nothing. 'Reassure him', said the doctor, 'his is a sensitive, nervous disposition; reassure him'. At this moment Matisse in his cab was making up his mind to be brave. He would belittle the accident. He felt rather grand about this, about the attitude he intended to adopt—he told the story himself you must remember—and so feeling reached his own door to be greeted by wife and daughter with cries of 'C'est rien, Henri', 'C'est rien, papa', 'le docteur dit que c'est rien'. It was a disappointing reception, you must admit, to one who had steeled himself for the rôle of stiff-lipped hero.

To return to my theme—Paris in 'the twenties',

which for my purpose begin in November 1919: it was then that *Les deux Magots* was in its glory. Derain was the presiding genius and Alice Derain the lovely and gracious queen. Braque and Madame Braque were faithful clients; André Salmon and Madame Salmon seldom failed to appear; Bernouard, the little printer who produced those elegant editions under the sign of *La rose de France*, never. Bernouard seemed to have known everyone and to have been present on all memorable occasions. Once I asked Cocteau how this could be, seeing that Bernouard was still young and had never been very important. He was so small, said Cocteau, that he slipped between everyone's legs and secured a front seat. Oberlé, the poet Gabory, the painter Gerbaud, came often to the apéritif; Segonzac and Despiau sometimes; Jean Marchand, Kisling, Marcoussis rarely; and when they chanced to be in Paris, Stravinsky and Ansermet dropped in. But these two I see most clearly at a restaurant in the rue Bonaparte where we sometimes dined. I recall with surprising distinctness—had I the gift I could make a drawing of the scene—a side room on a hot Sunday afternoon in the early 'twenties'. There we had lunched, and there we were sitting on and on, drinking tepid, sweet champagne, and moving round and round the table to dodge the sun that somehow would keep poking in. We—'we' were Derain and Alice, Stravinsky, Ansermet, an English lady and myself—we stayed because Derain had fallen into argument with Stravinsky about music. Ansermet joined the fray. And so great that afternoon was Stravinsky's lucidity and power of expression, or maybe so heady the wine, that for once in my life, and once only, I fancied that I understood music. Other musicians I remember meeting at the *Magots* were Satie and (once or twice) Poulenc. But it was not in my quarter that 'les six' were to be found: them I came to know (one intimately, the others slightly) through Jean Cocteau, and I associate them with *Le Boeuf sur le toit* and Cocteau's Saturday dinners.

In this exciting and delightful autumn—delightful it was though I believe it rained, and sometimes snowed as well, every day almost, I renewed my friendship with Copeau and Vildrac, whom Roger Fry had enticed to London in 1911 to represent 'the modern movement' in French literature and drama at the Post-Impressionist exhibition; and through them I met one or two writers and actors—Gide, Duhamel, Luc Durtain, Jules Romains, Jouvet: the enchanting Valentine Tessier I had already come to know and admire in London. None of these was ever to be seen at *Les Magots*. On the other hand, Léger, Lipchitz and Madame Lipchitz, Pascin and Metzinger made, I am inclined to think, rare appearances; certainly in the 'twenties' I knew them all, slightly. They were not, however, of the set to which I had been admitted—*la bande à Derain* as I believe it was called sometimes; neither were the dealers Zborowski and Basler who were often to be seen on the terrace and whom of course we knew. Basler was a figure of fun, a small Polish Jew with a bowler hat, who had taken on himself the sacred duty of making known the genius of a compatriot called Coubine. The story went that a delegation which had come to buy modern pictures for War-

AT THE FOIRE DE MONTMARTRE
Kisling, Fels, Gabory, Clive Bell, Alice Derain, Derain

saw visited Basler's gallery, his attic to be exact, and-
having made some purchases, refused to buy a work
by the protégé. In vain Basler implored. 'We have
exhausted our credit' explained the tactful leader of
the mission. 'Then', exclaimed Basler, trusting into
unwilling arms a substantial canvas by the neglected
master, 'then accept this as a tribute from La
France.' Zborowski, another Pole, was a different
sort of dealer. Cultivated and comely, he wrote poetry in his spare time, and was the friend of painters
and poets. He dealt especially in Modigliani and
Soutine, both of whom he knew well and helped
generously—neither of whom (alas!) did I ever meet.
He was also on the best of terms with Max Jacob,
whom I did know fairly well.

It was some time in November that I first met,
through the English dealer P. M. Turner, an artist
who, I am happy to say, remains one of my great
friends. Dunoyer de Segonzac is, as everyone knows,
a painter of class—in my opinion his water-colours,
pen-drawings and etchings are even better than his
oils: he is also one of the most charming men alive.
He is my notion of a gentleman of Gascony, and he
has a way with him that gets away with anything.
Stories in proof of this abound: for instance, it is
told how, on his first visit to England, staying at a
hotel in Mayfair, he came down to breakfast and
demanded what he understood from the writings of
Sir Walter Scott to be the correct fare—beef and
beer. The head-waiter tried to explain that the serving of such a meal at such an hour in the coffee-room
was not only unusual but inadmissible. All would not
do: Segonzac had his way, that is to say his flagon

of ale and cut off the cold sirloin. And only the other day—I record the incident to show that Segonzac has not lost the art of wheedling—returning with me after lunch to my hotel in the rue Condé he exclaimed—'Why, next door is my grandmother's house, where I played on Sunday afternoons as a child; I must show you over it'. Sure enough, he rang the bell, cajoled the old woman who answered it, and to the surprise, but also pleasure, of the tenants made a tour of their rooms describing exactly what was done in them and how it was done sixty years ago. In the 'twenties' Segonzac came sometimes to the *Magots* for an apéritif and every now and then stayed to dine with us. For you must not suppose that these gatherings ended at eight o'clock. As many as nine or ten—*la bande à Derain*—would go on to some bistrot or modest restaurant (Michaud, Establet or a place near *les halles de vins*) where, all other customers having retired, sometimes we ended the evening in song.

Othon Friesz, in whose house in la rue Notre Dame des Champs I have spent many pleasant evenings, never came to the *Magots*. I believe he had his own good reasons for not joining our party. So I believe had Vlaminck. He, as everybody knows, had a magnificent painting-gift, which, as some of us think, he squandered; and Friesz, too, never quite fulfilled his promise—at one moment he was amongst the most admired of the fauves. Vlaminck has written a couple of books which reveal a literary talent not to be denied; it is less generally known that Friesz too, could write effectively and wittily when he gave his mind to it: I doubt, however, whether

he published anything more substantial than an
article or preface.

Twice, and twice only, in my life did I meet James
Joyce, and our first encounter was on the terrace of
this famous café—still famous, or as some think in-
famous, haunted by Existentionalists and crowded
with tourists who come to see Existentionalists drink.
This meeting was not memorable; the second, if the
sitting of two people at the same table without ex-
changing a word can be called a meeting, was at
least on a memorable occasion. Kind Mr. Shiff gave
a supper-party in honour of Diaghileff after the first
night in Paris of some ballet or other. He invited
forty or fifty guests, members of the ballet and
friends of the ballet, painters, writers, dress-makers
and ladies of fashion; but that on which he had set
his heart was to assemble at his hospitable board—
in an upper room at the Majestic—the four living
men he most admired: Picasso, Stravinsky, Joyce
and Proust. About netting the first two there was no
difficulty: they pertained to the ballet. But when we
sat down to supper, well after midnight, there was
no sign of Joyce or Proust. However, about coffee-
time, appeared in the midst of the elegantly dressed
throng someone dressed otherwise, someone a good
deal the worse for wear. It turned out to be Joyce.
He seemed far from well. Certainly he was in no
mood for supper. But a chair was set for him on our
host's right, and there he remained speechless with
his head in his hands and a glass of champagne in
front of him. Between two and three o'clock appeared, to most people's surprise I imagine, a small dap-
per figure, not 'dressed' to be sure, but clad in ex-

quisite black with white kid gloves. It was Proust of course. He entered in the manner of one who should say 'I was passing by and happened to see a light in your room, so I just dropped in to shake hands'. He was given a chair on his host's left, and found himself next Stravinsky to whom, in his polite way, he tried to make himself agreeable. 'Doubtless you admire Beethoven', he began. 'I detest Beethoven' was all he got for answer. 'But, cher maître, surely those late sonatas and quartets . . . ?' 'Pires que les autres' growled Stravinsky. Ansermet intervened in an attempt to keep the peace; there was no row but the situation was tense. Joyce began to snore—I hope it was a snore. Marcelle Meyer, who sat next me, suggested that the Avenue de Breteuil lay not so far out of my way, which was hardly true, but I jumped at the excuse. Of course I should be delighted to drop her home; Mr. Shiff would understand; besides it really was very late.

How that party ended I have never cared to enquire; but it reminds me of another encounter with fame, in some ways similar. One Sunday in the late 'twenties' Nils de Dardel invited me to lunch in his studio on the heights of Montmartre—in la rue Lepic I fancy. It was a small party: Nils and his charming wife, Marcel Herrand, one or two more I suppose. Isadora Duncan was expected; but when she arrived, at the end of lunch, all she felt up to was a large glass of brandy. Having disposed of that, she fell back on the sofa and drew down beside her the first male object she could lay hands on, which happened to be me. Then, taking one of my hands, she ran it lovingly over her person, murmuring the

SKETCH BY NILS DE DARDEL
OF ISADORA DUNCAN AND THE AUTHOR

while, by way of excuse and in a strong American accent—'Je ne suis pas une femme, je suis un génie'. So she continued for some time, long enough at any rate for Nils to whip out his water-colours and sketch the scene. That drawing used to hang in my flat at 50 Gordon Square, and if I can find it I will publish it, 'to witness if I lie'.[1]

The one person never to be seen at Les deux Magots, nor at any other gathering of painters unless it were a private view or a first night, was Picasso. He lived apart, with his lady-wife and his little son Polo, in the rue la Boëtie above Paul Rosenberg's shop. There I used to visit him of a morning. As you may suppose, I was shy of disturbing the great artist at that time of day; but he would say 'drop in any time in the morning—besides no one ever caught me working'. And true it is I have rarely seen Picasso at work. I saw him make a drawing of which I shall have a word to say; in London, I saw him add a few touches to his curtain for *Le Tricorne*; and once I saw him do something to a plate in his pottery at Valauris. But I have seen him watching others work. One day when I called workmen were painting and graining a big *porte cochère* on the opposite side of the street. Picasso was fascinated. The elaboration of the technique enchanted him. He explained to me what they were about and that they were only at the beginning of their job (I had imagined that it was nearly finished). No, they would go on adding coats of paint and letting them dry; and then would come the delicate business of

[1] I have found it.

regraining and varnishing. It would take days. And so far as I could make out Picasso intended to stay at the window till it was done.

As I have said, in the years after his first marriage Picasso lived apart and saw more of the fashionable world than of pre-war acquaintances. But I recall a luncheon-party in his flat—a rare event—in the autumn of 1920 perhaps, to which were invited Derain, Jean Cocteau, Satie and myself. After lunch we were set in a row, for all the world as though we were posing for the village photographer, and Picasso 'took our likenesses'. I wish I could get hold of that drawing or a reproduction even. Years ago I asked Picasso what had become of it. He felt sure it was not lost; but as to where it was, of that he was far from sure: probably somewhere in the studio, not easily to be come at. Now, however, that he has two or three secretaries at his beck and call surely it should be possible to hunt it down.

Picasso kept himself to himself in the 'twenties'. I saw him from time to time in his studio or in the fashionable or quasi-fashionable world, at parties which generally had something to do with the ballet; for of the Russian ballet Olga Picasso was a loyal supporter. I remember pleasant lunches with him and Cocteau, Madame Picasso being sometimes of the party. She liked discreet places such as La Pérouse or Voisin, but was not averse from an occasional evening at 'Le Boeuf sur le toit', which, if not discreet, was gay and tolerably smart. And, having named this restaurant, may I, before describing it, take the opportunity of contradicting a lie which the name puts me in mind of? It is a paltry lie but vexatious. I should have scotched it long ago, but, being lazy, I procrastinated; and as it still rankles I will get the humour off my chest at the risk of being thought touchy and of wandering from my subject. The late Lord Derwent, under the pseudonym 'George Vandan' or 'Vanden'—Vandan or Vanden was I believe one of his Christian names—some years since published a book the name of which I forget; and in that book gave his version of a party at *Le Boeuf*. His version is incorrect. Here are the facts. Peter Johnstone, as he then was, longed to meet Picasso, and pestered me to bring about a meeting. I will commit almost any folly to avoid being pestered, or, when unescapably cornered, to bring the affliction to an end. I invited him to meet Picasso and Madame Picasso at dinner. I was not drunk: I see no harm in being tipsy on suitable occasions, but on this occasion it happens I was not. I did not pay Picasso extravagant compliments: our relations were not of a kind in which compliments are paid face to face. In any case I do not think Lord Derwent could have known what was Picasso's impression of the evening, for, to the best of my knowledge, they did not meet again for years—if ever. I suppose Picasso felt no call to improve the acquaintance.

Madame, I have said, preferred discreet restaurants; but I must not forget an evening on which a lady of whom both were fond enticed them with my help to dinner in Montmartre—on the Place du Tertre if you please. Recalling the event—for an event it was—I realise that as early as 'the twenties' Picasso had become a legendary figure. I shall not forget the date either, for not only was it Sunday,

Sunday in June, but Whit-Sunday, *La Pentecôte*. The streets were full of saunterers; the *Place* was packed; tables crept out into the road. It was beginning to look as though our plot to lure the shy master into the open would be foiled by a coincidence, when I had the luck to espy a free table by the door of a bistrot. Slowly, very slowly, we were served by a little boy with a genuine Montmartrois accent; and the accent maybe reminded Picasso of old days in the rue Ravignan. At any rate he seemed to take pleasure in making the child prattle. His spirits rose, he became wittier than ever, and I began to count on a late sitting. But it was Picasso—Picasso the legendary. It may have been as much as ten years since he was last seen outside or inside a bistrot. People eyed our table. There was whispering: 'c'est Picasso'. One or two almost forgotten acquaintances —whom I did not know—came up and shook hands. Madame became restless. It was time to call for the bill. So we too began to saunter. We sauntered down the hill towards the rue La Boëtie, and, as we were passing the Gare St. Lazare, Picasso, turning to his hostess, said 'Would you like to be shown over the station? It is one of the finest sights in Paris'. Stupidly I demurred: it was late, I said, and the better part of the station would be closed or in darkness at all events. So I shall never know what beauties and curiosities Picasso had discovered in the Gare St. Lazrae; and serve me right.

Now I must try to describe *Le Boeuf sur le toit*. This restaurant, café, café-chantant and 'dancing' combined was invented by Jean Cocteau and began life, modestly enough, as, unless I mistake, *La Cigogne*, in the rue Duphot. Soon, having become well known and much frequented, it migrated to roomier quarters in the rue Boissy d'Anglas. Here Cocteau reigned supreme. He made of it a sort of G.H.Q. for *Les six*—the six musicians: Darius Milhaud, Poulenc, Auric, Honneger, Germaine Taillefer and Marcelle Meyer. I believe I have named them correctly, though it seems odd that neither Satie nor Sauguet should have been of the company. The *Boeuf* cannot be described properly as a night-club or a 'dancing' though people did dance and drink champagne there, sometimes till four o'clock in the morning. But people also lunched there quietly, and dined unobtrusively in a side room. Of an afternoon you might find writers and journalists who wished to discuss seriously an article or a scene in a play, and in a corner some young American correcting proofs. Shabby painters dropped in for a look round at any hour of the day or night. Nevertheless it was smart; it was 'the place to go to', and a peculiar section of Tout Paris, Tout Londres and Tout New York went. English visitors would come straight from the train, sure of finding there someone they knew, some friend or friends with whom to make dates. It was a fashionable meeting-place, but peaceful enough till six o'clock in the evening.

After six the *Boeuf* became immensely gay and light-hearted. It was a 'show' in itself—a show in which waiters and chasseurs played their parts, while the girl who sold nosegays by the cloakroom door was always pretty and never stayed long. At the piano would be some hard up youth of talent, destined for fame—Wiener at one time. Freyel might

sing. Rubinstein might suddenly take it into his head
to play. On the floor were some of the most elegant
women and best dancers in Paris. The décor, always
amusing, was subject to surprising changes. For instance, struck by the decorative effect of fly-posters
stuck all over the town advertising a concert and
bearing on pink paper the single word 'RUBIN-
STEIN', Cocteau had printed fly-posters bearing
the names of favoured clients and stuck them all
over the café and restaurant. In discreet but magis-
terial control of all was the inimitable Moyse.

Gradually the *Boeuf* became one of those places,
which perhaps still exist in Paris, where the beau
monde and the ragamuffins can drop clan-conscious-
ness and mingle happily—more or less. And so it
remained for half a dozen years or more. In the
middle 'twenties' at any rate it was both fashionable
and what, for want of a better English word, I must
call Bohemian. Sometimes 'en smoking' with my
more elegant friends, French, English and American, sometimes in tweeds—en ragamuffin in fact—
with the painters, I have spent merry nights in the
rue Boissy d'Anglas. To be sure the painters affected
to despise the place, declaring that it was too *chic*,
and too dear and stank of American cigarettes
which, however, they always smoked when given
the chance. Nevertheless I have had as much fun
there with Derain, Segonzac, Villeboeuf and Kisling, as with Arthur Rubinstein and his decorative
public. And it was there that I heard Picasso (still
in the dinner-jacket period) deliver one of those
utterances as characteristically Picassonian as the
sentences of the majestic doctor are characteristic-

ally Johnsonian. Cocteau was at the time composing that brilliant piece, *Orphée*, and, turning to Picasso with whom I was sitting, enquired—'Do you see any objection to a miracle on the stage? I want to bring a miracle into my play'. 'A miracle', said Picasso, 'there's nothing surprising about a miracle. Why it's a miracle every morning that I don't melt in my bath'. Dare I add Derain's comment on this flight of fancy when I repeated it to him? 'A few years ago it would have been a greater miracle if Picasso had taken a bath at any hour of the day'.

Of all the French painters who illustrated the 'twenties' Derain was the one I knew best: he was the only one whom I 'tutoyed'. Of his art I have written elsewhere at length. It was as various as that of any artist of his time, and, like the little girl with the curl in the middle of her forehead, 'when it was good it was very, very good'. In the 'thirties' and 'forties' he painted plenty of bad pictures, and in consequence his art was decried. Now justice is being done by the more thoughtful critics, for instance by Mr. Douglas Cooper and Mr. Denys Sutton. I wonder what has become of the decorations he made for Halvorsen's dining-room: ballet décors apart, they are, I suspect, his finest achievement. But perhaps it was his character that most impressed his friends; it seemed exactly suited to his height and tremendous frame and noble Roman head. He was a man of natural authority, which he exerted without a glimmer of self-consciousness. He spoke slowly, as beseemed his bulk, and with distinction and humour; though a habit of talking with a pipe in his mouth sometimes muffled his voice and distressed his friends. Two stories may give a better notion of his character and style than any analysis of which I am capable.

I was walking with Derain in Seven Dials, where, at the time of *La Boutique fantasque*, he had a studio, or rather a floor above a warehouse—I think it was a warehouse. A stranger approached me and asked the way to some hotel with the name of which I was unfamiliar. Derain promptly took the matter in hand. With a magnificent gesture and sounds which presumably he took to be English words he indicated a direction. The authority was superb and it inspired absolute confidence. The stranger marched off, completely satisfied it seemed, down a street towards which the impressive arm was pointing. When he was gone Derain informed me with undiminished authority that the hotel he was seeking was 'The Shaftesbury': it did not sound in the least like that nor did what Derain said to me sound much like 'Shaftesbury'. However that was what he had in mind. He knew the place well, he said. Whether the stranger ever reached it we shall never know.

And here is another story that may help those who knew him not to savour Derain's character. It was decided at *Les Deux Magots* that Rubinstein should meet Kisling, since these two—who had never met—were reckoned amongst the greater glories of their country. They were to meet at the café after dinner. Now Arthur Rubinstein, who, besides being a great pianist, is a delightful companion, has or had this drawback: he took his public about with him. That was not his fault: his admirers adhered to him. Often their presence added to the

pleasure of his company; for amongst his faithful
followers were many attractive women and men
both sensitive and intelligent. But there were others.
On this Sunday evening arrived with Rubinstein in
fullest evening dress two tall 'rastas' from South
America with what Derain called their 'poules de
luxe'. The meeting at the *Magots* was not a success;
so unsuccessful was it that very soon Rubinstein invited those who would to come with him for a drink
chez Fox. Fox was 'a character', of English descent
presumably, who kept a small café-restaurant (a
snack-bar they would call it now) near the Gare
St-Lazare. A dozen of us perhaps, including the four
South Americans, took cabs and crossed the river.
Chez Fox the two rastas behaved abominably. They
insulted the old *patron* and his waiter, called them
spies, pulled out Fox's tie, and finally pelted his
looking glass and bottles with the hard-boiled eggs
that lay in a basket on the counter. They were not
drunk: they were simply hubristic; they were rich
and they were bloody. (I am bound to say they paid
for the damage). I could see that Derain was fur-
ious. Rubinstein I make no doubt suffered acutely.
But Derain took action, that is to say he took my
hand, observing—'as you know, I have the gift of
reading a man's future in his hand: I will tell your
fortune'. He proceeded to foretell the most exciting
and improbable adventures for me and for two or
three more of his friends, accompanied by caustic
comments on our characters and habits. The South
Americans stopped throwing eggs and crowded
round him. Of course they all wished to have their
fortunes told. Derain took the hand of the taller and

189

handsomer of the two men and gazed on it with terrifying intensity. Then in calm but awe-inspiring tones pronounced—'No: I dare not tell you what I see there'. The effect was magical; I could hardly believe my eyes. He had frightened the rastas out of their wits. They fled; and I suppose Rubinstein felt bound to accompany his public. But Derain, turning to Fox, said 'Now we will all have supper, and you and your waiter shall be our guests. I dare say there's plenty to eat in the house: I can see a few eggs still intact: anyhow there's plenty of wine. The evening ended as well as it had begun badly.

If I were to name all the odd and eminent Parisians I met in 'the twenties' but never came to know well, this chapter would grow as tedious as the social column of *The Times*—some may think it would not have far to go. For instance, one summer I did come to know Dufy quite well; for we used to lunch together of a Sunday in a restaurant near his studio in the Impasse Guelma. To my shame I have no vivid recollections of his conversation. I remember that he was an agreeable companion, and that his atelier was of an extraordinary neatness and factory-like precision. There was a room for silks and a room for cottons and a room for painting pictures, and in all his operations were so neat and cleanly that one felt he could have executed them in a drawing-room. Of the charm of his work, especially of his textiles, I need not speak: everyone knows them, and most people of taste admire. Another artist whom I wish I had known better was Christian Bérard. I used to meet him with Cocteau and later at our Embassy: once or twice he dined with me.

He was both eminent and odd, and in my opinion, one of the best stage-decorators of our time. And then there was that great man Rouault. Only once did I meet him; I sat next to him at dinner, but all he said, and kept on saying, was 'on ne peut pas dire que Vollard me tient', from which I concluded that Vollard le tenait. He is a great artist, but he might have been a greater. Apparently, some time early in the century, he gave up looking at things and invented clichés. There was a formula for Dives and a formula for Lazarus: clowns, judges, tycoons, saints, sinners and divine persons, he had them all taped. Trusting to his imagination and skill he has played beautifully with his formulae these forty years; but I wish he would sometimes go out of doors and look about him.

One of the people I met in Paris in 'the twenties' has become a life-long friend—Georges Duthuit. But to describe all the fun we have had, together and in company, in Paris and in London, in Barcelona, Venice and Aix-en-Provence, would need fifty pages and a pen more picturesque than mine. When he comes to write my obituary notice in *Nice-Matin*—I count on him for that—I hope he will not forget the racing fleas of Montparnasse nor Aldous Huxley's wry smile at Barcelona.

If, in the 'twenties' and 'thirties' I saw a good deal of Picasso, since the war I have seen little. That is explicable. Picasso, as all the world knows, is become a 'monument historique'. To reach him one must slip past secretaries on sentry-duty and the last time I penetrated the defences of his studio I should not have been surprised if someone had invited me

to fill up a card stating the object of my visit and
the number of my passport. But I do see him from
time to time, and since the war I have spent a long
afternoon with him which I like to remember because I found him unchanged, that is to say, witty,
charming, affectionate, and quite unlike anyone
else. It happened in this way. I was dining with the
Simon Bussys in their flat at Nice. The party, if I
remember right, besides our host and hostess and
daughter (Janie Bussy), were Mrs. St. John Hutchinson, Roger Martin du Gard and myself. It was a
Friday evening. Someone said—'What fun to surprise Picasso in his pottery at Vallauris'. A surprise
visit it had to be for no one could discover the telephone number. So next morning off we went by
omnibus, Mrs. Hutchinson, Simon Bussy and I, and
after many enquiries found the pretty little pottery
with its slightly medieval air, to learn that the master was not at home but was expected in the afternoon. Clearly the sensible thing to do was to lunch
somewhere in the village, then sit in the sun and
wait; and that is what we did. Soon to us appeared
this curious cortège: first Picasso, marching, in an
old grey sweater and espadrilles; next, a handsome
black car, driven by a chauffeur, otherwise empty;
then a troupe of workmen and girls most of whom
seemed to have questions to put which the master
found no difficulty in answering. I have rarely seen
Picasso surprised; but when he saw us sitting in a
row on the ground, or rather on my coat, his surprise was unmistakable. Also unmistakable was his
pleasure at seeing Mrs. Hutchinson, an old friend,
whom he had not met since before the war. The sun

blazed, Picasso was at his best, our courage and enterprise were rewarded. None of us had seen the pots, nor had we the faintest idea what they would be like; for they had not yet been shown or photographed nor, I think, had anything been written about them. As you may suppose, it was our turn to be surprised. I thought, and think, those pots extraordinary. Returning, we broke the journey at Antibes, to see the paintings presented to the museum, which was closed—by now it was evening—but opened instantly at the magic name. That, I think, was the last time I saw Picasso as he should be seen; but I do not despair of seeing him so again. Matisse in the 'twenties' and 'thirties' I did not see often. I met him now and then, and once or twice he wrote to me about things I had written about him: these, I suppose, had been translated by Janie Bussy. Since the war I have been more fortunate; I have seen him in Paris and whenever I was in the midi I made a point of calling as I was told he liked visits. At the time of his death I felt I had known him well enough to correct a few of the more glaring errors that occurred in *The Times*' obituary notice. One visit, when he was living at Vence, is perhaps worth recording. It was in the spring of '48. He was in bed but he did not seem ill; indeed he said of himself 'I am not a sick man, I am a wounded man —"un grand mutilé".' Of a morning he still worked a little in his studio, and in the afternoon lay in bed cutting out those marvellous paper decorations and drawing. (By the way, or partly by the way, I noticed a picture by Picasso on the wall). His guide, philosopher and friend, Madame Lydia, showed us his latest paintings, and he himself showed drawings for *Jazz* and the *Portuguese Nun*. 'Us', I say, because an English lady, to whom Matisse was deeply attached, was also paying a visit. With her, while Madame Lydia was showing me more drawings, he held a private colloquy, in which, it seems, he spoke feelingly of his life, ambitions and achievements, of his hopes and fears, in fact of 'life, death and the grand Forever'. His friend was touched, naturally, and possibly flattered. Who would not have been? Breathes there a woman with soul so dead . . . ? So it must have been a little disappointing when, some days later, at the Gare du Nord, she bought the *Figaro Littéraire* and discovered that precisely the same confidences had been imparted to a journalist who had been accorded an interview a day or two before her visit.

I saw Matisse several times in '51 and I must have seen him later: but the last visit I recall was in the spring of that year, when he was in bed at the hôtel Regina at Cimiez. I remember that Simon Bussy who was with me teased him into a perhaps unprofitable argument about religious art, during which it looked for a moment as though there had been only two religious painters. Fra Angelico was the other. On the ceiling above his bed—it was a very high room indeed—I noticed with surprise several characteristic drawings. 'How did you make them?' I enquired. 'With a fishing-rod' replied Matisse. And so he sent me off, with a note to the Mother Superior, to see his not quite finished chapel at Vence. It is finished now, and, though far from being the best thing Matisse ever did, that chapel deserves a visit. But may I advise anyone who contemplates making the pilgrimage to choose a sunny day?

INDEX

INDEX

Dardel, Nils de, 180, 181
Darwin, Charles, 88
Daumier, 55
Degas, 16, 20, 29, 152
Delacroix, 165
Delcassé, 140
Derain, Alice, 175
Derain, André, 138, 166–190
Derwent, Lord, 183
Despiau, 175
Diaghileff, 170–172, 179
Drieu la Rochelle, 172
Dryden, 68
Dufy, 190
Duff, 28
Dugardier, 151
Duhamel, Georges, 176
Duncan, Isadora, 180, 181
Durtain, Luc, 176
Duthuit, Georges, 138, 168, 191

Eastman, Max, 73
Eliot, George, 113
Eliot, T. S., 10, 119–125, 137
Emmons, Dr., 13, 18
Ethiopians (blameless), 23

Fabius Maximus, 48
Falstaff, Sir John, 9
Forster, E. M., 28, 131
Fort, Paul, 146
Freyel, 185
Friesz, Othon, 149, 150, 178
Fry, Roger, 10, 11, 15, 59, 60, 62–91, 104, 119, 130, 133, 134, 136, 138, 173, 176

Gabory, 175
Gard, Roger Martin du, 192
Garnett, David, 131, 136
Gauguin, 80–82, 165–167
Gautier, Théophile, 66
Gerbaud, 175
Gertler, 122
Gide, André, 146–148, 176
Gibbon, 32, 35, 36
Gladstone, 33
Goldoni, 17
Gourmont, Remy de, 165

Granier, Jeanne, 160
Grant, Duncan, 45, 49, 50, 54, 100, 101, 106, 130, 134, 172
Granta, The, 30
Greco, El, 167
Greek sculpture (Roger Fry on), 71
Grey, Sir Edward, 80
Guardian, The, 93

Halliday, Henry, 15
Hannibal, 48
Harpignies, 157
Harrison, Alexander, 151
Harrod, Roy, 46, 50, 51, 53
Hawtrey, R., 28, 42
Haynes, E.S.P., 141
Hayward, John, 11
Hazlitt, 161
Heredia, 152
Herrand, Marcel, 180
Honneger, 185
Horace, 17
Howard (Pompy), 151
Hudson, Geoffrey, 10
Huilmann (or Ulmann), 151
Hume, David, 88
Hutchinson, Mrs. St. John, 45, 122, 124, 192
Huxley, Aldous, 60, 122, 124, 131, 148, 172
Huxley, Maria (Mrs. Aldous Huxley, née Balthus), 122
Huysmans, 13, 162

Indian Art (Roger Fry on), 70
Ingres, 165
Irma, Madame, 151

Jacob, Max, 177
James, Henry, 14
Joachim, 28
Joad, Mrs., 105
Johnson, Dr., 36
Jouvet, Louis, 176
Joyce, James, 179, 180

Kelly, Sir Gerald, 139–144, 153–155, 163, 164

197

INDEX

Keynes, Lady (Lopokova), 56, 172
Keynes, Maynard, 11, 27, 42–61, 105, 119, 124, 130, 133, 135, 136, 171
Kisling, 175, 186, 188
Kite, 151
Klee, 113

La Bruyère, 124
Laforgue, 165
Lamb, Lady Caroline, 98
Lamb, Charles, 39
Lamb, Henry, 27
Laprade, 165
Lawrence, D. H., 43
Léger, 176
Leighton, Lord, 20
Lepage, Bastien, 67
Lewis, Lady, 106
Lipschitz, 176
Lloyd-George, 47, 57
London Clinic, The, 10
Low, David, 54–55
Lucas, F. L., 131, 133
Lydia, Madame, 193–194

Macaulay, Lord, 36
MacCarthy, Sir Desmond, 28, 30, 131
MacCarthy, Lady (Molly), 45, 100, 129–131
McKenna, R., 45
McLaren, 28
MacTaggart, 28
Mallarmé, 75, 122, 152, 153
Manet, 157
Mansfield, Katherine, 122
March, Richard, 11
Marcoussis, 175
Marchand, Jean, 175
Marshall, Alfred, 57
Martin, Kingsley, 54, 55
Massine, 170
Matisse, 12, 15, 82, 134, 138, 157, 158, 168, 174, 193, 194
Maugham, Somerset, 151–153
Melville, 28
Mérimée, 119, 165

Metzinger, 176
Meyer, Marcelle, 180, 185
Milhaud, Darius, 185
Milton, 76, 154
Modigliani, 177
Monet, 114, 157
Montagu, Edwin, 42
Moore, G. E., 28, 42, 133
Moréas, 146
Morgan, Pierpont, 87
Morley, Lord, 145
Morrell, Lady Ottoline, 104, 122
Morrell, Phillip, 44, 122
Morrice, J. W., 66, 67, 138–169 (passim)
Mortimer, Raymond, 108, 131, 133
Murray (House of), 10
Murry, Middleton, 122

Nation, The, 105, 106
New Age, The, 15
Newman, Cardinal, 33
New Republic, The, 147
New Statesman, The, 54, 55
Northcliffe, Lord, 47
Norton, H. T. J., 27, 46, 48, 130, 135

Oberlé, 175
O'Conor, Roderick, 138–169 (passim)
Olliviers, The, 44
Omega Workshop, 78
Orangerie, 16

Partridge, Ralph, 105, 131, 133
Partridge, Frances (née Marshall), 85, 86, 131, 133
Peacock, 39
Philipon, 55
Philippe, Charles-Louis, 152, 165
Picasso, 12, 15, 82, 113, 134, 137, 138, 170–173, 179, 181–184, 187, 191–193
Picasso, Olga, 171, 182, 184
Piot, 158, 159
Pope, 10, 29

198

INDEX

INDEX